Bayesian Risk Management

The Wiley Finance series contains books written specifically for finance and investment professionals as well as sophisticated individual investors and their financial advisors. Book topics range from portfolio management to e-commerce, risk management, financial engineering, valuation and financial instrument analysis, as well as much more. For a list of available titles, visit our website at www.WileyFinance.com.

Founded in 1807, John Wiley & Sons is the oldest independent publishing company in the United States. With offices in North America, Europe, Australia and Asia, Wiley is globally committed to developing and marketing print and electronic products and services for our customers' professional and personal knowledge and understanding.

Bayesian Risk Management

A Guide to Model Risk and Sequential Learning in Financial Markets

MATT SEKERKE

WILEY

Published by John Wiley & Sons, Inc., Hoboken, New Jersey.
Published simultaneously in Canada.

Library of Congress Cataloging-in-Publication Data:

Sekerke, Matt.
Bayesian risk management : a guide to model risk and sequential learning in financial markets / Matt Sekerke.
pages cm. — (The Wiley finance series)
Includes bibliographical references and index.
ISBN 978-1-118-70860-6 (cloth) – ISBN 978-1-118-74745-2 (epdf) – ISBN 978-1-118-74750-6 (epub)
1. Finance—Mathematical models. 2. Financial risk management—Mathematical models. 3. Bayesian statistical decision theory. I. Title.
HG106.S45 2015
332'.041501519542–dc23

2015013791

Cover Design: Wiley
Cover Image: Abstract background © iStock.com/matdesign24

Printed in the United States of America

10 9 8 7 6 5 4 3 2 1

Contents

Preface

Most financial risk models assume that the future will look like the past. They don't have to. This book sketches a more flexible risk-modeling approach that more fully recognizes our uncertainty about the future.

Uncertainty about the future stems from our limited ability to specify risk models, estimate their parameters from data, and be assured of the continuity between today's markets and tomorrow's markets. Ignoring any of these dimensions of model risk creates an illusion of mastery and fosters erroneous decision making. It is typical for financial firms to ignore all of these sources of uncertainty. Because they measure too little risk, they take on too much risk.

The core concern of this book is to present and justify alternative tools to measure financial risk without assuming that time-invariant stochastic processes drive financial phenomena. Discarding time-invariance as a modeling assumption makes uncertainty about parameters, models, and forecasts accessible and irreducible in a way that standard statistical risk measurements do not. The constructive alternative offered here under the slogan *Bayesian Risk Management* is an online sequential Bayesian modeling framework that acknowledges all of these sources of uncertainty, without giving up the structure afforded by parametric risk models and asset-pricing models.

Following an introductory chapter on the far-reaching consequences of the time-invariance assumption, Part One of the book shows where Bayesian analysis opens up uncertainty about parameters and models in a static setting. Bayesian results are compared to standard statistical results to make plain the strong assumptions embodied in classical, "objective" statistics. Chapter 2 begins by discussing prior information and parameter uncertainty in the context of the binomial and normal linear regression models. I compare Bayesian results to classical results to show how the Bayesian approach nests classical statistical results as a special case, and relate prior distributions under the Bayesian framework to hypothesis tests in classical statistics as competing methods of introducing nondata information. Chapter 3 addresses uncertainty about models and shows how candidate models may be compared to one another. Particular focus is given to the relationship between prior information and model complexity, and the manner in which model uncertainty applies to asset-pricing models.

Part Two extends the Bayesian framework to sequential time series analysis. Chapter 4 introduces the practice of discounting as a means of creating adaptive models. Discounting reflects uncertainty about the degree of continuity between the past and the future, and prevents the accumulation of data from destroying model flexibility. Expanding the set of available models to entertain multiple candidate discount rates incorporates varying degrees of memory into the modeling enterprise, avoiding the need for an a priori view about the rate at which market information decays. Chapters 5 and 6 then develop the fundamental tools of sequential Bayesian time series analysis: dynamic linear models and sequential Monte Carlo (SMC) models. Each of these tools incorporates parameter uncertainty, model uncertainty, and information decay into an online filtering framework, enabling real-time learning about financial market conditions.

Part Three then applies the methods developed in the first two parts to the estimation of volatility in Chapter 7 and the estimation of a commodity forward curve under the risk-neutral measure subject to arbitrage restrictions in Chapter 8. My goal here is to show the applicability of the methods developed to two problems which represent two extremes in our level of modeling knowledge. Additional applications are also possible. In Chapter 8 especially, I discuss how other common models may be reformulated and estimated using the same sequential Bayesian toolkit.

Chapter 9, the sole chapter of Part Four, synthesizes the results of the first three parts and begins the transition from a risk *measurement* framework based on Bayesian principles to a properly Bayesian risk *management.* I argue that the sequential Bayesian framework offers a coherent mechanism for organizational learning in environments characterized by incomplete information. Bayesian models allow senior management to make clear statements of risk policy and test elements of strategy against market outcomes in a direct and rigorous way. One may wish to begin reading at the final chapter: A glimpse of the endgame could provide useful orientation while reading the rest of the text.

The genesis of this book is multifold. As an undergraduate student in economics, I was impressed by the divide between the information-processing capacity assumed for individuals and firms in economic theory and the manner in which empirical individuals and firms actually learn. While economics provided many powerful results for the ultimate market outcomes, the field had less to say about the process by which equilibria were reached, or the dynamic stability of equilibrium given large perturbations from fixed points. Given a disruption to the economy, it seemed as though economic agents would have to find their way back to equilibrium over time, and on the basis of incomplete and uncertain information. With the notable exception of Fisher (1983) and some works by the Austrian economists, I quickly discovered that the field furnished few ready answers.

As I began my career consulting in economic litigations, I had two further experiences that find their theme in this book. The first involved litigation over a long-term purchase contract, which included a clause for renegotiation in the event that a "structural change" in the subject market had occurred. In working to find econometric evidence for such a structural change, I was struck, on the one hand, by the dearth of methods for identifying structural change in a market as it happened; identification seemed to be possible mainly as a forensic exercise, though there were obvious reasons why a firm would want to identify structural change in real time. On the other hand, after applying the available methods to the data, it seemed that it was more likely than not to find structural change wherever one looked, particularly in financial time series data at daily frequency. If structural change could occur at any time, without the knowledge of those who have vested interests in knowing, the usual methods of constructing forecasts with classical time series models seemed disastrously prone to missing the most important events in a market. Worse, their inadequacy would not become evident until it was probably too late.

The second experience was my involvement in the early stages of litigation related to the credit crisis. In these lawsuits, a few questions were on everyone's mind. Could the actors in question have seen significant changes in the market coming? If so, at what point could they have known that a collapse was imminent? If not, what would have led them to believe that the future was either benign or unknowable? The opportunity to review confidential information obtained in the discovery phase of these litigations provided innumerable insights into the inner workings of the key actors with respect to risk measurement, risk management, and financial instrument valuation. I saw two main things. First, there was an overwhelming dependence on front-office information—bid sheets, a few consummated secondary-market trades, and an overwhelming amount of "market color," the industry term for the best rumor and innuendo on offer—and almost no dependence on middle-office modeling. Whereas certain middle-office modeling efforts could have reacted to changes in market conditions, the traders on the front lines would not act until they saw changes in traded prices. Second, there were interminable discussions about how to weigh new data on early-stage delinquencies, default rates, and home prices against historical data. Instead of asking whether the new data falsified earlier premises on which expectations were built, discussions took place within the bounds of the worst-known outcomes from history, with the unstated assurance that housing market phenomena were stable and mean-reverting overall. Whatever these observations might imply about the capacity of the actors involved, it seemed that a better balance could be struck between middle-office risk managers and front-office traders, and that gains could be had by making the expectations of all involved explicit in the context of models grounded in the relevant fundamentals.

However, it was not until I began my studies at the University of Chicago that these themes converged around the technical means necessary to make them concrete. Nick Polson's course in probability theory was a revelation, introducing the Bayesian approach to probability within the context of financial markets. Two quarters of independent study with him followed immediately in which he introduced me to the vanguard of Bayesian thinking about time series. A capstone elective on Bayesian econometrics with Hedibert Lopes provided further perspective and rigor. His teaching was a worthy continuation of a tradition at the University of Chicago going back to Arnold Zellner.

The essay offered here brings these themes together by offering sequential Bayesian inference as the technical integument, which allows an organization to learn in real time about "structural change." It is my provisional and constructive answer to how a firm can behave rationally in a dynamic environment of incomplete information.

My intended audience for this book includes senior management, traders and risk managers in banking, insurance, brokerage, and asset management firms, among other players in the wider sphere of finance. It is also addressed to regulators of financial firms who are increasingly concerned with risk measurement and risk governance. Advanced undergraduate and graduate students in economics, statistics, finance, and financial engineering will also find much here to complement and challenge their other studies within the discipline. Those readers who have spent substantial time modeling real data will benefit the most from this book.

Because it is an essay and not a treatise or a textbook, the book is pitched at a relatively mature mathematical level. Readers should already be comfortable with probability theory, classical statistics, matrix algebra, and numerical methods in order to follow the exposition and, more important to appreciate the recalcitrance of the problems addressed. At the same time, I have sought to avoid writing a mathematical book in the usual sense. Math is used mainly to exemplify, calculate, and make a point rather than to reach a painstaking level of rigor. There is also more repetition than usual so the reader can keep moving ahead, rather than constantly referring to previous formulas, pages, and chapters. In almost every case, I provide all steps and calculations in an argument, hoping to provide clarity without becoming tedious, and to avoid referring the reader to a list of hard-to-locate materials for the details necessary to form an understanding. That said, I hardly expect to have carried out my self-imposed mandates perfectly and invite readers to email me at BayesianRiskManagement@gmail.com with typos and other comments.

Acknowledgments

It is hard to express my gratitude to Nick Polson adequately. Certainly, this book would not exist without him. His intellectual fingerprints are all over it, and I hope I have proven myself a worthy student. More than any lecture or guidance in the thicket of the statistical literature, the many hours spent with Nick (more often than not, over burgers at Medici on 57th in Hyde Park) thinking through the ways in which people attempt to learn about financial markets from data helped me not only to grasp the Bayesian manner of thinking about probability but also to gain the confidence necessary to test it against the prevailing orthodoxy. His intuitive way of proceeding and his fantastic sense of humor also made it great fun to set off in an exciting new field. For all I have absorbed from him, I am still overwhelmed by the many brilliant new directions of his thinking, and will have much to learn from him for many years to come.

This book also bears traces of many years working with Steve Hanke, first as his research assistant and as an ongoing collaborator in writing and consulting. Professor Hanke first introduced me to the importance of time and uncertainty in economic analysis by encouraging me to read the Austrians, and especially Hayek. These pages are part of an ongoing process of coming to grips with the wealth of ideas to which Professor Hanke exposed me. Professor Hanke has also supported my writing efforts from the very beginning and continues to be a source of encouragement and wise counsel to me in virtually all matters of importance.

Chris Culp has been incredibly supportive to me for nearly 15 years as a mentor and a colleague. His boundless productive energy and generosity of spirit have been an inspiration to me from the beginning. ("Ask Culp" was one of the more common prescriptions heard in Professor Hanke's office.) The insightful ways in which Chris connects problems in risk management with fundamental problems in economics and corporate finance were decisive in sparking my interest in the subject. More directly, without his introduction to Bill Falloon at Wiley, this project would have remained in the realm of wishful thinking.

Bill Falloon has shown me a staggering degree of support with this book and more generally in developing as an author. I look forward to more projects with him and his fantastic team, especially Meg Freeborn, who kept my developing manuscript on the rails despite multiple interruptions and radical, wholesale revisions.

Most important, I am grateful for the unflagging support of my incredible wife, Nancy. She kept me going on this project whenever the going got tough, and patiently auditioned my many attempts to distill my thesis to a simple and forthright message. Whatever clarity may be found in a book dense with mathematics and quantitative finance is probably due to her. All of the shortcomings of the book are, however, mine alone.

Bayesian Risk Management

CHAPTER 1

Models for Discontinuous Markets

The broadening and deepening of markets for risk transfer has marked the development of financial services perhaps more than any other trend. The past 30 years have witnessed the development of secondary markets for a wide variety of financial assets and the explosion of derivative instruments made possible by financial engineering. The expansion of risk transfer markets has liquefied and transformed the business of traditional financial firms such as banks, asset managers, and insurance companies. At the same time, markets for risk transfer have enabled nontraditional players to enter financial services businesses, invigorating competition, driving down prices, and confounding the efforts of regulators. Such specialist risk transfer firms occupy a number of niches in which they can outperform their more diversified counterparts in the regulated financial system by virtue of their specialized knowledge, transactional advantages, and superior risk management.

For all firms operating in risk transfer markets, traditional and nontraditional alike, the ability to create, calibrate, deploy, and refine risk models is a core competency. No firm, however specialized, can afford to do without models that extract information from market prices, measure the sensitivity of asset values to any number of risk factors, or forecast the range of adverse outcomes that might impact the firm's financial position.

The risk that a firm's models may fail to capture shifts in market pricing, risk sensitivities, or the mix of the firm's risk exposures is thus a central operational risk for any financial services business. Yet many, if not most, financial services firms lack insight into the probabilistic structure of risk models and the corresponding risk of model failures. My thesis is that most firms lack insight into model risk because of the way they practice statistical modeling. Because generally accepted statistical practice provides thin means for assessing model risk, alternative methods are needed to take model risk seriously. Bayesian methods allow firms to take model risk seriously—hence a book on Bayesian risk management.

RISK MODELS AND MODEL RISK

Throughout this book, when I discuss risk models, I will be talking about parametric risk models. Parametric risk models are attempts to reduce the complexity inherent in large datasets to specific functional forms defined completely by a relatively low-dimensional set of numbers known as parameters. Nonparametric risk models, by contrast, rely exclusively on the resampling of empirical data, so no reduction of the data is attempted or accomplished. Such models ask: Given the risk exposures I have today, what is the distribution of outcomes I can expect if the future looks like a random draw from some history of market data? Nonparametric risk models lack model specification in the way we would normally understand it, so that there is no risk of misspecification or estimation error by construction. Are such models therefore superior? Not at all. A nonparametric risk model cannot represent any outcome different from what has happened, including any outcomes more extreme than what has already happened. Nor can it furnish any insight into the ultimate drivers of adverse risk outcomes. As a result, nonparametric risk models have limited use in forecasting, though they can be useful as a robustness check for a parametric risk model.

Parametric risk models begin life as a probability distribution, which is a statement of the likelihood of seeing different values conditional only on the parameters of the distribution. Given the parameters and the form of the distribution, all possibilities are encompassed. More parameters create more flexibility: A Weibull distribution is more flexible than an exponential distribution. Many risk models rely heavily on normal and lognormal distributions, parameterized by the mean and variance, or the covariance matrix and mean vector in the multivariate case. A great deal has been written on the usefulness of heavier-tailed distributions for modeling financial data, going back to Mandelbrot (1963) and Fama (1965).

Undoubtedly, the unconditional distributions of most financial returns have heavier tails than the normal distribution. But to solve the problem of heavy tails solely through the choice of a different family of probability distributions is to seek a solution at a very low level of complexity.

More complex risk models project a chosen risk distribution onto a linear system of covariates that helps to articulate the target risk. Regression models such as these seek to describe the distribution of the target variable conditional on other available information. The functional form of the distribution is subsumed as an error term. Familiar examples include the following:

- *Linear regression with normally distributed errors*, widely used in asset pricing theory and many other applications.

- *Probit and logit models*, which parameterize the success probability in binomial distributions.
- *Proportional hazard models from insurance and credit risk modeling*, which project a series of gamma or Weibull distributions onto a linear system of explanatory factors.

Parameters are added corresponding to each of the factors included in the projection. The gain in power afforded by projection raises new questions about the adequacy of the system: Are the chosen factors sufficient? Unique? Structural? What is the joint distribution of the system parameters, and can that tell us anything about the choice of factors?

It seems the pinnacle in financial risk modeling is achieved when parameters governing several variables—a yield curve, a forward curve, a volatility surface—may be estimated from several time series simultaneously, where functional forms are worked out from primitives about stochastic processes and arbitrage restrictions. Such models pass over from the physical probability measure P to the risk-neutral probability measure Q. In terms of the discussion above, such models may be seen as (possibly nonlinear) transformations of a small number of factors (or state variables) whose distributions are defined by the nature of the underlying stochastic process posited for the factors. When the number of time series is large relative to the parameters of the model the parameters are overidentified, permitting highly efficient inference from the data. Such models are the ultimate in powerful description, offering the means to capture the dynamics of dozens of interest rates or forward contracts with a limited number of factors and parameters.

Our hierarchy of risk models thus includes as elements probability distributions, parameters, and functional forms, which may be linear or nonlinear, theoretically motivated or *ad hoc*. Each element of the description may not conform to reality, which is to say that each element is subject to error. An incorrect choice of distribution or functional form constitutes specification error on the part of the analyst. Errors in parameters arise from estimation error, but also collaterally from specification errors. The collection of all such opportunities for error in risk modeling is what I will call model risk.

TIME-INVARIANT MODELS AND CRISIS

The characteristics enumerated above do not exhaust all dimensions of model risk, however. Even if a model is correctly specified and parameterized inasmuch as it produces reliable forecasts for currently observed data, the possibility remains that the model may fail to produce reliable forecasts in the future.

Two assumptions are regularly made about time series as a point of departure for their statistical modeling:

1. Assuming the joint distribution of observations in a time series depends not on their absolute position in the series but only on their relative position in this series is to assume that the time series is *stationary*.
2. If sample moments (time averages) taken from a time series converge in probability to the moments of the data-generating process, then the time series is *ergodic*.

Time series exhibiting both properties are said to be ergodic stationary. However, I find the term *time-invariant* more convenient. For financial time series, time-invariance implies that the means and covariances of a set of asset returns will be the same for any T observations of those returns, up to sampling error. In other words, no matter when we look at the data, we should come to the same conclusion about the joint distribution of the data, and converge to the same result as T becomes large.

Standard statistical modeling practice and classical time series analysis proceed from the underlying assumption that time series are time-invariant, or can be made time-invariant using simple transformations like detrending, differencing, or discovering a cointegrating vector (Hamilton 1994, pp. 435–450, 571). Time series models strive for time-invariance because reliable forecasts can be made for time-invariant processes. Whenever we estimate risk measures from data, we expect those measures will be useful as forecasts: Risk only exists in the future.

However, *positing* time-invariance for the sake of forecasting is not the same as *observing* time-invariance. Forecasts from time-invariant models break down because time series prove themselves not to be time-invariant. When the time-invariance properties desired in a statistical model are not found in empirical reality, unconditional time series models are no longer a possibility: Model estimates must be conditioned on recent history in order to supply reasonable forecasts, greatly foreshortening the horizon over which data can be brought to bear in a relevant way to develop such estimates.

In this book, I will pursue the hypothesis that the greatest obstacle to the progress of quantitative risk management is the assumption of time-invariance that underlies the naïve application of statistical and financial models to financial market data. A corollary of this hypothesis is that extreme observations seen in risk models are not extraordinarily unlucky realizations drawn from the extreme tail of an unconditional distribution describing the universe of possible outcomes. Instead, extreme observations are manifestations of inflexible risk models that have failed to adapt to shifts in the market data. The quest for models that are true for all time and for all eventualities actually frustrates the goal of anticipating the range of likely adverse outcomes within practical forecasting horizons.

Ergodic Stationarity in Classical Time Series Analysis

To assume a financial time series is ergodic stationary is to assume that a fixed stochastic process is generating the data. This data-generating process is a functional form combining some kind of stochastic disturbance summarized in a parametric probability distribution, with other parameters known in advance of the financial time series data being realized. The assumption of stationarity therefore implies that if we know the right functional form and the values of the parameters, we will have exhausted the possible range of outcomes for the target time series. Different realizations of the target time series are then just draws from the joint distribution of the conditioning data and the stochastic disturbance. This is why a sample drawn from any segment of the time series converges to the same result in an ergodic stationary time series.While we cannot predict where a stationary time series will go tomorrow, we can narrow down the range of possible outcomes and make statements about the relative probability of different outcomes. In particular, we can make statements about the probabilities of extreme outcomes.

Put differently, when a statistical model is specified, stationarity is introduced as *an auxiliary hypothesis about the data* that allows the protocols of statistical sampling to be applied when estimating the model. Stationarity implies that parameters are constant and that further observations of the data improve their estimates. Sampling-based estimation is so widely accepted and commonplace that the extra hypothesis of stationarity has dropped out of view, almost beyond criticism. Consciously or unconsciously, the hypothesis of stationarity forms a basic part of a risk manager's worldview—if one model fails, there must be another encompassing model that would capture the anomaly; some additional complication must make it possible to see what we did not see in the past.

Yet stationarity remains an assumption, and it is important to understand its function as the glue that holds together classical time series analysis. The goal in classical time series econometrics is to estimate parameters and test hypotheses about them. Assuming stationarity ensures that the estimated parameter values converge to their "correct" values as more data are observed, and tests of hypotheses about parameters are valid.

Both outcomes depend on the law of large numbers, and thus they both depend on the belief that when we observe new data, those data are sampled from the same process that generated previous data. In other words, only if we assume we are looking at a unitary underlying phenomenon can we apply the law of large numbers to ensure the validity of our estimates and hypothesis tests. Consider, for the example, the discussion of 'Fundamental Concepts in Time-Series Analysis' in the textbook by Fumio Hayashi (2000, pp. 97–98) concerning the 'Need for Ergodic Stationarity':

> *The fundamental problem in time-series analysis is that we can observe the realization of the process only once. For example, the sample on the U.S. annual inflation rate for the period from 1946 to 1995 is a string of 50 particular numbers, which is just one possible outcome of the underlying stochastic process for the inflation rate; if history took a different course, we would have obtained a different sample ....*
>
> *Of course, it is not feasible to observe many different alternative histories. But* if the distribution of the inflation rate remains unchanged *[my emphasis] (this property will be referred to as stationarity), the particular string of 50 numbers we do observe can be viewed as 50 different values from the* same *distribution.*

The discussion is concluded with a statement of the ergodic theorem, which extends the law of large numbers to the domain of time series (pp. 101–102).

The assumption of stationarity is dangerous for financial risk management. It lulls us into believing that, once we have collected enough data, we have completely circumscribed the range of possible market outcomes, because tomorrow will just be another realization of the process that generated today. It fools us into believing we know the values of parameters like volatility and equity market beta sufficiently well that we can ignore any residual uncertainty from their estimation. It makes us complacent about the choice of models and functional forms because it credits hypothesis tests with undue discriminatory power. And it leads us again and again into crisis situations because it attributes too little probability to extreme events.

We cannot dismiss the use of ergodic stationarity as a mere simplifying assumption, of the sort regularly and sensibly made in order to arrive at an elegant and acceptable approximation to a more complex phenomenon. A model of a stationary time series approximates an object that can never be observed: a time series of infinite length. This says nothing about the model's ability to approximate a time series of any finite length, such as the lifetime of a trading strategy, a career, or a firm. When events deemed to occur 0.01 percent of the time by a risk model happen twice in a year, there may be no opportunity for another hundred years to prove out the assumed stationarity of the risk model.

Recalibration Does Not Overcome the Limits of a Time-Invariant Model

Modern financial crises are intimately connected with risk modeling built on the assumption of stationarity. For large actors like international banks, brokerage houses, and institutional investors, risk models matter a lot for the formation of expectations. When those models depend on the assumption of stationarity, they lose the ability to adapt to data that are inconsistent with the assumed data-generation process, because any other data-generation process is ruled out by fiat.

Consider what happens when an institution simply recalibrates the same models, without reexamining the specification of the model, over a period when economic expansion is slowing and beginning to turn toward recession. As the rate of economic growth slows the assumption of ergodicity dissolves new data signaling recession into a long-run average indicating growth. Firms and individuals making decisions based on models are therefore unable to observe the signal being sent by the data that a transition in the reality of the market is under way, even as they recalibrate their models. As a result, actors continue to behave as if growth conditions prevail, even as the market is entering a process of retrenchment.

Thinking about a series of forecasts made during this period of transition, one would likely see forecast errors consistently missing in the same direction, though no information about the forecast error would be fed back into the model. When models encompass a large set of variables, small changes in the environment can lead to sharp changes in model parameters, creating significant hedging errors when those parameters inform hedge ratios. Activity is more at odds with reality as the reversal of conditions continues, until the preponderance of new data can no longer be ignored; through successive recalibrations the weight of the new data balances and overtakes the old data. Suddenly actors are confronted by a vastly different reality as their models catch up to the new data. The result is a perception of discontinuity. The available analytics no longer support the viability of the financial institution's chosen risk profile. Management reacts to the apparent discontinuity, past decisions are abruptly reversed, and consequently market prices show extreme movements that were not previously believed to be within the realm of possibility.

Models staked on stationarity thus sow the seeds of their own destruction by encouraging poor decision making, the outcomes of which later register as a realization of the nearly-impossible. *Crises are therefore less about tail events "occurring" than about model-based expectations failing to adapt*. As a result, perennial efforts to capture extreme risks in stationary models as if they were simply given are, in large part, misguided. They are as much *effect* as they are *cause*. Financial firms would do much better to confront the operational task of revising risk measurements continuously, and using the outputs of that continuous learning process to control their business decisions. Relaxing the assumption of stationarity within one's risk models has the goal of enabling revisions of expectations to take place smoothly, to the extent that our expectations of financial markets are formed with the aid of models, in a way that successive recalibrations cannot.

BAYESIAN PROBABILITY AS A MEANS OF HANDLING DISCONTINUITY

The purpose of this book is to set out a particular view of probability and a set of statistical methods that untether risk management calculations from the foundational assumption of time-invariance. Such methods necessarily move away from the classical analysis of time series, and lay bare the uncertainties in statistical and financial models that are typically papered over by the assumption of ergodic stationarity. Thus, our methods will allow us to entertain the possibilities that we know the parameters of a model only within a nontrivial range of values, multiple models may be adequate to the data, and different models may become the best representation of the data as market conditions change. It is the author's conjecture (and hope) that introducing flexibility in modeling procedures along these multiple dimensions will reduce or even eliminate the extreme discontinuities associated with risk models in crisis periods.

Efforts to deal with nonstationarity within the realm of classical time series have centered around—and foundered on—the problems of unit roots, cointegration, and structural change (Maddala and Kim 1998). Unit roots and cointegration both deal with nonstationary time series by transforming them into stationary time series. Unit root econometrics achieves stationarity by differencing, whereas the analysis of cointegrated time series depends on the discovery of a linear combination of nonstationary series which becomes stationary. Still other methods rely on fractional differencing or other methods of removing deterministic or seasonal trends. Yet all of these classically-motivated methods for dealing with nonstationarity run into the problem of structural change. The possibility of structural change means unit root processes and cointegrating relations, among other data relationships, may not persist over the entirety of an observed period of data. When estimated models fail to detect and cope with structural changes, forecasts based on those models can become completely unreliable.

Bayesian probability methods may be used to overcome the assumptions that render classical statistical analysis blind to discontinuities in market conditions. As a result, we anticipate that firms operating in risk transfer markets can remain more sensitive to shifts in the market landscape and better understand the risks which form their core business focus by adopting a Bayesian modeling regime.

The choice of a Bayesian toolkit will tempt many readers to dismiss out of hand the alternatives presented here. I will plead pragmatism and try to mollify such readers by showing the conditions under which Bayesian results converge with classical probability. These skeptical readers can then decide whether they prefer to remain within the bounds of classical time series analysis or, better yet, choose to adapt their deployments of classical time series models to remain more sensitive to weaknesses in those models. For readers who are not burdened by such preconceptions, I will be unashamed of showing where Bayesian methods allow for possibilities ruled out a priori by classical probability and statistics.

In the previous section, we identified a taxonomy of model risks, which included parameter uncertainty, model specification uncertainty, and breakdowns in forecasting performance. In other words, models can lead us to incorrect conclusions because unknown parameters are known imprecisely, because the form of the model is incorrect, or because the form of the model no longer describes the state of affairs in the marketplace. Bayesian probability is predicated on the existence and irreducibility of all of these forms of model risk, and as a result, it furnishes resources for quantifying and monitoring each of these aspects of model risk.

Accounting for Parameter and Model Uncertainty

Let's consider a basic model. Denote the data by $\{x_t\}$ (we can assume they are continuously compounded large-cap equity returns) and the unknown parameters within the model as θ. If the model were the normal distribution, for example, we would have

$$p(x_t \mid \theta) = \frac{1}{\sqrt{2\pi\sigma^2}} \exp\left[-\frac{1}{2}\frac{(x_t-\mu)^2}{\sigma^2}\right],$$

with $\theta = \{\mu, \sigma^2\}$, the unknown mean and variance of the return series. Classical statistics would treat θ as unknown constants to be found by computing sample moments from $\{x_t\}$. Any uncertainty about θ is held to arise from sampling error, which implies that uncertainty can be reduced to a negligible amount by observing ever more data.

The basic insight of Bayesian probability comes from Bayes' rule, a simple theorem about conditional probability. If we consider the joint probability of x and θ, both of the following statements are true:

$$\begin{aligned} p(x,\theta) &= p(x \mid \theta)p(\theta) \\ &= p(\theta \mid x)p(x). \end{aligned}$$

Hence, if we equate the two statements on the right-hand side with each other and rearrange, we obtain another true statement, which is Bayes' rule:

$$\begin{aligned} p(\theta \mid x)p(x) &= p(x \mid \theta)p(\theta) \\ p(\theta \mid x) &= \frac{p(x \mid \theta)p(\theta)}{p(x)}. \end{aligned}$$

Setting aside the unconditional probability of the data $p(x)$ for the time being, we have the following expression of Bayes' rule as a statement about proportionality:

$$p(\theta \mid x) \propto p(x \mid \theta)p(\theta).$$

A particular interpretation is attached to this last expression. The term on the right $p(\theta)$ is a probability distribution expressing beliefs about the value of θ before observing the data. Rather than treating θ as a set of unknown constants, uncertainty about θ is explicitly recognized by assigning a probability distribution to possible values of θ. Here, we might break $p(\theta) = p(\mu, \sigma^2)$ into $p(\mu \mid \sigma^2)\, p(\sigma^2)$. Since μ can be anywhere on the real line, an appropriate prior distribution $p(\mu \mid \sigma^2)$ could be another normal distribution with parameters μ_0 and σ_0^2. An inverse-gamma distribution is useful as a model for $p(\sigma^2)$ because it is defined on the interval $[0, \infty)$ and variance cannot be negative in a normal distribution.

At the same time $p(\theta)$ recognizes uncertainty about the values of θ, it also provides a vehicle for introducing knowledge we already have about θ. Such knowledge is 'subjective' in that it is not based on the data. But that does not mean that it is arbitrary. For a lognormal model of large-cap equity returns at daily frequency, we may believe μ is centered on zero, with some greater or lesser degree of confidence, expressed through the specification of σ_0^2. The mode for the distribution of σ^2 might be $(50\%)^2/252$.

Specifying $p(\theta)$ also places useful restrictions on the parameter space, such as requiring σ^2 to be positive, while also indicating which values for θ would be surprising. A large nonzero value for the mean of a large-cap equity return series would be surprising, as would a volatility of 5 percent or 5,000 percent. Results such as these would lead a classical statistician to question his computations, data, and methods. The information in $p(\theta)$ may be interpreted as an indication of which results would be so contrary to sense as to be nearly impossible. However $p(\theta)$ has a failsafe, since $p(\theta) > 0$ everywhere along its support; no valid value of θ can be completely excluded a priori.

Because $p(\theta)$ is determined before seeing x on the basis of nondata knowledge, it is known as the *prior distribution* for the parameters θ. The prior distribution captures knowledge obtained from sources other than the data at hand, while recognizing the provisional and imperfect nature of such knowledge.

The distribution $p(x \mid \theta)$ will be familiar to students of statistics as the *likelihood* of seeing the data x conditional on the parameters θ. Maximum-likelihood techniques search for the θ that maximizes $p(x \mid \theta)$, bypassing prior information $p(\theta)$. Working the other way around, for fixed θ the likelihood is a statement about how surprising x is. The likelihood captures the information contained in the data. Moreover, most statisticians subscribe to the *likelihood principle*, which states that *all* information in the data is captured by the likelihood.

Given these elements, Bayes' theorem tells us that the *posterior distribution* of parameter values $p(\theta \mid x)$ is proportional to the prior distribution of parameter values $p(\theta)$ times the likelihood $p(x \mid \theta)$. The posterior distribution refines the knowledge introduced by the prior distribution on the basis of information contained in the likelihood. Thus, for unknown parameters within a given statistical model, we begin and end with a probabilistic expression for the model parameters that acknowledges the uncertainty of our knowledge about the parameters. We know before and after seeing the data what degree of uncertainty applies to our parameter estimates. If the data are consistent with our prior estimates, the location of the parameters will be little changed and the variance of the posterior distribution will shrink. If the data are surprising given our prior estimates, the variance will increase and the location will migrate. In Chapter 2, we explore the consequences of introducing prior information in this way, and compare the Bayesian approach to classical methods for handing prior information via hypothesis tests.

Now consider alternative model specifications. Instead of x and θ, we could just as easily consider (formally) the joint probability of x and M_i, where M_i is a candidate model specification:

$$p(M_i \mid x) \propto p(x \mid M_i)p(M_i)$$

The notation suppresses θ, but that is not to say that $p(\theta)$ and $p(\theta \mid x)$ do not matter to the determination of model probabilities. We defer dealing with these subtleties for now.

The explicit recognition of multiple models with competing claims to being true on the basis of the data is in sharp contrast to classical statistical practice, which merely permits the acceptance or rejection of individual model specifications against unspecified alternatives, or as hypothesis tests within the context of an encompassing model. If the idea of attaching numeric probabilities to models seems unnatural, think of the probabilities as expressions of the odds model i is a better representation of the data than model j, $p(M_i)/p(M_j)$, subject to the constraint $\sum_i p(M_i) = 1$.

Just as in the specification of $p(\theta)$, $p(M_i)$ for each model i expresses existing beliefs about the adequacy of different models, which recognizes uncertainty about the best representation of the data-generation process. The axioms of probability ensure that $p(M_i) > 0$ for any model within the set of models being considered. On the other hand, closure of the set of models is not as straightforward as closure of the set of possible parameter values: We implicitly set $p(M_i) \equiv 0$ for any model not entertained. However, efforts to close the set of models are neither possible nor practical.

Posterior model probabilities are updated on the basis of the data from their prior values, also as in the case of prior and posterior parameter distributions. As a result, the adequacy of the model is explicitly evaluated on the basis of the available data, relative to the adequacy of other models. Further, with the aid of posterior model probabilities, an expectation may be computed over an ensemble of models, so that forecasts need not depend exclusively on a particular specification. Instead of assuming stationarity, a Bayesian approach with multiple models admits the possibility that a variety of data-generating processes—all of which are known only approximately—may be responsible for current observations. The manner in which Bayesian probability accounts for uncertainty about data-generating processes is discussed at greater length in Chapter 3.

Responding to Changes in the Market Environment

The passage from prior to posterior probability via the likelihood suggests a sequential approach to modeling in which inferences are progressively updated as more data are observed. Sequential model implementation in turn suggests a means of coping with the third aspect of model risk, the risk of discontinuity. Part Two of the book is concerned with extending the Bayesian framework for handling parameter and model uncertainty to a dynamic form, which allows for ongoing monitoring and updating. The goal of Part Two is to construct adaptive models that remain sensitive to anomalous data and learn from their forecasting mistakes, and to identify metrics that will show the evolution of parameter and model uncertainty as new data are encountered.

With the construction of adaptive models, our approach to modeling financial time series switches from the *batch analysis* perspective of classical time series to an *online* perspective that updates inferences each time new data are observed. The shift in perspective is essential to abandoning the assumption of a time-invariant data-generation process. When we model a financial time series with classical methods, time series data are batched without knowing if the same process generated all of the data. If transitions between processes go undetected, the time series model will average parameter values on either side of the transition, glossing over the change in the process. The resulting model would not have produced valid forecasts on either side of the transition, and its ability to forecast out-of-sample would be anyone's guess.

The primary obstacle to making Bayesian analysis sequential is its own tendency in the face of accumulating data to reproduce the *ignorant certainty* inherent in classical statistics. If all observed data are regarded as being sampled from the same data-generation process, the relative weight on the likelihood converges to unity, while the weight on the prior goes to zero. Asymptotically, Bayesian estimates are equivalent to maximum-likelihood estimates unless we explicitly recognize the possibility that current observations are not sampled from the same process as past observations. The technique of discounting, introduced in Chapter 4, ensures that current observations have a greater role in reevaluating parameter distributions and model probabilities than the accumulated weight of observations in the distant past.

Discounting past data is already common practice and is implemented in standard risk management software. When new data enter the observation window, models are recalibrated on the reweighted data set. However, reweighting the data introduces new problems and does not nullify the problems associated with recalibration. First, the weight that current data deserve relative to past data cannot be specified a priori. Efforts to estimate "optimal" discount rates via maximum likelihood are once again misguided, because the result will be sensitive to the data set and may paper over important differences. Second and more important, model recalibration fails to carry any useful information about parameters or models from one date to the next. The results from previous calibrations are simply thrown away and replaced with new ones. Often, the result is that model parameters jump discontinuously from one value to another.

In Chapters 5 and 6, dynamic state-space models are introduced as a means of carrying inferences through time without the profligate waste of information imposed by recalibration. Dynamic models thus allow discounting to take place without erasing what has been learned from earlier data. Indexing models by alternative discount rates then allows for uncertainty about discount rates to be handled through the computation of posterior model probabilities. When the world looks more like a long-run average, models that give less relative weight to current data should be preferred, whereas models that forget the past more rapidly will be preferred in times of rapid change.

TIME-INVARIANCE AND OBJECTIVITY

Bayesian methods view probability as a degree of justified belief, whereas classical methods define probability as frequency, or the expected number of outcomes given a large number of repetitions. Classical statisticians trumpet the "objectivity" of their approach against the "subjectivity" of Bayesians, who speak unabashedly about belief, rather than "letting the data speak." So-called objective Bayesians aim to split the difference by using *uninformative priors,* which have minimal influence on inferences, though disagreements exist about which priors are truly uninformative. To the extent that classical statisticians will arrive at the same result if they apply the same protocol, their process is "objective."

However, it is rarely the case that everyone with access to the same data draws the same conclusion from it—they test different hypotheses, use different models, and weigh the results against other knowledge (justified belief?) before coming to a (provisional) conclusion. Bayesian probability makes these subjective prior commitments explicit and produces an outcome which weighs the prior commitment and the data in a completely transparent way. Two Bayesians applying the same prior and model to the same data will arrive at the same result. So is the Bayesian process "subjective" because it makes a summary of non-data-based knowledge explicit, whereas "objective" statistics leave such things unstated?

Given an unlimited amount of data, any prior belief expressed by a Bayesian will be swamped by the evidence—the relative weight accorded to the prior belief goes to zero. Hence, from the point of view of Bayesian probability, objectivity is a kind of limit result that is only possible under the strong assumption of unlimited data drawn from a time-invariant data-generating process. In the realm of classical time series analysis, objectivity requires stationarity, as well as a possibly unlimited amount of time to permit ergodicity (the law of large numbers) to take hold. We should be wary of a protocol that requires everyone to ignore the possibility that the world does not accord with our modeling assumptions, and to suspend our disbelief about short-term results in the faith that in the limit, our measurements of relative frequency will be correct. If accounting for these possibilities introduces subjectivity, then so be it.

Dispersion in prior probabilities is the essence of trading and entrepreneurship. New trading ideas and new ventures do not get under way without a strong prior belief that something is the case within a market. These ideas and ventures are new and entrepreneurial precisely because they are out of sync with what is generally accepted. Different prior probabilities will most certainly generate different posterior probabilities, particularly when data are scarce, and when decisions are being made on the basis of posterior probabilities, dispersion in beliefs will generate dispersion in actions. Competition and speculation both depend on the heterogeneity of opinions and actions.

A protocol that encourages market participants to agree on "objective" estimates and take identical actions in response to those estimates enforces homogeneity, crowding, and ossification (Chincarini 2012). Multiple firms acting on the same "objective" conclusion from the same data herd into markets pursuing the same value proposition. Consider the universe of statistical arbitrage hedge funds that mine the CRSP and Compustat databases—among other standard data sources—to discover asset-pricing anomalies and build "riskless" portfolios to exploit them. Starting from the same data and the same set of models, they should buy and sell the same universes of securities in pursuit of value. When results break down, as they did in August 2007, it is impossible for all traders to obtain liquidity at a reasonable price, and an entire segment of the asset management industry can get crushed at once (Khandani and Lo 2007, Section 10). Objectivity does not lead to robustness at a systemic level, and objective statistics cannot generate competition or support new ideas, so their enduring value within the financial firm is circumscribed, at best.

It is also striking, on deeper examination, how "objective" statistical practice buries subjective elements deep within methodology as *ad hoc* choices and rationalizing simplifications. So-called objective classical statistics not only rely on the dogma of uniform data-generation processes already discussed; they also enforce certain beliefs about nondata knowledge and loss functions about which most people would express different views, if they were free to do so.

We already know that risk is subjective. Different people have different risk tolerances, and their willingness to bear risk depends crucially on their relative knowledge endowments. Thus, if the goal of a risk specialist firm is to identify and exploit a particular opportunity within the universe of financial risks, a modeling framework that provides a vehicle for that firm's particular knowledge is to be greatly preferred to a modeling framework that enforces the same conclusions on all users. On the other hand, if a firm, its management, and its regulators are eager to follow the herd, even if it means going over the precipice, they are welcome to take refuge in the "objective" of their conclusions.

PART
One

Capturing Uncertainty in Statistical Models

CHAPTER 2

Prior Knowledge, Parameter Uncertainty, and Estimation

Bayesian probability treats data as known conditioning information and the unknown parameters of statistical models as probability distributions. Classical statistics follows the opposite approach, treating data as random samples from a population distribution and parameters as constants known up to sampling error. While Bayesian probability regards parameter uncertainty as irreducible, classical statistics generally ignores sampling error in estimates after any interesting hypothesis tests have been conducted. An important dimension of model risk is therefore lost in the classical approach.

Bayesian parameter estimates are also distinguished by the incorporation of prior information about parameter values via a prior probability distribution. Prior information is also important for classical statistics, though it is introduced through hypothesis tests rather than prior distributions. To compare the handling of prior knowledge in the two approaches, we must examine the process of hypothesis testing closely. We will show that classical hypothesis tests are inadequate vehicles for introducing useful prior knowledge, and that their neglect of prior knowledge leads to inconsistent decisions and uncontrolled error rates. Thus, not only are classical estimates misleading as to their precision and reliability, they also fail to carry as much information as their Bayesian counterparts.

The problem of hypothesis testing also yields some initial insight into the model selection problem. Since model selection is typically framed as a matter of reducing an "encompassing" model through a series of individual hypothesis tests, subject to assumptions on the collinearity of the regressors, any weaknesses in hypothesis testing will impact model selection. The irreducibility of parameter uncertainty thus leads to a first source of model uncertainty. Other dimensions of model uncertainty will be discussed in Chapter 3.

ESTIMATION WITH PRIOR KNOWLEDGE: THE BETA-BERNOULLI MODEL

We saw in Chapter 1 that the hallmark of the Bayesian approach is a posterior distribution of parameter values that combines likelihood information with prior information. Classical statistics, on the other hand, has developed a variety of different estimators that depend solely on the data. Where explicit formulations of the likelihood are possible, maximum-likelihood estimators find optimal choices for parameter values given a sample of data. Least squares estimation follows a similar optimization approach in minimizing the sum of squared residuals for a chosen model. The generalized method of moments (GMM) estimator finds the best approximation to a moment condition whenever instrumental variables are used to deal with endogeneity. In all cases, prior information is not brought to bear until the hypothesis testing stage.

To draw out the contrast between the Bayesian approach and classical statistics, we begin with a very simple estimation setting in which the data are generated by Bernoulli trials. In such a simple setting, maximum likelihood is a natural choice to represent the classical statistical approach (Hendry and Nielsen 2007).

In a Bernoulli trial, two outcomes are possible for a given observation: success or failure. Denoting success as 1 and failure as 0, for a trial x_i we have $x_i \in \{0, 1\}$. Success occurs with probability s, implying that failure occurs with probability $1 - s$. We observe n trials, from which we count $x = \sum_i x_i$ successes.

The probability of seeing an observation x_i conditional on the success probability s is

$$p(x_i \mid s) = s^{x_i}(1 - s)^{1-x_i}$$

which is equal to s when $x_i = 1$ and $1 - s$ when $x_i = 0$. Assuming n trials are sampled independently from an identical distribution, the likelihood of seeing $x = \sum_i x_i$ successes in n trials is given by

$$L(x \mid n, s) = \prod_{i=1}^{n} p(x_i \mid s) = \prod_{i=1}^{n} s^{x_i}(1 - s)^{1-x_i} = s^{\sum x_i}(1 - s)^{n-\sum x_i} = s^{x}(1 - s)^{n-x}.$$

This result for the joint likelihood of n trials is known as the binomial distribution with parameter s. The independence assumption allows us to work with products that aren't conditioned on the other observations. Assuming that samples are drawn from an identical distribution ensures that the form of the likelihood and the parameters are common to all of the observations.

Note, finally, that we have explicitly conditioned the number of successes observed on the number of trials and the success probability.

The maximum-likelihood approach of classical statistics finds s by differentiating the expression for the likelihood:

$$\frac{\partial L(x \mid n, s)}{\partial s} = xs^{x-1}(1-s)^{n-x} - s^x(n-x)(1-s)^{n-x-1} = 0$$

$$xs^{x-1}(1-s)^{n-x} = s^x(n-x)(1-s)^{n-x-1}$$

$$x(1-s) = s(n-x)$$

$$x - sx = sn - sx$$

$$s = \hat{s}_{ML} = \frac{x}{n} = \frac{\sum x_i}{n}$$

The calculation follows the usual approach of maximizing by setting the first-order derivative to zero. The third line follows from the second by canceling common terms under the exponent.

The maximum-likelihood estimate $\hat{s}_{ML} = \frac{x}{n}$ is the empirical rate of successes seen in the data. Since parameter uncertainty arises in classical statistics as a result of sampling, evaluating parameter uncertainty requires solving for the sampling variance, $Var(\hat{s}_{ML})$:

$$Var\left(\frac{x}{n}\right) = n^{-2} \cdot Var(x) = n^{-2} \cdot \sum_n Var(x_i) = n^{-1} \cdot Var(x_i)$$

$$Var\left(\frac{x}{n}\right) = \frac{\hat{s}_{ML}(1-\hat{s}_{ML})}{n}$$

which goes to zero as n increases without limit. The last equality in the first line again uses the i.i.d. assumption to conclude

$$\sum_n Var(x_i) = n \cdot Var(x_i).$$

Encoding Prior Knowledge in the Beta-Bernoulli Model

Now suppose that we already have some beliefs about the value of s. We know s must be between 0 and 1. So let's imagine we believe s is about 0.3, and we have as much conviction about our guess as if we had seen 100 Bernoulli trials with 30 successes before the current set of trials.

Bayesian probability represents prior beliefs about parameters such as s through probability distributions. In this case, our prior knowledge can be encoded in the form of the beta distribution, which is defined on the interval [0, 1] and which has two parameters that control the location and scale of the distribution. The beta distribution (Johnson, Kotz, and Balakrishnan [JKB] 1995, p. 210) is given by

$$B(x \mid a, b) = \frac{\Gamma(a+b)}{\Gamma(a)\Gamma(b)} x^{a-1}(1-x)^{b-1}$$

Note the similarity of the beta distribution to the binomial distribution. In fact the beta distribution is the integral of the binomial likelihood with some slight reparameterization (JKB 1995, p. 211). The terms in front expressed as gamma functions are a normalizing constant that ensures $\int_0^1 B(x \mid a, b)dx = 1$.

We would like to set the prior parameters so that $E(x) = 0.3$, our prior estimate of s. The mean of $B(x \mid a, b)$ is $\frac{a}{a+b}$ (JKB 1995, p. 217). Comparing this expression with $\hat{s}_{ML} = \frac{x}{n}$ suggests that a plays the same role as x in counting successes, whereas $a + b$ captures the number of trials n. Since $n = x + (n - x)$ and a is analogous to x, we can interpret b as $n - x$ or the number of failures. Thus, for 100 observations, $a = 30$ and $b = 100 - 30 = 70$.

Clearly, any scale multiple of a and b will lead to the same mean. If we wanted to express our prior knowledge with less conviction, we could choose values that imply a small number of observations, such as $\{a, b\} = \{3, 7\}$ or $\{15, 35\}$. If we were more certain, we could choose $\{a, b\} = \{90, 210\}$. These choices also have consequences for the variance of the beta distribution, which is equal to (JKB 1995, p. 217)

$$\frac{ab}{(a+b)^2(a+b+1)}.$$

Thus, choosing $\{a, b\} = \{3, 7\}$ implies a variance around the mean of 0.0191, or a standard deviation of 0.138, while $\{a, b\} = \{90, 210\}$ implies a standard deviation of only 0.026. Our chosen parameters $\{a, b\} = \{30, 70\}$ imply a standard deviation of 0.046. For the beta distribution, it is evident that the equivalent sample size also determines the variance.

We now have a probability distribution that summarizes our prior knowledge about the success probability s, or $p(\theta)$. In this case it is a beta distribution with $a = 30$ and $b = 70$, or B(30,70). We also have the expression derived previously for the likelihood of seeing different realizations of Bernoulli trial data $p(x \mid \theta)$. For a Bayesian estimate conditional on the data, we want to find $p(\theta \mid x)$, the posterior distribution of the parameters after seeing the data. Recalling Bayes' rule,

$$p(\theta \mid x) \propto p(x \mid \theta)p(\theta)$$

where the proportionality sign $\propto$ means we can ignore normalizing constants, since proportionality is equality up to a constant. Thus, we can write

$$\begin{aligned} p(\theta \mid x) &\propto s^x(1-s)^{n-x}\bar{s}^{a-1}(1-\bar{s})^{b-1} \\ &\propto s^{x+a-1}(1-s)^{n-x+b-1} \\ &\propto \mathrm{B}(x+a, n-x+b) \\ &\propto \mathrm{B}(A, B) \end{aligned}$$

In the first line, we changed the parameter of the prior distribution to $\bar{s}$ in order to emphasize that the prior distribution is modeling the same variable as the likelihood. The overbar tracks its origin from the prior distribution. We drop the distinction and the overbar in the second line and combine exponents. The transition from the second line to the third line notes that our result is in the form of another beta distribution, whereas the fourth line rewrites the parameters of the posterior beta distribution as $A = a + x$ and $B = b + (n - x)$. Clearly, we could reintroduce the normalizing constant as

$$\frac{\Gamma(A+B)}{\Gamma(A)\Gamma(B)}$$

to turn the proportionality sign into an equality.

Impact of the Prior on the Posterior Distribution

Because the posterior distribution for the Bernoulli inference problem is a beta distribution, its expected value is

$$\frac{A}{A+B} = \frac{a+x}{a+x+b+(n-x)} = \frac{a+x}{a+b+n} = \frac{a}{a+b+n} + \frac{x}{a+b+n}.$$

The last step shows that the mean of the posterior distribution is a weighted combination of the prior success count a and the success count observed in the data $x = \sum_i x_i$. The relative weights of a and x in the mean depend on how large n is relative to $a + b$, the data-equivalent weight of the prior distribution. As n becomes large relative to $a + b$, the mean is increasingly determined by the maximum-likelihood estimate $\hat{s}_{ML} = \frac{x}{n}$. For large n, the quantity $\frac{a}{a+b+n}$ will go to zero, whereas $\frac{x}{a+b+n}$ will approach $\frac{x}{n}$, the maximum-likelihood estimate. Alternatively, if we expressed a high degree of conviction in our prior distribution with a large value of $a + b$, the mean will be more completely determined by $\frac{a}{a+b}$.

When does the mean Bayesian estimate of s coincide with the "objective" maximum-likelihood result? Putting $a = b = 0$ gives no data-equivalent weight to the prior and ensures that $\hat{s} = \hat{s}_{ML} = \frac{x}{n}$. With $a = b = 0$ the prior beta distribution is degenerate, with undefined mean and infinite variance. Because the distribution is degenerate, it is an *improper* prior; because the distribution supplies no information about s, it is also an *uninformative* prior (Bernardo and Smith 2000, pp. 357–367). Nevertheless, the statement $p(\theta \mid x) \propto p(x \mid \theta)p(\theta)$ is still true, whether $p(\theta)$ is informative or not. So-called objective Bayesians prefer uninformative prior distributions because they allow the apparatus of Bayesian probability to be used consistently without introducing information from sources other than the data. For our purposes, we note that the mean of the posterior distribution of a parameter will coincide with its maximum-likelihood estimate only when we begin from a state of complete ignorance about the parameters of interest.

However, it is important to emphasize that even when we begin from an improper, uninformative prior we still arrive at a posterior distribution for the parameter of interest, rather than a point estimate. To the extent that classical statistics makes no use of information other than the mode of the distribution, information about the uncertainty of the estimate is lost due to the conviction that the uncertainty reliably and quickly approaches zero.

Shrinkage and Bias Though we have developed the concepts in a deliberately simple probability setting, the previous results are completely general for Bayesian inference. Bayesian parameter estimates will always be a weighted combination of prior knowledge and the data, or, more precisely, a weighted combination of prior knowledge and the information contained in the likelihood function. The analyst has control over how these elements are weighted, as well as how prior knowledge is encoded.

Because of the weighted-average quality of the posterior distribution, Bayesian estimates are said to exhibit *shrinkage,* owing to the fact that the maximum-likelihood estimators are "shrunk" toward the mode of the prior distribution. (Some authors use the term *shrinkage* only in connection with a prior estimate of zero.) From a classical point of view, shrinkage estimators are subjective and biased, two very bad words in science and in the vernacular. In particular, classical statisticians fear that unscrupulous investigators will use the prior distribution to steer results to a desired outcome. In this sense, the data speak for themselves in the classical framework because there is no outside influence in one direction or the other. We let the data speak for themselves in an "objective Bayesian" context by using an uninformative prior. The absence of outside information gets a nice designation: the property of being unbiased.

However much we like an absence of bias, the statistical property of being unbiased does not come without costs. One cost of "unbiased" estimates is the loss of efficiency, meaning that the likelihood is less peaked at the mode of the parameter sampling distribution than at the mode of the posterior distribution. Suppose we observed only 10 Bernoulli trials, in which there were three successes. If we had existing information that suggested $s \approx 0.3$, the posterior distribution for s would be more peaked in the Bayesian case than in the maximum-likelihood case. The maximum-likelihood estimate would indeed be $\hat{s}_{ML} = 3/10 = 0.3$ and its sampling distribution would have a standard deviation of $\sqrt{3 \cdot 7}/\sqrt{10} = 1.449$. If instead we had relied on our prior B(30,70), the mean of the posterior distribution would be the same as the maximum-likelihood estimate, but with a standard deviation of $\sqrt{33 \cdot 77}/\sqrt{(110)^2(111)} = 0.043$. Clearly, if good prior knowledge is available, it can vastly increase the efficiency of estimates.

One must also consider the yardstick by which an estimator is deemed to be unbiased. An unbiased estimator will, on average, be equal to its theoretical value as specified by the probability model. If there is any doubt about the form of the likelihood, convergence to the theoretical value won't necessarily result in an optimal estimate. The unbiased estimate is only optimal if the probability model is correct. In certain contexts, prior knowledge can offer some quality control against the risk of a misspecified model, particularly when an empirical interpretation can be attached to a parameter value, as is often the case in finance.

The charge of manipulation is a serious one. Without a doubt, one can manipulate results by changing a prior. Had we used $B(3 \times 10^6, 7 \times 10^6)$ as our prior distribution, even 10,000 observations with $x = 9000$ would have very little influence on the outcome. But a prior may be exposed to criticism every bit as much as the posterior result. One who routinely uses farfetched or tendentious priors will draw faulty conclusions and lose credibility every bit as much as one who produces incorrect results or dogmatically refuses to consider the data. What is gained in every case is an explicit representation of what is taken to be true at the outset, or a disclosure of existing belief (or, if you like, bias) in an extremely straightforward way. Compare the Bayesian procedure to, say, the decision to exclude certain influential observations as outliers on the grounds that they are at odds with "more sensible results," or to reject a model because estimates have "the wrong sign."

Efficiency The second key result of the previous example is that maximum-likelihood estimators are the most efficient estimator only if no prior knowledge is available, or if prior knowledge is entirely uninformative. As such, an inferential framework that is built exclusively on maximum likelihood is the most wasteful framework possible whenever data are scarce. Data are used up reestablishing knowledge that could have been introduced at the outset through the prior distribution. In the previous example, we would have needed 11 times as much data to arrive at the same results as when prior knowledge was incorporated. Indeed, if it is even a possibility that data of interest may be relatively scarce or costly to collect one would benefit from using prior knowledge to improve the efficiency of estimators.

The gain in efficiency afforded by the prior distribution will be particularly important to us later in the development when we begin to discuss sequential estimation and learning. Sequential estimation maintains its ability to adapt to new data by operating with a relatively small equivalent sample size at all times. Thus, in a sequential setting, the challenge of effectively employing prior knowledge becomes a problem of managing the trade-off between the efficiency gain afforded by relevant prior knowledge, and the tendency of accumulated prior knowledge to drown out the information contained in more recent data. The alternative to sequential analysis is periodic recalibration on small (possibly reweighted) data sets, which coincides with the relatively inefficient maximum-likelihood case. Because recalibration throws away information that could be used in forming an efficiency-enhancing prior, it uses new information less effectively than a sequential Bayesian model does.

The last point can be further appreciated by considering a few examples in which we vary the quality of the prior knowledge and the number of equivalent observations. Three sets of data are simulated for which the success probability is varied from 0.3 to 0.5 to 0.7. Each data set contains 1000 observations. The prior estimate of success probability is likewise varied from 0.3 to 0.5 to 0.7, with equivalent sample sizes of 100, 1000, and 2000. As a result, we can easily see the consequences of whether prior knowledge is in accord with the data, as well as the impact of different relative weights for prior knowledge. The sampling distribution of the maximum-likelihood estimator is also computed for comparison.

Figure 2.1 plots the results for a simulated data set with $s = 0.3$. The nine panels in the figure are arranged so that the equivalent sample size for the prior distribution increases from left to right, whereas the mean of the prior distribution increases from top to bottom. We can see that in instances where the prior mean agrees with the data (top row), the posterior distribution is narrower and more peaked around the mean value than the maximum-likelihood estimator. Perhaps surprisingly, this is also true when the prior mean does not coincide with the data. This reflects both the weight given to prior information as well as the information gained by restricting the parameter space to $[0, 1]$. Similar results are seen in Figure 2.2, which uses a simulated data set with $s = 0.5$, and Figure 2.3, which uses data with $s = 0.7$.

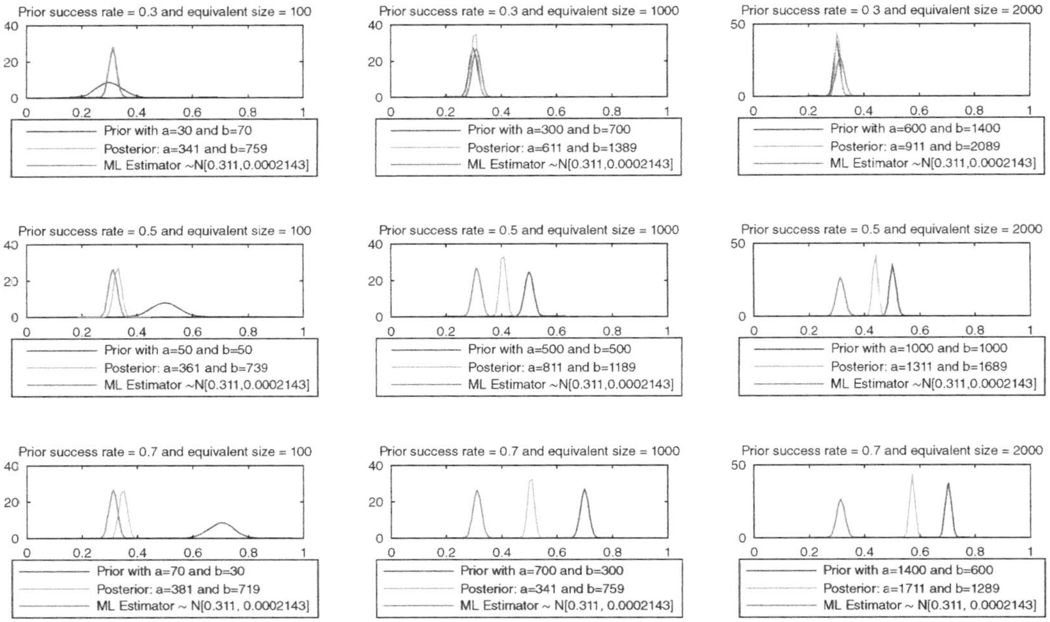

FIGURE 2.1 Posterior Distribution of Success Probability: Random Data with $s = 0.3$

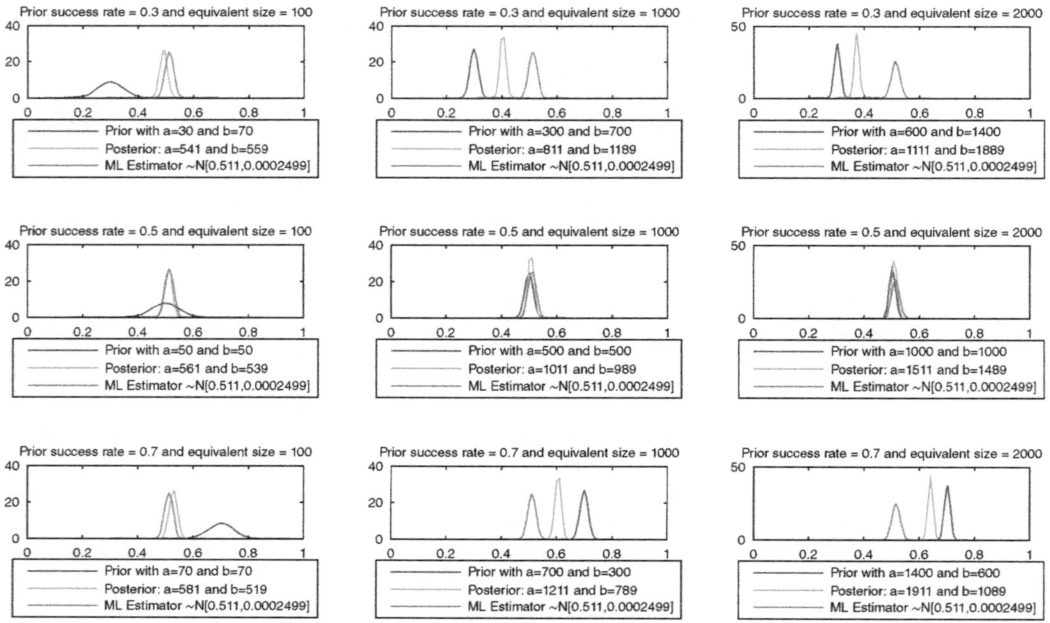

FIGURE 2.2 Posterior Distribution of Success Probability: Random Data with $s = 0.5$

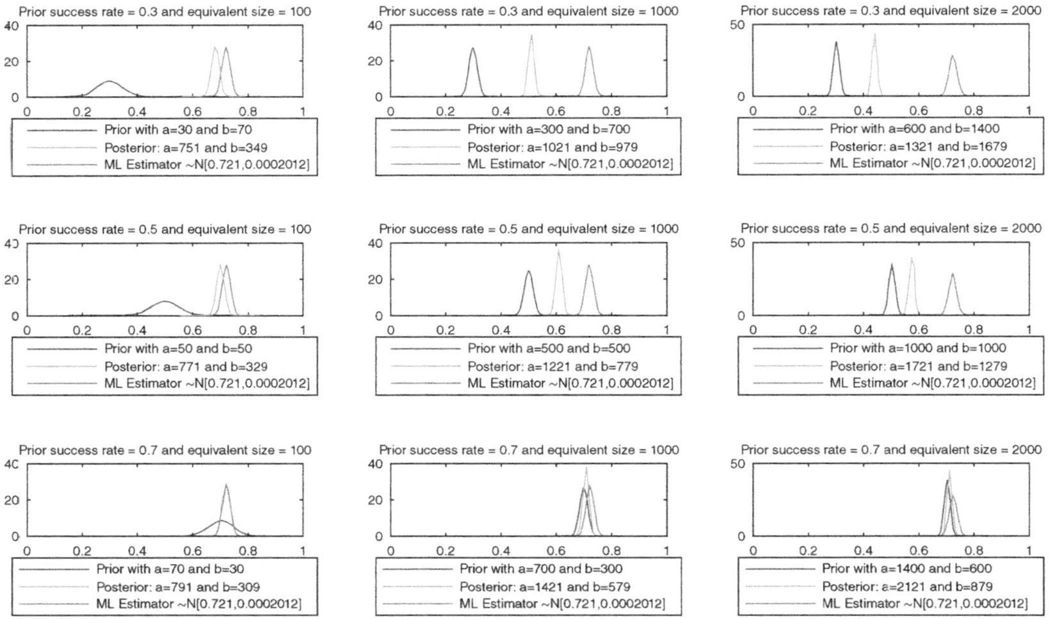

FIGURE 2.3 Posterior Distribution of Success Probability: Random Data with $s = 0.7$

Posterior estimates clearly gravitate away from maximum-likelihood estimates when prior and likelihood information are at odds with each other, and more so when greater weight is given to the prior. Whether this is a problem is a question we will explore at the end of the chapter.

Hyperparameters and Sufficient Statistics

A further point can be made from the Bernoulli trial example. Once we hit on the beta distribution representation of the parameters, all of the relevant information about the prior distribution was contained in the choice of the parameters a and b. Likewise, when given the form of the likelihood, all of the relevant information was contained in n and $\sum x_i = x$. Special names are given to these situations where a few quantities exhaust all the available information. In the case of the likelihood, n and x are called sufficient statistics. So long as we know n and x following a run of Bernoulli trials, we know everything we need to know about the data to evaluate the likelihood. Someone could, for example, tell us the exact order in which the trials came out, but that would not change $\sum x_i = x$. As a result, the order of the x_i would not change the conclusions that we draw from the data about s, whether we use the maximum-likelihood estimator $\hat{s}_{ML} = \frac{x}{n}$ or the Bayesian analogue $\frac{a+x}{a+b+n}$. In fact we can throw out the complete set of information $\{x_1, \ldots, x_n\}$ *without loss* so long as we retain the sufficient statistics n and x. Not all likelihoods have low-dimension sufficient statistics, so it is often the case that the sufficient statistics comprise the entire data set. In these situations ongoing storage of the data set is necessary. However, many parametric likelihoods admit sufficient statistics.

Similarly, a and b completely parameterize and uniquely define a probability distribution $p(\theta) = \mathrm{B}(a, b)$. As parameters that control parameters, a and b are commonly called *hyperparameters*. Hyperparameters stand in the same relation to the prior distribution as sufficient statistics stand with respect to the likelihood. They, too, provide for a concise, low-dimensional, and exhaustive specification of the distribution of prior parameter estimates.

Our result for the posterior was a beta distribution $\mathrm{B}(A, B)$ with new parameters $A = a + x$ and $B = b + (n - x)$. Thus, our update of $\mathrm{B}(a, b)$ to $\mathrm{B}(A, B)$ is determined by a simple operation involving the combination of hyperparameters and sufficient statistics. We can therefore call a and b the prior hyperparameters and A and B the posterior hyperparameters. One updates the prior hyperparameters with sufficient statistics to obtain posterior hyperparameters. Because of the properties of sufficient statistics, no information is lost in updating.

The ability of hyperparameters to absorb information from data into a low-dimensional vector permits efficient transmission of information from one instance of observed data to the next. Hence they, too, are key to maintaining efficiency in a sequential setting. Hyperparameters also give us a reason to strongly favor parametric models over nonparametric alternatives, which offer no corresponding reduction of dimension or complexity.

Conjugate Prior Families

Finally, we were able to deal with our Bernoulli trial data using sufficient statistics and hyperparameters because our prior distribution and likelihood had forms that resulted in a known probability distribution for the posterior. In this case, the posterior distribution was in the same class of distributions as the prior, since both are beta distributions. Thus, for Bernoulli likelihoods, beta distributions provide a *conjugate prior*. With a conjugate prior distribution, the posterior lies in the same class and updates can be made using hyperparameters and sufficient statistics. Conjugacy also aids in the interpretation of prior distributions in terms of data-equivalence (Bernardo and Smith 2000, pp. 269–279).

Not all likelihoods have conjugate prior distributions, but it is clear that calculations are incredibly convenient for those likelihoods that do. Bayesian inference can proceed without conjugacy, but it will require changes of tactics to be discussed later.

PRIOR PARAMETER DISTRIBUTIONS AS HYPOTHESES: THE NORMAL LINEAR REGRESSION MODEL

Classical statistical practice seeks to incorporate an analyst's prior information as a maintained or null hypothesis. Once formulated, the maintained hypothesis is tested against the data and a test statistic is computed. If the test statistic exceeds a certain critical level, the null hypothesis is rejected in favor of an alternative hypothesis that is the logical complement of the null. If the null hypothesis is $\beta = 0$, for example, the alternative is $\beta \neq 0$. Otherwise one *fails to reject* the maintained hypothesis. Hypothesis testing thus takes an all-or-nothing stance against prior knowledge: The null hypothesis either lives to fight another day or is declared wrong and discarded. Hypothesis tests also ask an overly narrow question. If we fail to reject our null hypothesis $\beta = 0$ on the basis of the data, are there other null hypotheses we might equally well fail to reject? If the null hypothesis *is* rejected, on the other hand, what value of β should be maintained afterward?

In business situations, hypothesis testing generally takes a back seat to estimation when statistical models are used, and those hypotheses that are tested are usually of the $\beta = 0$ variety. In fact, most hypothesis tests are likely conducted out of view by automated model-selection procedures like forward or backward regression and their related counterparts. Even so, there are reasons to keep the prior knowledge implied by hypothesis tests in view. If one fails to reject $\beta = 0$, one might also fail to reject $\beta = 0.05$ or $\beta = -0.05$. Adopting one or the other for decision-making purposes may have a meaningful impact. It may also be wise to reserve judgment while gathering more data.

Further, given an alternative means of expressing prior knowledge, practitioners may develop greater interest in testing their beliefs than what is practiced within the ground rules of classical statistics. Someone who is uncomfortable asserting that parameters take on a certain value may be more at ease expressing his beliefs as a range. Hence, the relative absence of hypothesis testing from common practice doesn't imply it is not useful; in fact, the implication may be that it is *not useful enough* in the form it has been given by classical statistics.

Since there are compelling reasons to evaluate and reevaluate prior information about model estimates, we must address the question of whether prior information is better handled within the classical hypothesis testing framework or by the explicit specification of prior parameter distributions. Since linear regression is perhaps the most familiar setting for hypothesis testing, we introduce the ordinary least squares and Bayesian analyses of the normal linear regression model. Besides being extremely useful for other applications in the book, the derivations allow us to compare classical and Bayesian properties on equal analytical footing. After comparing the two approaches, we bring out the ways in which the Bayesian analysis maintains continuity with the prior information, and what priors would have to look like in order to preserve classical conclusions intact.

Classical Analysis of the Normal Linear Regression Model

In order to specify hypothesis tests of coefficients in the normal linear regression model, we need to derive an estimator for the coefficients and their sampling distributions. Following these derivations, we walk through the construction of test statistics from the estimation output and the decisions that follow from them.

Estimation Derivation of a classical estimator $\hat{\beta}_{ML}$ is easiest from the perspective of ordinary least squares, which can be shown to coincide with the maximum-likelihood result obtained directly from the likelihood function (Hayashi 2000). For n observations and k regressors (one of which may be a vector of ones), define y as an $n \times 1$ vector, X as an $n \times k$ matrix in which there are k regressors observed for each y, $\boldsymbol{\beta}$ as a $k \times 1$ vector, and $\boldsymbol{\varepsilon}$ as the $n \times 1$ error vector. Then, of course,

$$\mathrm{y} = \mathrm{X}\boldsymbol{\beta} + \boldsymbol{\varepsilon}$$

with $E[\boldsymbol{\varepsilon}] = 0$ and $E(\boldsymbol{\varepsilon}\boldsymbol{\varepsilon}') = \sigma^2 I_n$, so that $\boldsymbol{\varepsilon} \sim N[0, \sigma^2 I_n]$. The expression I_n is the n-dimensional identity matrix.

We want to minimize the sum of squared errors,

$$\boldsymbol{\varepsilon}'\boldsymbol{\varepsilon} = (\mathrm{y} - \mathrm{X}\boldsymbol{\beta})'(\mathrm{y} - \mathrm{X}\boldsymbol{\beta}).$$

Since our decision variable is $\boldsymbol{\beta}$, we find the first derivative with respect to $\boldsymbol{\beta}$ and set it equal to zero:

$$\begin{aligned}
ESS &= \boldsymbol{\varepsilon}'\boldsymbol{\varepsilon} = (\mathrm{y} - \mathrm{X}\hat{\boldsymbol{\beta}})'(\mathrm{y} - \mathrm{X}\hat{\boldsymbol{\beta}}) = \mathrm{y}'\mathrm{y} - 2\hat{\boldsymbol{\beta}}\mathrm{X}'\mathrm{y} + \hat{\boldsymbol{\beta}}'\mathrm{X}'\mathrm{X}\hat{\boldsymbol{\beta}} \\
\frac{\delta ESS}{\delta \hat{\boldsymbol{\beta}}} &= -2\mathrm{X}'\mathrm{y} + 2\mathrm{X}'\mathrm{X}\hat{\boldsymbol{\beta}} = 0 \\
\mathrm{X}'\mathrm{X}\hat{\boldsymbol{\beta}} &= \mathrm{X}'\mathrm{y} \\
\hat{\boldsymbol{\beta}}_{ML} &= (\mathrm{X}'\mathrm{X})^{-1}\mathrm{X}'\mathrm{y} = \mathrm{var}(\mathrm{X})^{-1}\mathrm{cov}(\mathrm{X}, \mathrm{y}).
\end{aligned}$$

In order to test hypotheses about $\hat{\boldsymbol{\beta}}_{ML}$ the classical approach requires that we find the sampling distribution to quantify how much $\hat{\boldsymbol{\beta}}_{ML}$ could wander from the estimate we have just obtained, in the event that another sample of size n were taken for y and X. Writing $\boldsymbol{\beta}$ for the "true" value of the coefficient vector, the deviation of the maximum-likelihood estimate from its true value is

$$\begin{aligned}
\hat{\boldsymbol{\beta}}_{ML} - \boldsymbol{\beta} &= (\mathrm{X}'\mathrm{X})^{-1}\mathrm{X}'\mathrm{y} - \boldsymbol{\beta} \\
&= (\mathrm{X}'\mathrm{X})^{-1}\mathrm{X}'(\mathrm{X}\boldsymbol{\beta} + \boldsymbol{\varepsilon}) - \boldsymbol{\beta} \\
&= (\mathrm{X}'\mathrm{X})^{-1}\mathrm{X}'\mathrm{X}\boldsymbol{\beta} + (\mathrm{X}'\mathrm{X})^{-1}\mathrm{X}'\boldsymbol{\varepsilon} - \boldsymbol{\beta} \\
&= \boldsymbol{\beta} + (\mathrm{X}'\mathrm{X})^{-1}\mathrm{X}'\boldsymbol{\varepsilon} - \boldsymbol{\beta} \\
&= (\mathrm{X}'\mathrm{X})^{-1}\mathrm{X}'\boldsymbol{\varepsilon}.
\end{aligned}$$

Then the variance of $\hat{\boldsymbol{\beta}}_{ML}$ conditional on X is equal to the variance of $\hat{\boldsymbol{\beta}}_{ML} - \boldsymbol{\beta}$ because $\boldsymbol{\beta}$ is a constant:

$$\begin{aligned}
\mathrm{var}(\hat{\boldsymbol{\beta}}_{ML} - \boldsymbol{\beta}) &= \mathrm{var}((\mathrm{X}'\mathrm{X})^{-1}\mathrm{X}'\boldsymbol{\varepsilon} \mid \mathrm{X}) \\
&= \left[(\mathrm{X}'\mathrm{X})^{-1}\mathrm{X}'\right] \mathrm{var}(\boldsymbol{\varepsilon} \mid \mathrm{X}) \left[(\mathrm{X}'\mathrm{X})^{-1}\mathrm{X}'\right]' \\
&= \left[(\mathrm{X}'\mathrm{X})^{-1}\mathrm{X}'\right] (\sigma^2 I_n) \left[(\mathrm{X}'\mathrm{X})^{-1}\mathrm{X}'\right]' \\
&= \sigma^2 \cdot (\mathrm{X}'\mathrm{X})^{-1}\mathrm{X}'\mathrm{X}(\mathrm{X}'\mathrm{X})^{-1} \\
&= \sigma^2 \cdot (\mathrm{X}'\mathrm{X})^{-1}.
\end{aligned}$$

Since $\sigma^2 = Var(\boldsymbol{\varepsilon} \mid \mathbf{X})$ is unknown, we must find an estimator for it as well. We do not observe $\boldsymbol{\varepsilon}$, but we do have the estimated residuals $\mathbf{e}$. Start by finding the fitted values $\hat{\mathbf{y}} = \mathbf{X}\hat{\boldsymbol{\beta}}_{ML} = \mathbf{X}(\mathbf{X}'\mathbf{X})^{-1}\mathbf{X}'\mathbf{y} = \mathbf{P}\mathbf{y}$. This defines $\mathbf{P} = \mathbf{X}(\mathbf{X}'\mathbf{X})^{-1}\mathbf{X}'$. Then, since $\mathbf{e} = \mathbf{y} - \hat{\mathbf{y}}$, we know $\mathbf{e} = \mathbf{y} - \mathbf{P}\mathbf{y} = (\mathbf{I}_n - \mathbf{P})\mathbf{y} = \mathbf{M}\mathbf{y}$, defining $\mathbf{M} = (\mathbf{I}_n - \mathbf{P})$, which is symmetric and idempotent.

Now, recalling the original definition of the regression model, we can relate $\mathbf{e}$ and $\boldsymbol{\varepsilon}$:

$$\begin{aligned}
\mathbf{e} &= \mathbf{M}\mathbf{y} \\
&= \mathbf{M}(\mathbf{X}\boldsymbol{\beta} + \boldsymbol{\varepsilon}) \\
&= \mathbf{M}\mathbf{X}\hat{\boldsymbol{\beta}}_{ML} + \mathbf{M}\boldsymbol{\varepsilon} \\
&= (\mathbf{I}_n - \mathbf{X}(\mathbf{X}'\mathbf{X})^{-1}\mathbf{X}')\mathbf{X}(\mathbf{X}'\mathbf{X})^{-1}\mathbf{X}'\mathbf{y} + \mathbf{M}\boldsymbol{\varepsilon} \\
&= \mathbf{X}(\mathbf{X}'\mathbf{X})^{-1}\mathbf{X}'\mathbf{y} - \mathbf{X}(\mathbf{X}'\mathbf{X})^{-1}\mathbf{X}'\mathbf{y} + \mathbf{M}\boldsymbol{\varepsilon} \\
&= \mathbf{M}\boldsymbol{\varepsilon}.
\end{aligned}$$

The fourth line follows from the definitions of $\mathbf{M}$, $\mathbf{P}$, and $\hat{\boldsymbol{\beta}}_{ML}$. Using the symmetry and idempotence of $\mathbf{M}$, $\mathbf{e}'\mathbf{e} = \boldsymbol{\varepsilon}'\mathbf{M}'\mathbf{M}\boldsymbol{\varepsilon} = \boldsymbol{\varepsilon}'\mathbf{M}^2\boldsymbol{\varepsilon} = \boldsymbol{\varepsilon}'\mathbf{M}\boldsymbol{\varepsilon}$. The variance of the residuals thus becomes

$$E[\mathbf{e}'\mathbf{e} \mid \mathbf{X}] = E[\boldsymbol{\varepsilon}'\mathbf{M}\boldsymbol{\varepsilon} \mid \mathbf{X}] = \sum_i \sum_j m_{ij} E[\varepsilon_i \varepsilon_j \mid \mathbf{X}] = \sum_i m_{ii} E[\varepsilon_i \varepsilon_i \mid \mathbf{X}]$$

with the last line following because $E[\varepsilon_i \varepsilon_j \mid \mathbf{X}] = 0$ for $i \neq j$. Using the definition of the trace operator, it follows that $E[\mathbf{e}'\mathbf{e} \mid \mathbf{X}] = \sigma^2 \cdot tr(\mathbf{M})$. Then using various properties of the trace operator,

$$tr(\mathbf{M}) = tr(\mathbf{I}_n - \mathbf{P}) = tr(\mathbf{I}_n) - tr(\mathbf{P}) = n - k.$$

Because $\mathbf{P}\mathbf{X} = \mathbf{X}(\mathbf{X}'\mathbf{X})^{-1}\mathbf{X}'\mathbf{X} = \mathbf{X}$, it is evident that $tr(\mathbf{P}) = k$. We therefore obtain

$$s^2 = \frac{\mathbf{e}'\mathbf{e}}{n - k}$$

as a consistent estimator for σ^2 and $s^2 \cdot (\mathbf{X}'\mathbf{X})^{-1}$ as a consistent estimator for $\text{var}(\hat{\boldsymbol{\beta}}_{ML} - \boldsymbol{\beta})$.

Hypothesis Testing Constructing a test statistic for $\hat{\boldsymbol{\beta}}_{ML}$ involves evaluating the difference of $\hat{\boldsymbol{\beta}}_{ML}$ from its hypothetical value $\boldsymbol{\beta}_0$ relative to the sampling error for $\hat{\boldsymbol{\beta}}_{ML}$. To make things simple, we limit our attention to a single parameter in the set $i = 1, \ldots, k$ so the quantities of interest are $\hat{\boldsymbol{\beta}}_{i(ML)}$

and $\boldsymbol{\beta}_{i(0)}$. Converting the sampling variance to the same units as $\hat{\boldsymbol{\beta}}_{ML}$, we obtain the test statistic

$$t = \frac{\hat{\boldsymbol{\beta}}_{i(ML)} - \boldsymbol{\beta}_{i(0)}}{\sqrt{s^2 \cdot ((\mathbf{X}'\mathbf{X})^{-1})_{ii}}}$$

which has the Student t distribution with $n - k$ degrees of freedom. The analyst specifies a desired significance level, and finds the critical value associated with that significance level for the Student t distribution with $n - k$ degrees of freedom. If the test statistic exceeds the critical value, the null hypothesis is rejected. One often associates a p-value with the test statistic, indicating the amount of probability beyond the critical value in the test distribution.

Note the appearance of $(\mathbf{X}'\mathbf{X})^{-1}$ in the denominator of the test statistic. The double subscript in the denominator refers to the ith diagonal of the $(\mathbf{X}'\mathbf{X})^{-1}$ matrix. Hence, information about covariances between the regressors is thrown away in constructing the test statistic, so that test results are unchanged if one of the regressors in $\mathbf{X}$ is discarded. It is typical in the classical analysis of the linear regression model to assume the absence of multicollinearity so that these off-diagonal elements of $(\mathbf{X}'\mathbf{X})^{-1}$ are equal to zero a priori.

Bayesian Analysis of the Normal Linear Regression Model

The Bayesian analysis of the normal linear regression model begins from the same primitives about $\mathbf{y}$, $\mathbf{X}$, and the error distribution $\boldsymbol{\varepsilon} \sim N[0, \sigma^2 I_n]$. Because $\boldsymbol{\beta}$ and σ^2 are unknown parameters, prior distributions for the parameters must also be specified. Since the likelihood for the normal linear regression model is part of the exponential family of distributions, a conjugate prior family exists (Bernardo and Smith 2000, pp. 265–279), which, in this case, is the normal-inverse gamma prior.

The derivation will be simple, but long. It pays to follow every step to understand how to arrive at the posterior distribution. Along the way, we will also learn the useful technique of completing the square.

The prior distribution $p(\boldsymbol{\beta}, \sigma^2)$ gets broken up into the conditionals $p(\boldsymbol{\beta} \mid \sigma^2)$ and $p(\sigma^2)$:

$$\begin{aligned} p(\boldsymbol{\beta} \mid \sigma^2) &\sim N\left[\mathbf{b}_0, \sigma^2\mathbf{B}_0\right] \\ &= (2\pi\sigma^2)^{-k/2} \exp\left[-\frac{1}{2\sigma^2}(\boldsymbol{\beta} - \mathbf{b}_0)'\mathbf{B}_0^{-1}(\boldsymbol{\beta} - \mathbf{b}_0)\right] \end{aligned}$$

$$p(\sigma^2) \sim IG[n_0, n_0S_0]$$
$$= \frac{(n_0S_0/2)^{n_0/2}}{\Gamma(n_0/2)}(\sigma^2)^{n_0/2-1} \exp\left[-\frac{1}{2\sigma^2}\left(n_0S_0\right)\right]$$

The likelihood $p(\mathbf{y} \mid \mathbf{X}, \boldsymbol{\beta}, \sigma^2)$ follows directly from the definition of the linear regression model. Since $\mathbf{y} = \mathbf{X}\boldsymbol{\beta} + \boldsymbol{\varepsilon}$ and $\boldsymbol{\varepsilon} \sim N[0, \sigma^2 I_n]$,

$$p(\mathbf{y} \mid \mathbf{X}, \boldsymbol{\beta}, \sigma^2) \sim N[\mathbf{X}\boldsymbol{\beta}, \sigma^2 I_n]$$
$$= (2\pi\sigma^2)^{-n/2} \exp\left[-\frac{1}{2\sigma^2}(\mathbf{y} - \mathbf{X}\boldsymbol{\beta})'(\mathbf{y} - \mathbf{X}\boldsymbol{\beta})\right]$$
$$= (2\pi\sigma^2)^{-n/2} \exp\left[-\frac{1}{2\sigma^2}\left(\mathbf{y}'\mathbf{y} - 2\boldsymbol{\beta}'\mathbf{X}'\mathbf{y} + \boldsymbol{\beta}'\mathbf{X}'\mathbf{X}\boldsymbol{\beta}\right)\right]$$

Finding the posterior follows from applying Bayes' rule. Multiply the prior and the likelihood to obtain:

$$p(\boldsymbol{\beta}, \sigma^2 \mid \mathbf{y}, \mathbf{X}) \propto p(\mathbf{y} \mid \mathbf{X}, \boldsymbol{\beta}, \sigma^2) \times p(\boldsymbol{\beta} \mid \sigma^2) \times p(\sigma^2)$$
$$\propto (2\pi\sigma^2)^{-n/2} \exp\left[-\frac{1}{2\sigma^2}\left(\mathbf{y}'\mathbf{y} - 2\boldsymbol{\beta}'\mathbf{X}'\mathbf{y} + \boldsymbol{\beta}'\mathbf{X}'\mathbf{X}\boldsymbol{\beta}\right)\right]$$
$$\times (2\pi\sigma^2)^{-k/2} \exp\left[-\frac{1}{2\sigma^2}(\boldsymbol{\beta} - \mathbf{b}_0)'\mathbf{B}_0^{-1}(\boldsymbol{\beta} - \mathbf{b}_0)\right]$$
$$\times \frac{(n_0S_0/2)^{n_0/2}}{\Gamma(n_0/2)}(\sigma^2)^{n_0/2-1} \exp\left[-\frac{1}{2\sigma^2}\left(n_0S_0\right)\right]$$

Since we are working under the proportionality sign, we can drop the 2π terms in the normalizing constants, as well as the normalizing constant for the inverse-gamma distribution. Grouping the terms in σ^2 and the exponentials:

$$p(\boldsymbol{\beta}, \sigma^2 \mid \mathbf{y}, \mathbf{X}) \propto (\sigma^2)^{-((n+k+n_0)/2+1)}$$
$$\times \exp\left[-\frac{1}{2\sigma^2}\left(\mathbf{y}'\mathbf{y} - 2\boldsymbol{\beta}'\mathbf{X}'\mathbf{y} + \boldsymbol{\beta}'\mathbf{X}'\mathbf{X}\boldsymbol{\beta}\right)\right]$$
$$\times \exp\left[-\frac{1}{2\sigma^2}\left(\boldsymbol{\beta}'\mathbf{B}_0^{-1}\boldsymbol{\beta} - 2\boldsymbol{\beta}'\mathbf{B}_0^{-1}\mathbf{b}_0' + \mathbf{b}_0'\mathbf{B}_0^{-1}\mathbf{b}_0 + n_0S_0\right)\right]$$

We leave the problem of the exponent on σ^2 to one side and concentrate on the kernel for the posterior $p(\boldsymbol{\beta}|\sigma^2, \mathbf{y}, \mathbf{X})$, which will be determined by the expressions in the exponential term. We will be free to divide up the exponent on σ^2 however is convenient later when we look for an inverse-gamma kernel for the posterior $p(\sigma^2 \mid \mathbf{y}, \mathbf{X})$.

For the exponential term, we now have

$$\exp\left[-\frac{1}{2\sigma^2}\{(\mathbf{y}'\mathbf{y} - 2\boldsymbol{\beta}'\mathbf{X}'\mathbf{y} + \boldsymbol{\beta}'\mathbf{X}'\mathbf{X}\boldsymbol{\beta}) + (\boldsymbol{\beta}'\mathbf{B}_0^{-1}\boldsymbol{\beta} - 2\boldsymbol{\beta}'\mathbf{B}_0^{-1}\mathbf{b}_0' + \mathbf{b}_0'\mathbf{B}_0^{-1}\mathbf{b}_0 + n_0S_0)\}\right].$$

Because we are seeking a kernel for $\boldsymbol{\beta} \mid \sigma^2$, we can ignore all terms that are not a function of $\boldsymbol{\beta}$, leaving

$$\exp\left[-\frac{1}{2\sigma^2}\{(-2\boldsymbol{\beta}'\mathbf{X}'\mathbf{y} + \boldsymbol{\beta}'\mathbf{X}'\mathbf{X}\boldsymbol{\beta}) + (\boldsymbol{\beta}'\mathbf{B}_0^{-1}\boldsymbol{\beta} - 2\boldsymbol{\beta}'\mathbf{B}_0^{-1}\mathbf{b}_0')\}\right]$$

Reserve the other terms $\mathbf{y}'\mathbf{y}$, $\mathbf{b}_0'\mathbf{B}_0^{-1}\mathbf{b}_0$ and n_0S_0 for working out the exponential term in the posterior distribution for σ^2, $p(\sigma^2 \mid \mathbf{y}, \mathbf{X})$. Regrouping the terms in $\boldsymbol{\beta}$, a quadratic form in $\boldsymbol{\beta}$ becomes apparent:

$$\exp\left[-\frac{1}{2\sigma^2}\{(\boldsymbol{\beta}'\mathbf{X}'\mathbf{X}\boldsymbol{\beta} + \boldsymbol{\beta}'\mathbf{B}_0^{-1}\boldsymbol{\beta}) + (-2\boldsymbol{\beta}'\mathbf{X}'\mathbf{y} - 2\boldsymbol{\beta}'\mathbf{B}_0^{-1}\mathbf{b}_0)\}\right]$$

$$\exp\left[-\frac{1}{2\sigma^2}\{\boldsymbol{\beta}'(\mathbf{X}'\mathbf{X} + \mathbf{B}_0^{-1})\boldsymbol{\beta} - 2\boldsymbol{\beta}'(\mathbf{X}'\mathbf{y} + \mathbf{B}_0^{-1}\mathbf{b}_0)\}\right]$$

In order to complete the square in $\boldsymbol{\beta}$, it helps to define some new variables. Recalling that the prior $p(\boldsymbol{\beta} \mid \sigma^2)$ was a quadratic form in $\boldsymbol{\beta}$, it seems sensible to guess that the posterior will be as well. Hence, put $\mathbf{B}_1^{-1} = \mathbf{X}'\mathbf{X} + \mathbf{B}_0^{-1}$ and, to preserve the quadratic form (now in $\boldsymbol{\beta}$ and $\mathbf{B}_1^{-1}$), multiply the second term by one using $\mathbf{B}_1^{-1}\mathbf{B}_1$:

$$\exp\left[-\frac{1}{2\sigma^2}\{\boldsymbol{\beta}'\mathbf{B}_1^{-1}\boldsymbol{\beta} - 2\boldsymbol{\beta}'\mathbf{B}_1^{-1}\mathbf{B}_1(\mathbf{X}'\mathbf{y} + \mathbf{B}_0^{-1}\mathbf{b}_0)\}\right].$$

Then, define $\mathbf{b}_1 = \mathbf{B}_1(\mathbf{X}'\mathbf{y} + \mathbf{B}_0^{-1}\mathbf{b}_0)$ to obtain

$$\exp\left[-\frac{1}{2\sigma^2}\{\boldsymbol{\beta}'\mathbf{B}_1^{-1}\boldsymbol{\beta} - 2\boldsymbol{\beta}'\mathbf{B}_1^{-1}\mathbf{b}_1\}\right].$$

Now the square can be completed by adding and subtracting $\mathbf{b}_1'\mathbf{B}_1^{-1}\mathbf{b}_1$:

$$\exp\left[-\frac{1}{2\sigma^2}\{\boldsymbol{\beta}'\mathbf{B}_1^{-1}\boldsymbol{\beta} - 2\boldsymbol{\beta}'\mathbf{B}_1^{-1}\mathbf{b}_1 + \mathbf{b}_1'\mathbf{B}_1^{-1}\mathbf{b}_1 - \mathbf{b}_1'\mathbf{B}_1^{-1}\mathbf{b}_1\}\right]$$

$$= \exp\left[-\frac{1}{2\sigma^2}\left\{(\boldsymbol{\beta} - \mathbf{b}_1)'\mathbf{B}_1^{-1}(\boldsymbol{\beta} - \mathbf{b}_1) - \mathbf{b}_1'\mathbf{B}_1^{-1}\mathbf{b}_1\right\}\right]$$

which, setting aside the final term (which is not a function of $\boldsymbol{\beta}$ and which will be used in working out the posterior for σ^2), provides the kernel of the posterior $p(\boldsymbol{\beta} \mid \sigma^2, \mathbf{y}, \mathbf{X})$. Because the kernel has dimension k the exponent on σ^2 in the expression for $p(\boldsymbol{\beta} \mid \sigma^2, \mathbf{y}, \mathbf{X})$ must be $-k/2$. Thus, we can summarize the posterior as

$$p(\boldsymbol{\beta} \mid \sigma^2, \mathbf{y}, \mathbf{X}) \propto (\sigma^2)^{-k/2} \exp\left[-\frac{1}{2\sigma^2}\left\{(\boldsymbol{\beta} - \mathbf{b}_1)'\mathbf{B}_1^{-1}(\boldsymbol{\beta} - \mathbf{b}_1)\right\}\right]$$

or $p(\boldsymbol{\beta} \mid \sigma^2, \mathbf{y}, \mathbf{X}) \sim N[\mathbf{b}_1, \sigma^2\mathbf{B}_1]$, with $\mathbf{b}_1 = \mathbf{B}_1(\mathbf{X}'\mathbf{y} + \mathbf{B}_0^{-1}\mathbf{b}_0)$ and $\mathbf{B}_1$ defined implicitly by $\mathbf{B}_1^{-1} = \mathbf{X}'\mathbf{X} + \mathbf{B}_0^{-1}$.

Gathering up what remains, the starting point for the posterior $p(\sigma^2 \mid \mathbf{y}, \mathbf{X})$ is the expression

$$(\sigma^2)^{-((n+n_0)/2+1)} \exp\left[-\frac{1}{2\sigma^2}\left(\mathbf{y}'\mathbf{y} + \mathbf{b}_0'\mathbf{B}_0^{-1}\mathbf{b}_0 + n_0S_0 - \mathbf{b}_1'\mathbf{B}_1^{-1}\mathbf{b}_1\right)\right].$$

The initial σ^2 term is the result of allocating $(\sigma^2)^{-k/2}$ to the posterior for $\boldsymbol{\beta}$. In the exponential term, $\mathbf{y}'\mathbf{y}$, $\mathbf{b}_0'\mathbf{B}_0^{-1}\mathbf{b}_0$ and n_0S_0 were dropped before completing the square in $\boldsymbol{\beta}$, while $-\mathbf{b}_1'\mathbf{B}_1^{-1}\mathbf{b}_1$ arose after defining $\mathbf{b}_1$ and completing the square. The expression can be cleaned up by first expanding out the last term in the exponential:

$$\mathbf{b}_1 = \mathbf{B}_1(\mathbf{X}'\mathbf{y} + \mathbf{B}_0^{-1}\mathbf{b}_0)$$

$$\mathbf{B}_1^{-1}\mathbf{b}_1 = \mathbf{X}'\mathbf{y} + \mathbf{B}_0^{-1}\mathbf{b}_0$$

$$\mathbf{b}_1'\mathbf{B}_1^{-1}\mathbf{b}_1 = \mathbf{b}_1'\mathbf{X}'\mathbf{y} + \mathbf{b}_1'\mathbf{B}_0^{-1}\mathbf{b}_0$$

so that we obtain the final expression for $p(\sigma^2 \mid \mathbf{y}, \mathbf{X})$:

$$(\sigma^2)^{-((n+n_0)/2+1)} \exp\left[-\frac{1}{2\sigma^2}\left(\mathbf{y}'\mathbf{y} + \mathbf{b}_0'\mathbf{B}_0^{-1}\mathbf{b}_0 + n_0S_0 - \mathbf{b}_1'\mathbf{X}'\mathbf{y} - \mathbf{b}_1'\mathbf{B}_0^{-1}\mathbf{b}_0\right)\right]$$

$$= (\sigma^2)^{-((n+n_0)/2+1)} \exp\left[-\frac{1}{2\sigma^2}\{((\mathbf{y} - \mathbf{X}\mathbf{b}_1)'\mathbf{y} + (\mathbf{b}_0 - \mathbf{b}_1)'\mathbf{B}_0^{-1}\mathbf{b}_0 + n_0S_0)\}\right].$$

The posterior $p(\sigma^2 \mid \mathbf{y}, \mathbf{X})$ is therefore distributed $IG[n_1, n_1 S_1]$ with

$$n_1 = n_0 + n$$
$$n_1 S_1 = n_0 S_0 + (\mathbf{y} - \mathbf{X}\mathbf{b}_1)'\mathbf{y} + (\mathbf{b}_0 - \mathbf{b}_1)'\mathbf{B}_0^{-1}\mathbf{b}_0$$

so we now have a complete set of updates from the set of prior hyperparameters $\{\mathbf{b}_0, \mathbf{B}_0, \mathbf{n}_0, \mathbf{n}_0\mathbf{S}_0\}$ to the posterior hyperparameters $\{\mathbf{b}_1, \mathbf{B}_1, \mathbf{n}_1, \mathbf{n}_1\mathbf{S}_1\}$ via the sufficient statistics

$$\{\mathbf{X}'\mathbf{X}, \mathbf{X}'\mathbf{y}, n, \mathbf{y}, \mathbf{X}\}.$$

Collecting results, the complete updating rules are

$$\mathbf{B}_1^{-1} = \mathbf{X}'\mathbf{X} + \mathbf{B}_0^{-1}$$
$$\mathbf{b}_1 = \mathbf{B}_1(\mathbf{X}'\mathbf{y} + \mathbf{B}_0^{-1}\mathbf{b}_0)$$
$$n_1 = n_0 + n$$
$$n_1 S_1 = n_0 S_0 + (\mathbf{y} - \mathbf{X}\mathbf{b}_1)'\mathbf{y} + (\mathbf{b}_0 - \mathbf{b}_1)'\mathbf{B}_0^{-1}\mathbf{b}_0.$$

The term S_1 defined implicitly by the last term $n_1 S_1$, is the expectation of σ^2 using the distribution $IG[n_1, n_1 S_1]$. Note that when it is decomposed in the manner above it incorporates the prior estimate, an adjustment based on the posterior regression residuals $(\mathbf{y} - \mathbf{X}\mathbf{b}_1)$, and an adjustment based on the change in the variance of the prior uncertainty about the coefficients as a result of updating the mean of the coefficient estimate $(\mathbf{b}_0 - \mathbf{b}_1)\mathbf{B}_0^{-1}\mathbf{b}_0$.

Note also that the mean of the estimate for $\boldsymbol{\beta}$ is a variance-weighted average of the prior mean and the ordinary least squares estimate $(\mathbf{X}'\mathbf{X})^{-1}\mathbf{X}'\mathbf{y}$. Just as in the binomial model, the maximum-likelihood value is shrunk toward the prior value, which is now standing in the role of the "null hypothesis."

Hypothesis Testing with Parameter Distributions By integrating σ^2 out of the posterior $p(\boldsymbol{\beta} \mid \sigma^2, \mathbf{y}, \mathbf{X})$, we obtain a marginal posterior distribution $p(\boldsymbol{\beta} \mid \mathbf{y}, \mathbf{X})$ that may be analogized to the estimator and sampling variance found by classical methods. It can be shown that

$$p(\boldsymbol{\beta} \mid \mathbf{y}, \mathbf{X}) \sim T_{n_1}[\mathbf{b}_1, S_1 \cdot \mathbf{B}_1],$$

a Student t distribution with mean $\mathbf{b}_1$, variance $S_1 \cdot \mathbf{B}_1$, and n_1 degrees of freedom (Poirier 1995, pp. 547–548). Since we once again have a t distribution for the coefficient vector, for a particular coefficient b_1 we can construct the pseudo test statistic

$$t^{pseudo}_{posterior} = \frac{\mathbf{b}_{i1} - \boldsymbol{\beta}_i}{\sqrt{(S_1 \cdot \mathbf{B}_1)_{ii}}} = \frac{\mathbf{b}_{i1} - \mathbf{b}_{i0}}{\sqrt{S_1 \cdot ((\mathbf{X}'\mathbf{X} + \mathbf{B}_0^{-1})^{-1})_{ii}}}$$

Thus in place of the classical estimator s^2 we have S_1, the expectation of the posterior distribution $p(\sigma^2|\mathrm{y}, \mathbf{X})$, and in place of the SSCP matrix $\mathbf{X}'\mathbf{X}$ we have the posterior coefficient variance $\mathbf{X}'\mathbf{X} + \mathbf{B}_0^{-1}$, which is very intuitive.

We can just as easily compute the same pseudo test statistic using prior information. In this case, we would have

$$t^{pseudo}_{prior} = \frac{\mathbf{b}_{i0} - \boldsymbol{\beta}_i}{\sqrt{(S_0 \cdot \mathbf{B}_0)_{ii}}}.$$

While the pseudo test statistics facilitate comparison with the classical results, they throw away important information about the posterior distribution of $\boldsymbol{\beta}$ by only employing the mean of the parameter distribution.

Using the Bayesian expression for the marginal distribution of $\boldsymbol{\beta}_i$, one can evaluate the probability of any hypothesis for $\boldsymbol{\beta}_i$ simply by integrating over the marginal distribution. Hence, the posterior probability $P(\beta_i \leq 0)$ is given by

$$\int_{-\infty}^{0} t[\mathbf{b}_i, S \cdot \mathbf{B}_{ii}]d\mathbf{b}_i.$$

Employing the obvious alternative hypothesis, the evidence in the data in favor of the null hypothesis is given by the likelihood ratio

$$\frac{\int_{-\infty}^{0} t[\mathbf{b}_i, S \cdot \mathbf{B}_{ii}]d\mathbf{b}_i}{1 - \int_{-\infty}^{0} t[\mathbf{b}_i, S \cdot \mathbf{B}_{ii}]d\mathbf{b}_i} = \frac{\int_{-\infty}^{0} t[\mathbf{b}_i, S \cdot \mathbf{B}_{ii}]d\mathbf{b}_i}{\int_{0}^{\infty} t[\mathbf{b}_i, S \cdot \mathbf{B}_{ii}]d\mathbf{b}_i} = \frac{P(\mathbf{b}_i \leq 0)}{P(\mathbf{b}_i > 0)}.$$

Probabilities may be associated with hypotheses prior to observing the data in the same way. If one wishes to express 95 percent confidence that $\boldsymbol{\beta}_i > 0$, choose $\mathbf{b}_0$ and $\mathbf{B}_0$ such that $\int_0^\infty t[\mathbf{b}_{0i}, S \cdot (\mathbf{B}_0)_{ii}]d\mathbf{b}_{0i} = 0.95$. Generalizing the null hypothesis to $\boldsymbol{\beta}_i > k$, we can evaluate $\int_k^\infty t[\mathbf{b}_{0i}, S \cdot (\mathbf{B}_0)_{ii}]d\mathbf{b}_{0i}$ for any k to obtain the corresponding probability that $\boldsymbol{\beta}_i > k$.

The prior distribution, we see, *is* the hypothesis. However, it is framed in a markedly different way than in the classical analysis. Instead of concentrating all of the probability on a single value, a continuous distribution of values for the null hypothesis is entertained. Then, after observing the data, the probability that the alternative hypothesis is true may be simply read off, and the probability that the coefficient lies in any particular interval may be found by integration.

Comparison

Now consider the same analysis from a classical perspective.

First, assume that the mean of the posterior distribution for $\boldsymbol{\beta}$ is identical to the maximum-likelihood estimate ($\hat{\boldsymbol{\beta}}_{ML} = \mathbf{b}_1$) and the mean of the prior distribution is equal to the null hypothesis value ($\boldsymbol{\beta}_0 = \mathbf{b}_0$) to focus attention on the uncertainty term in the test statistics. The classical test statistic for parameter i is

$$t = \frac{\hat{\boldsymbol{\beta}}_{i(ML)} - \boldsymbol{\beta}_{i(0)}}{\sqrt{s^2 \cdot ((\mathbf{X}'\mathbf{X})^{-1})_{ii}}}$$

while the Bayesian pseudo test statistic is

$$t^{pseudo}_{posterior} = \frac{\hat{\boldsymbol{\beta}}_{i(ML)} - \boldsymbol{\beta}_{i(0)}}{\sqrt{S_1 \cdot ((\mathbf{X}'\mathbf{X} + \mathbf{B}_0^{-1})^{-1})_{ii}}}$$

The only way that the pseudo test statistic will coincide with the classical test statistic is if $\mathbf{B}_0^{-1} = 0$ and $s^2 = S_1$, which implies that prior parameter uncertainty is infinite.

If there is any useful information available about $\boldsymbol{\beta}$ so that $\mathbf{B}_0^{-1} > 0$, we will have $\left|t^{pseudo}_{posterior}\right| < |t|$. As a result, for the same choice of critical value, the pseudo test statistic based on the posterior distribution will *always* be less likely to reject the null hypothesis, unless there is infinite prior uncertainty about the coefficients. If and only if there is no prior information at all about $\boldsymbol{\beta}$ will the p-values used in classical hypothesis testing correspond to the conclusions obtained from a Bayesian analysis. When prior uncertainty about the value of $\boldsymbol{\beta}$ is *not* infinite, hypothesis tests under the classical statistical regime will not have the desired *size* or Type I error rate. The less prior uncertainty there is about $\boldsymbol{\beta}$, the greater the Type I error rate, as classical hypothesis tests overreject the null.

Relaxing the assumption that $\hat{\boldsymbol{\beta}}_{ML} = \mathbf{b}_1$, the probability of erroneously rejecting the null is increased further. Prior information about the location of $\boldsymbol{\beta}$ will shrink $\mathbf{b}_1$ toward $\mathbf{b}_0$, whereas $\hat{\boldsymbol{\beta}}_{ML}$ does not vary with $\boldsymbol{\beta}_0$, the maintained hypothetical value. The numerator of the pseudo test statistic $\mathbf{b}_{i1} - \mathbf{b}_{i0}$ will always be smaller than $\hat{\boldsymbol{\beta}}_{i(ML)} - \boldsymbol{\beta}_{i(0)}$ whenever $\boldsymbol{\beta}_0 = \mathbf{b}_0$. A smaller numerator combined with a larger denominator widens the gap between the classical and Bayesian pseudo test statistics, exacerbating problems with size.

Seen from the Bayesian viewpoint, it also becomes obvious how useless tests of point hypotheses are. In the classical framework the hypothesis $\theta_i = 0$ has a particular pride of place, as tests of it are calculated automatically by most statistical packages and these results are the ones most frequently published in academic journals. An integral of a probability distribution over a single point has zero probability, so the hypothesis $\theta_i = 0$ is essentially unintelligible from a Bayesian standpoint. Instead, one might evaluate

$$\frac{\int_{-\varepsilon}^{\varepsilon} p(\theta_i \mid x) d\theta_i}{1 - \int_{-\varepsilon}^{\varepsilon} p(\theta_i \mid x) d\theta_i}$$

to decide whether $\theta_i = 0$ is approximately true for a chosen margin of error $\varepsilon > 0$.

Unless $p(\theta_i \mid x) \equiv 0$ with probability one, for increasingly large samples and smaller values of ε the numerator $\int_{-\varepsilon}^{\varepsilon} p(\theta_i \mid x) d\theta_i$ will converge to zero, so that the hypothesis $\theta_i = 0$ will be rejected every time (Berger 1985). Thus, the conventional tests of significance regularly applied to select variables for inclusion in a statistical model will overreject the null, particularly when data are abundantly available. When tests such as these are used for model selection, models will tend to be overfit to the data and thus overly complex.

DECISIONS AFTER OBSERVING THE DATA: THE CHOICE OF ESTIMATORS

An innocent but excellent question following a classical hypothesis test is: What value of $\boldsymbol{\beta}_i$ should I adopt? Classical statisticians usually assert the null hypothesis value should be used if we fail to reject it, and the maximum-likelihood value should be adopted otherwise. In contrast to the either-or classical decision rule, Bayesians use a blend of the null hypothesis values (the prior distribution) and the information in the likelihood to arrive at a distribution of possible values for $\boldsymbol{\beta}_i$ after seeing the data. Consider the expression for $\mathbf{b}_1$,

$$\mathbf{b}_1 = \mathbf{B}_1(\mathbf{X}'\mathbf{y} + \mathbf{B}_0^{-1}\mathbf{b}_o) = (\mathbf{X}'\mathbf{X} + \mathbf{B}_0^{-1})^{-1}(\mathbf{X}'\mathbf{y} + \mathbf{B}_0^{-1}\mathbf{b}_o)$$

which shows that the mean of the Bayesian estimate is a weighted average of the maximum-likelihood estimator $(\mathbf{X}'\mathbf{X})^{-1}\mathbf{X}'\mathbf{y}$ and the prior $\mathbf{b}_0$, with the weighting determined by the relative variances of the data $\mathbf{X}'\mathbf{X}$ and the prior $\mathbf{B}_0^{-1}$. Because of the shrinkage inherent in Bayesian inference, the mean of $\mathbf{b}_{i1}$ must lie between the maximum-likelihood estimate $\hat{\boldsymbol{\beta}}_{i(ML)}$ and the null hypothesis value $\mathbf{b}_{i0}$. As a result, the information in the null hypothesis is preserved by the Bayesian approach.

Decisions and Loss

Inquiring into which treatment of $\boldsymbol{\beta}_i$ is the better decision principle requires an explicit consideration of loss functions (Berger 1985). Let Θ be the set of possible "correct" values for θ (or the parameter space) and let a be the choice of θ made by the statistician. From a classical perspective we have $a = \delta(x)$ since the decision is to be made on the basis of the sampled data. Classical statisticians seek to minimize the loss $L[\theta, \delta(x)]$ averaged over possible values of x, or

$$R[\theta, \delta(x)] = \int_X L[\theta, \delta(x)]p(x \mid \theta)$$

which is known as the *frequentist risk*. It can be shown that the accept-reject decision of classical statistics corresponds to an all-or-nothing loss function, where losses are zero if the parameter lies in the confidence interval and an arbitrary value otherwise. Note, however, that even with a definite loss function the decision criterion is meaningless, since it still depends on the unknown θ.

Bayesians average over the source of uncertainty θ rather than over the data, which are known. Then the decision criterion depends on minimizing the following expected loss, known as the *Bayes risk*:

$$\int_\theta L[\theta, a]p(\theta \mid x)$$

where a is the value to be chosen as the "correct" value. The term on the right is the posterior parameter distribution, so the decision criterion says to minimize expected loss averaged over the distribution of posterior parameter values. This allows us to evaluate specific loss functions that are more realistic than the all-or-nothing loss that rationalizes classical hypothesis testing. In addition, because the integral is taken over the posterior distribution, the corresponding decision takes into account information contained in the prior distribution, whereas classical decisions ignore prior information.

A common choice for the loss function is the quadratic loss $L[\theta, a] = (\theta - a)^2$, or for multivariate problems, $L[\boldsymbol{\theta}, \mathrm{a}] = (\boldsymbol{\theta} - \mathrm{a})'\mathrm{Q}(\boldsymbol{\theta} - \mathrm{a})$, where Q is a weighting matrix. In such cases, error increases with the square of the distance from the "true" parameter value, and the optimal estimator is the mode of the posterior distribution, which Berger calls the generalized maximum-likelihood estimator (Berger 1985).

However, in financial applications it is often the case that loss functions are more complicated. The loss to underestimating a quantity may exceed the loss from overestimating it—for instance, if the quantity is the value-at-risk (VaR) that determines holdings of economic capital. The loss function may also be extremely complicated—for instance, when a large portfolio is exposed in a nonlinear way to a common risk factor. The Bayes risk provides a means for a financial institution to translate all of the information in the posterior distribution into a decision with the aid of an explicit loss function. The decision sought is the single value a that should be chosen to summarize the posterior distribution in an optimal way. The quantity a can be called the Bayes estimator (Robert 2007, pp. 60–77, 173–180). When downstream calculations require discrete numbers, a Bayes estimator should be developed; otherwise it is usually helpful to preserve the full posterior distribution of values. Since the Bayes risk will often be intractable analytically, one can search numerically for the value a that minimizes the Bayes risk for a simulation of values from the posterior distribution, $\frac{1}{N}\sum_N L[\theta_i, a] p_N(\theta_i \mid x)$.

Loss and Prior Information

Both the loss function $L[\theta, a]$ and the prior distribution $p(\theta)$ contain subjective information that is relevant for decision making. The loss function expresses subjective views about the cost of different estimation errors, while the posterior distribution incorporates subjective prior views on parameter values. Both are suppressed in classical estimation and hypothesis testing. The dependence of decisions on both $L[\theta, a]$ and $p(\theta)$ makes it difficult to separate their importance analytically (Jaynes 2003, pp. 419–425). A decision may have a large expected loss because $L[\theta, a]$ attains its maximum at a given pair (θ, a), or because the prior information $p(\theta)$ concentrates mass at a high-value region for $L[\theta, a]$, regardless of the choice of a. Because it is usually harder to specify $L[\theta, a]$ than $p(\theta)$, one would likely do best to work with a simple $L[\theta, a]$. Then standard results on simple loss functions (quadratic loss, absolute loss, asymmetric absolute loss) may be invoked to justify summary statistics such as the mean, median, or a chosen quantile of the distribution as the Bayes estimator.

One can then craft $p(\theta)$ intuitively in a way that will help to avoid large losses. For example, if there are greater losses from underestimating than overestimating, $p(\theta)$ should be chosen to pull the likelihood-based estimate upward. If losses are greater from overstating diversification, the prior estimate for the covariance matrix should understate diversification by putting more weight on the diagonal. The interpretation of the prior in terms of expected loss is thus an important tool for decision making, allowing a Bayes estimator to be used without explicitly specifying the loss function.

The Bayes estimator furnishes an answer to the question posed at the beginning of the section, from the point of view of Bayesian analysis. From a classical point of view, the same simple loss functions are used to justify using certain summary statistics of the sampling distribution. Since there are relatively few situations in which explicit consideration of one's loss function will be worthwhile, the difference between estimator choice and decision in the classical and Bayesian approaches reduces to the source of uncertainty over which expectations are taken. Bayes risk evaluates decisions over the range of uncertainty captured in the posterior parameter distribution, whereas frequentist risk considers sampling to be the relevant source of uncertainty. A sufficiently large series of independent, identically distributed alternative samples taken to answer the same question is suggestive as a thought experiment, but meaningless in practice. Why choose an estimator based on its expected performance over an infinite amount of data when only one data set is at hand? By contrast, posterior distributions cover a knowable source of uncertainty that can be circumscribed on the basis of available information.

Classical statistics does not eliminate prior knowledge from estimation. Instead, it handles prior knowledge in a severe, all-or-nothing way. By contrast, Bayesian probability incorporates prior knowledge in a theoretically rigorous way that conserves prior knowledge to the extent it conforms to the data, through the lens of a chosen model. Only when data are unlimited and there is no doubt that all data have been sampled from the same generating process can classical estimates be justified on rigorous grounds. Since it is prudent not to assume that the world works this way when analyzing time series, one is led to prefer Bayesian estimates.

The treatment of prior information by classical statistics leads to suboptimal choices of estimators, the loss of information on parameter uncertainty, indeterminate error rates in hypothesis tests, and a tendency to overreject maintained hypotheses. Thus, even within the relatively simple context of a single, static model, the use of classical statistics for estimation and model reduction introduces multiple sources of model risk, while providing no indicia to record traces of such risk. Bayesian parameter estimation provides a faithful accounting of these model risks and offers a consistent framework for reducing distributional information to a single number when a single number is required.

It is somewhat striking to realize that so much potential error can be introduced simply by the choice of estimation method and the practice of classical hypothesis testing. However, this is only the first dimension of model risk we will consider. The next chapter widens the frame of reference to incorporate risks involved in choosing a particular statistical model from a universe of possible models. Once again, we will see that Bayesian methods provide a means of seeing a risk to which classical methods are essentially blind.

CHAPTER 3

Model Uncertainty

In addition to the risk that unknown model parameters are imperfectly known, there is the risk that a model has been incorrectly specified, meaning that its form does not conform to the process generating the observed data. (Though we are skeptical of the classical time series notion of an ultimate "data-generation process" operative in nature, we retain use of the term as a placeholder for the reality that is imperfectly captured by our models.) Decisions about model form include the selection of conditioning data series, as well as a variety of choices about the functional form of the joint probability distribution. Though analysts will regularly audition a variety of model specifications in the course of analyzing a data set, it is rare that the final model specification is closely interrogated. As a result, a highly subjective and perhaps arbitrary choice is allowed to stand virtually beyond criticism in many, if not most, empirical investigations. Not only does this call into question the supposed objectivity of classical statistics, but it also arouses interest as to whether methods that accept subjectivity as an irreducible fact of statistical modeling can shed greater light on the relative merits of different model specifications.

Classical statistics tends to imagine model selection as a reduction of a highly inclusive "encompassing" model to a minimal subset of covariates via a series of hypothesis tests (Hendry and Nielsen 2007). Such an approach makes model selection only as good as classical hypothesis testing, which is not very good. In the previous chapter we saw that classical hypothesis tests ignore prior information, lead to inconsistent decisions, and produce results that can only be rationalized by very artificial loss functions. Both factors lead classical tests to overreject null hypotheses. As a result, the use of hypothesis tests to select a model from a larger, encompassing model will usually lead to an overly complex model.

We might also wonder whether model choice is best conceived as a once-and-for-all problem of reduction, just as we questioned the all-or-nothing decision theory underlying the choice of a classical estimator. Bayesian analysis allows us to think of the parameter set as a joint probability distribution, which makes plain the hazards of thinking uncritically in terms of the marginal distributions. For certain configurations of the other parameters, any given parameter may predictably take on a range of values that is sufficiently different from zero to merit the inclusion of another regressor. This is our first clue that a more global analysis of model adequacy is needed. Tests based on truncated marginal parameter distributions only lead to correct inferences about the joint parameter distribution when all marginal distributions are independent.

Bayesian model comparisons evaluate models on their ability to generate useful predictions, while penalizing more complex models. The trade-off between complexity and predictive power is evaluated by integrating over the joint distribution of the parameters—that is, the entire parameter space. Models are permitted to expand in complexity based on their ability to sustain a higher-dimensional parameter space without a corresponding loss of information along individual dimensions. Because information may be introduced from either the data or prior information, it is possible that more complex models may be preferred because they can mediate richer prior information sets. Bayesian model comparisons may be conducted pairwise or across entire sets of models. It is also possible within the Bayesian framework to eliminate choices about individual models entirely by integrating over the space of available models. This process of Bayesian model averaging treats models as *nuisance parameters* that have only instrumental value in forming a forecast. The practices of comparing entire sets of models or taking expectations over a set of models raise questions about the completeness of the space of models. Hence, we devote some thought to the sense in which a space of models may be complete.

Two further questions are explored before concluding this chapter. The first concerns the relationship between statistical models generally and the pricing models used in trading and hedging financial instruments. The latter are not generally thought of as statistical models. Thus, we seek to bring out the ways in which these models are also subject to parameter and model uncertainty, and how their calibration to market data becomes a more pressing concern the longer one's horizon is. The second question, concerning backtesting, begins a transition to the third dimension of model risk—namely, the risk that the model does not conform to the generation process for market data on a dynamic basis. In order to address the possibility that a currently well-corroborated model may eventually break down, more tools are needed to monitor the adequacy of models on an ongoing basis. These tools are developed in Part Two of the book.

BAYESIAN MODEL COMPARISON

Bayesian methods employ basic tools of probability theory to assess alternative model specifications relative to each other. One can test whether the evidence in the data strongly favors a given model specification by computing a posterior model probability or a posterior odds ratio expressing the relative performance of any two models. In both cases, the quantity of primary interest is the *marginal likelihood*, or the probability of seeing the data conditional on the model (Koop 2003).

Bayes Factors

Define prior and posterior model probabilities $p(M_i)$ and $p(M_i|x)$ by analogy with prior and posterior parameter distributions. Then by Bayes' rule, we know

$$p(M_i|x) = \frac{p(x|M_i)p(M_i)}{p(x)}.$$

The odds of an event A occurring are defined as $P(A)/(1 - P(A))$. Consequently, if we had another candidate model M_j, then the odds for or against M_i would be

$$\frac{p(M_i|x)}{1-p(M_i|x)} = \frac{p(M_i|y)}{p(M_j|y)} = \frac{p(x|M_i)p(M_i)}{p(x)} \cdot \frac{p(x)}{p(x|M_j)p(M_j)} = \frac{p(x|M_i)}{p(x|M_j)} \cdot \frac{p(M_i)}{p(M_j)}.$$

This important formula tells us that the *posterior odds* of M_i relative to M_j is equal to the *prior odds* of the two models times the ratio

$$\frac{p(x|M_i)}{p(x|M_j)},$$

which is known as the *Bayes factor*. It captures the relative evidence in favor of the models M_i and M_j contained in the data. A Bayes factor greater than one increases the posterior odds of M_i, whereas a Bayes factor less than one reduces the posterior odds. The terms $p(x|M_i)$ and $p(x|M_j)$ are the marginal likelihoods of M_i and M_j, which will be defined in the next section. Just as in the case of parameter estimation, the model comparison is conditioned on the particular data set x rather than all possible data sets. Given alternative data sets x, the evidence can therefore swing in favor of one model or the other. The more strongly one of the models captures aspects of the data relative to the other, the more the Bayes factor will differ from one and tip the balance in favor of the better model.

Making evaluations of a model in relative terms forces the analyst to specify at least one alternative model and assign a nonzero probability to it. Examining the formula again in its final form

$$\frac{p(M_i|x)}{p(M_j|x)} = \frac{p(x|M_i)}{p(x|M_j)} \cdot \frac{p(M_i)}{p(M_j)}$$

one can ask if there is ever a situation in which the posterior odds of a model would be zero or infinite, suggesting that either M_i or M_j is the "correct" model. Both $p(x|M_i)$ and M_i are probability distributions, so they must be positive everywhere. As a result, posterior odds ratios of zero or infinity are impossible. The only way one model could receive exclusive support is if the prior odds assign zero probability to one of the models. In such a situation, no amount of evidence in the Bayes factor can result in support for an alternative model.

Though common practice routinely works exclusively with a single model, Bayes factors will always be computable for the chosen model relative to any conceivable alternative specification, so long as informative priors are used. The importance of prior parameter distributions for model comparison will also be discussed in a subsequent section. Bayes factors capture accumulating evidence that, in principle, may serve to increase or reduce the odds that a chosen model is well-supported by the data. Relying on a single model, on the other hand, ignores the evidence accumulated by the Bayes factor. If one is seriously interested in knowing when models are in danger of breaking down—or equivalently, when the dynamics of markets are undergoing a significant change relative to recent history—the information contained in the Bayes factor is crucially important.

Marginal Likelihoods

The Bayes factor is a ratio of marginal likelihoods. The marginal likelihood is obtained from a likelihood conditional on both the parameters and the model by integrating over the parameter distributions, as we now show. Start by rewriting Bayes' rule for the model parameters, but now introduce the choice of model M_i into the conditioning information for all of the probability distributions. Evidently, the set of parameters and their values are determined by the choice of M_i, so denote the corresponding parameters θ_i:

$$p(\theta_i|x, M_i) = \frac{p(x|\theta_i, M_i)p(\theta_i|M_i)}{p(x|M_i)}.$$

Integrating over θ_i we find

$$\int_{\theta_i} p(\theta_i|x, M_i) = \int_{\theta_i} \left[\frac{p(x|\theta_i, M_i)p(\theta_i|M_i)}{p(x|M_i)}\right]$$

$$1 = \frac{\int_{\theta_i} p(x|\theta_i, M_i)p(\theta_i|M_i)}{p(x|M_i)}$$

$$p(x|M_i) = \int_{\theta_i} p(x|\theta_i, M_i)p(\theta_i|M_i).$$

The second equality follows because $p(\theta_i|x, M_i)$ is a probability distribution and $p(x|M_i)$ is independent of θ_i. In the last line, we see the marginal likelihood of the model is the probability of observing the data, conditional on the model, after integrating out *prior* uncertainty about the parameters.

The evidence for or against a model is therefore a function of both the prior model probability and any prior knowledge about the parameters. Since the set of parameters is closely intertwined with the model specification, it is intuitive that both prior information sets should contribute to the posterior model probability.

In the classical analysis where θ_i is set to a constant vector, the marginal likelihood is an integral over a delta function and reduces to the likelihood. Under these circumstances the Bayes factor becomes a simple likelihood ratio of the sort routinely used to compare non-nested models in the classical approach. Once again, classical techniques can be captured as a special case of the Bayesian analysis in which important sources of uncertainty are overlooked.

Returning to the expression for the marginal likelihood, it is clear that evidence in favor of a model can come from two sources. The first and more obvious source of evidence in favor of the model comes from its conformity with the data-generating process, as captured by $p(x|\theta_i, M_i)$. But the marginal likelihood will also depend on the prior distribution for the model parameters $p(\theta_i|M_i)$. Hence, a model's mettle is proven not only by its fit to the data but also by *the ability of the model to capture and articulate useful prior information* that adds to the power of the inference.

The marginal likelihood's dependence on prior information may appear to be a weakness, since the evidence in favor of the model will not be determined purely by the data. However this is not the case for two reasons.

First, think of $p(x|M_i)$ as a forecast. Given M_i, one may be able to specify $p(\theta_i|M_i)$ such that the forecast $p(x|M_i)$ exactly reproduces the distribution of the data x to be observed in the future. With good enough prior information, the weaknesses of a misspecified model can be canceled out. This observation bears out the claim made in Chapter 2 that a well-specified prior parameter distribution can help to mitigate the risk that the chosen model does not conform to the actual data-generating process.

Parsimony

A second benefit of using the prior parameter distribution is that it actually enforces parsimony in the model (Jaynes 2003). The more parameters there are in the model, the more the mass in $p(\theta_i|M_i)$ will be spread out over the parameter space relative to a more parsimonious model. In order to overcome this leakage of probability into extra dimensions, a larger model has to do one of two things—either it must capture more prior information by better specifying the joint distribution of the parameters in the larger model or it must do a much better job of capturing variation in the data because the joint distribution of the data is better described by a larger model.

To see how the marginal likelihood penalizes overly complex models, suppose that parameters are already known—for instance, by setting them to their maximum-likelihood values. Then, we posit that the marginal likelihood can be decomposed as

$$p(x|M_i) = (L_i)_{\max} W_i$$

where $(L_i)_{\max} = p(x|\theta_i = \hat{\theta}_{ML}, M_i)$ and W_i is as yet undefined. Since we have already defined

$$p(x|M_i) = \int_{\theta_i} p(x|\theta_i, M_i)p(\theta_i|M_i)$$

we can write $L(x|\theta_i, M_i) = p(x|\theta_i, M_i)$ in analogy with $(L_i)_{\max}$ to arrive at

$$W_i \approx \int_{\theta_i} \frac{L(x|\theta_i, M_i)}{(L_i)_{\max}} p(\theta_i|M_i) = \int_{\theta_i} \frac{L(x|\theta_i, M_i)}{L(x|\theta_i = \hat{\theta}_{ML}, M_i)} p(\theta_i|M_i).$$

Jaynes (2003, pp. 601–605) calls W_i an *Ockham factor*. The following ratio provides an indication of how much the likelihood is moved from its maximum-likelihood value by the prior distribution:

$$\frac{L(x|\theta_i, M_i)p(\theta_i|M_i)}{L(x|\theta_i = \hat{\theta}_{ML}, M_i)}$$

The overall Ockham factor "is essentially just the amount of prior probability contained in the high-likelihood region picked out by the data" (p. 605). Thus, a larger Ockham factor signals the introduction of prior probability, which enhances the efficiency of estimation, whereas a smaller Ockham factor signals that prior information diminishes efficiency.

Using Ockham factors, the Bayes factor may be decomposed into

$$\frac{p(x|M_i)}{p(x|M_j)} = \frac{(L_i)_{\max}}{(L_j)_{\max}} \cdot \frac{W_i}{W_j}.$$

Assuming parameters are set to their maximum-likelihood values, a model with an extra parameter will have a likelihood no smaller than the base model. If M_i is the larger model, then we have

$$\frac{(L_i)_{\max}}{(L_j)_{\max}} \geq 1.$$

The advantage afforded M_i will be offset by the Ockham factor ratio W_i/W_j if the prior information corresponding to M_i is more diffuse than the prior information for M_j.

Bayes Factors versus Information Criteria The decomposition of the marginal likelihood

$$p(x|M_i) = (L_i)_{\max} W_i$$

also affords some perspective on the information criteria most commonly employed in model selection. Taking logs and multiplying by −1, the log marginal likelihood is:

$$-\ln p(x|M_i) = -\ln (L_i)_{\max} - \ln W_i.$$

Models with greater marginal likelihoods will have lower values $-\ln p(x|M_i)$. In this form, we prefer a greater log likelihood $-\ln (L_i)_{\max}$ and a greater Ockham factor W_i.

The Akaike Information Criterion (AIC), Schwarz Information Criterion (SIC), and Hannon-Quinn Information Criterion (HQIC) have all been proposed as criteria for penalizing models that are overly complex relative to the gain in explanatory power (Lütkepohl 2004a, pp. 33–34). For a model with k regressors and a data set with T observations,

$$AIC = \log \sigma + \frac{2}{T}k$$

$$SIC = \log \sigma + \frac{\log T}{T}k$$

$$HQIC = \log \sigma + \frac{2 \log \log T}{T}k$$

Each criterion contains a likelihood term in σ and a parsimony term in k. Each criterion implies that larger data sets will support more complex models.

Differentiating with respect to k and rearranging, each criterion implies a threshold variance reduction, which must be achieved to justify an additional regressor k, for fixed T:

$$AIC: \quad \frac{\partial \log \sigma}{\partial k} \leq -\frac{2}{T}$$

$$SIC: \quad \frac{\partial \log \sigma}{\partial k} \leq -\frac{\log T}{T}$$

$$HQIC: \quad \frac{\partial \log \sigma}{\partial k} \leq -\frac{2 \log \log T}{T}$$

When compared to Ockham factors, these expressions imply a fixed threshold rate of inference on the modeled data series from additional observations. However, improvements in the modeling of the data cannot be assured simply by having more data. The quality of prior information affects the efficiency of inference in a manner the standard information criteria cannot describe.

Bayes Factors versus Likelihood Ratios Bayes factors may also be compared to the likelihood ratios commonly employed for non-nested model comparisons. Rewriting and fully decomposing the entire expression for posterior model odds,

$$\frac{p(M_i|x)}{p(M_j|x)} = \frac{(L_i)_{\max}}{(L_j)_{\max}} \cdot \frac{W_i}{W_j} \cdot \frac{p(M_i)}{p(M_j)}$$

it is clear that model comparison based solely on likelihood ratios is incorrect for two reasons. Model comparison based on likelihood ratios does not account for the penalty for parsimony captured by the Ockham factor ratio. (Information criteria capture this penalty, albeit in a haphazard way.) More important, however, likelihood ratios assume even prior odds (an odds ratio of unity) for the models being compared. If we have any reason to prefer one model or the other on prior grounds, likelihood ratios are not sufficient to decide posterior odds. This basic error in reasoning is known as the base rate fallacy, and it applies in full force to model comparisons.

Computing marginal likelihoods and Bayes factors allows for a comparison of alternative models that rewards parsimony and upbraids models which do a better job of describing the data. A model may do a better job describing the data either because it better conforms to the data-generating process or because it provides a more effective vehicle for introducing prior information. Thus, if an additional factor is introduced into a model on the intuition that it implies a directional effect over and above the effects already captured by the existing model, the viability of the extra factor becomes a question of whether the directional effect is determined precisely enough by prior information to overcome the leakage of likelihood along an additional dimension. Prior information and model specification are closely intertwined in a way not appreciated by classical model comparisons.

Further, it bears repeating that model comparison with Bayes factors cannot reduce the posterior probability of any model to 0 or 1. The possibility always remains that new data or new prior information will increase the relevance of a model previously thought to be a highly unlikely description of the data. Transitions such as these furnish bona fide signals of breakdown in the incumbent model and should be the primary concern of any model risk analysis.

MODELS AS NUISANCE PARAMETERS

Previously, we found the marginal likelihood by integrating over the prior parameter distribution. Could we not go a step further to somehow integrate over the set of candidate models to arrive at a predictive density for the data

$$p(x) = \int_M p(x|M)?$$

Our intuition suggests that if we can arrive at posterior model probabilities $p(M_i|x)$, the weighted-average forecast

$$p(\hat{y}) = \sum_M p(\hat{y}|x, M_i)p(M_i|x)$$

would incorporate the posterior estimates from all available models. Conditioning on any particular model would vanish, leaving us with only a range of expected values for the data. Under certain assumptions, we can do exactly that: The models can be treated as *nuisance parameters*, which are of no interest in themselves but useful for their instrumental role in making predictions.

Using the law of total probability, it is possible to derive an explicit expression for the posterior probability of a model:

$$p(M_i|x) = \frac{p(x|M_i)p(M_i)}{p(x)} = \frac{p(x|M_i)p(M_i)}{\sum_M p(x|M_i)p(M_i)}.$$

One often sees Bayes' rule written in the latter form. Given a closed set of models M, one can compute numeric posterior probabilities for each model. Then predictions for y can be obtained in the anticipated manner by averaging over all models:

$$p(\hat{y}) = \sum_{M} p(\hat{y}|x, M_i)p(M_i|x).$$

Integrating over models in this way is known as Bayesian model averaging (Hoeting et al. 1999). The Bayesian model averaging formulation offers an interpretive advantage over Bayes factors and odds ratios. Multiple models may be appraised on the basis of prior and posterior probabilities. Fixing probabilities simplifies comparisons across ensembles of models. Instead of computing pairwise odds ratios, direct comparisons are possible. However odds ratios are easily recovered from individual model probabilities whenever desired.

The Space of Models

Taking expectations over an ensemble of models forces us, however, to confront the sense in which the distribution of probabilities over models forms a legitimate probability distribution. In particular, many authors worry about the completeness of the model space in much the same way model specification analysis is traditionally approached. Thus, if a candidate model includes eight regressors, one is obliged to consider all permutations of those eight regressors as other candidate models. For any but the leanest model specifications model averages will quickly become overwhelming to compute, particularly if one adjusts the prior parameter distribution for all combinations of regressors. If combinations are left out, on the other hand, a degree of model uncertainty will go unacknowledged.

Madigan and Raftery (1994) propose a search strategy that eliminates models with minimal probability in order to reduce the universe of all model permutations to a more manageable subset. Their approach acknowledges that there is often little value in considering small variations on a few specifications that capture the majority of the variation in the data. However, it leaves unanswered the possibility that models that have low posterior probability today may emerge as more probable on the basis of future data.

To the author's knowledge, no approach to statistics offers a definitive conceptualization or prescription concerning the "completeness of the model space," or the ability of an analyst to claim they have exhausted the universe of possible model specifications. Leamer (1983) points out the practical impossibility of even attempting such a search, once time and computational cost are taken into account.

As a practical, albeit *ad hoc*, solution to the problem, we recommend that the universe of alternatives be defined as a minimal set of incommensurable or "orthogonal" models, so that overlap between models is minimized and the broadest set of alternatives is canvassed. In other words, the framework of encompassing models is to be avoided in defining the model space as much as possible. Our discussion of hypothesis testing suggests that there is little to be gained from agonizing over the reduction of an encompassing model. There may be reasons to retain extra variables in a model, even if their significance is an open question.

More can be learned by trying out alternatives that are intended to be mutually exclusive. In the world of interest rate modeling, one might audition models based on macroeconomic data and models based on short- and long-term rate factors. Their claim to exclusivity is that one is based on economic fundamentals while the other has a reduced-form or no-arbitrage justification. Within the set of reduced-form models, it would be more productive to see whether short rates follow a diffusion process or a square-root process rather than seeing whether two or three diffusion processes are needed to fit all regions of the term structure. Here, the claim to exclusivity is based on different modeling primitives rather than the appropriate dimension of the model.

We would also suggest the inclusion of an extremely simple model within the set of candidate models as a best practice and a sort of "backstop" view of the data. This backstop model would be primed with a prior parameter distribution consistent with a distressed outcome. Its role is to be the canary in the coal mine. Within the world of interest rate modeling, one might posit a steady drift downward in levels spurred by a flight to quality if modeling government bonds; if modeling credit spreads, the corresponding assumption would be the risk of a substantial jump upward. Other examples would include a version of an asset-pricing model in which "pricing to worst" assumptions are incorporated, a model for equities in which all securities move downward in lockstep, or even an unconditional probability distribution with fat tails and a negative skew. In distress situations complexity vanishes, so the universe of models being entertained ought to include at least one alternative that is a vehicle for such an outcome.

Model comparisons should be less concerned with the reduction of encompassing models and more focused on entertaining wholly different perspectives on the data. In any event, it is anticipated that consideration of multiple models will improve on the practice of relying on a single model, even if the set of candidate models is far from exhaustive. Multiple models may also have an instrumental benefit as a way of characterizing more complex probability distributions as mixtures.

Mixtures of Models

It is straightforward to reinterpret Bayesian model averages in terms of approximations. Returning to an earlier expression:

$$p(\hat{y}) = \sum_{M} p(\hat{y}|x, M_i)p(M_i|x)$$

may be viewed as a superposition of multiple models according to a certain weighting scheme. It is well known, for instance, that many highly complex probability distributions may be represented as a location-scale mixture of normals, or an ensemble of normal models with different means and variances. The specification of the candidate models need not be different; they may just use different prior parameter distributions and prior model weights to achieve an approximation to a skewed, fat-tailed, multimodal, or otherwise unorthodox posterior distribution. Here the art lies in keeping the components sufficiently separate so they do not converge on the same asymptotic result.

A particular class of distributions that is well-represented as a location-scale mixture of normals is the class of hyperbolic distributions (Barndorff-Nielsen 1978). Such distributions do an excellent job representing financial returns due to their skewness and heavy tails (Eberlein and Keller 1995). However, working directly with hyperbolic distributions in a Bayesian framework is difficult due to the lack of a conjugate family and difficulty in simulating from hyperbolic distributions. Thus, working with model averages as an approximation to these distributions furnishes a tractable alternative.

UNCERTAINTY IN PRICING MODELS

Having come this far in an orthodox discussion of the uncertainty in statistical models from a Bayesian point of view, risk practitioners and financial engineers are likely wondering whether the points developed, which are clearly applicable to statistical inference under the physical probability measure (P), have anything to do with modeling under the risk-neutral measure (Q). In fact, it may be less than obvious whether modeling under the Q-measure involves inference at all, and the sense in which such models exhibit uncertainty might be of a different nature than the uncertainty associated with overtly statistical models. Surely once parameters have been determined in a way that reproduces current market prices, there can be no residual doubt that these are the only possible parameter values?

Showing the existence of parameter and model uncertainty in asset-pricing models is basic to establishing the relevance of Bayesian probability to financial risk management. If Bayesian principles had no practical importance outside of traditional actuarial or econometric settings, many financial firms might just as well get on without them. However, we claim that pricing models parameterized under the Q-measure do indeed involve inferences about parameters that are known less than perfectly. Further, the more that pricing models are used for forecasting purposes (as distinguished from static uses like finding very short-term arbitrage opportunities), the more practical relevance parameter uncertainty has for pricing models. The risk management of positions in financial instruments is one such setting where the goal is more akin to forecasting than to exploiting short-term price distortions.

Risk-neutral pricing models are also subject to observational error and overparameterization, which makes them accessible analytically under the lens of Bayesian model comparison. It is possible, in principle, to obtain useful feedback from market data concerning which pricing model, of a set of pricing models, is most likely to be consistent with the market data-generation process. Such feedback is useful when there is no shortage of competing models for the term structure, option prices, commodity forwards, and any number of other instruments. Since each model implies a different dynamic hedging strategy, differentiating between models can also help to lower P&L risk.

Front-Office Models

The pricing models used by front-office traders are designed to fit the prevailing structure of market prices as closely as possible, and in general they do a good job of achieving that goal. Accordingly, it might not be immediately obvious why model uncertainty or parameter uncertainty would be a concern for traders when pricing instruments or hedging their positions. For the discussion that follows, I draw on the thoughtful work of Rebonato, McKay, and White (2009, pp. 205–210), though I end up at a conclusion distinct from theirs. We also anticipate some themes about time series to be taken up in Part Two.

It is probably fair to say that the Black (1976b) model forms an industry-standard starting point in the interest-rate and commodity derivatives markets. Traders aim first to reproduce the forward curve (if it isn't taken as given), and then solve for implied volatilities using at-the-money options prices at each available tenor. The results can then be interpolated and repurposed to price other nonstandard instruments based on the same underlyings.

If the Black model were an adequate description of the underlying price dynamics, the only relevant state variable for the entire system of plain-vanilla derivative instruments would be the spot price, or possibly the future or forward contract closest to expiration. Changes in the spot price would shift the forward curve, and the constant volatility of the underlying would determine the value of options at all tenors. Under these conditions it is possible to hedge any outstanding derivatives using a self-financing portfolio of the underlying asset and the risk-free instrument, and all of the parameters of the model are properly parameters under the risk-neutral measure. The only variability in the model is that of the spot price, so the delta of the position would almost completely determine the necessary hedging strategy, with gamma (second-order sensitivity to the spot price) and theta (the change in value with respect to time) playing lesser roles.

However, the Black model is not an adequate description of the underlying price dynamics of any market. Green and Figlewski (1999) show that the average returns of writing options on equities, interest rates, and exchange rates when hedging with the Black model are often highly negative, with wide variance and egregious worst-case realizations. A market maker taking the Black model at its word would be sunk before long.

There are also solid theoretical reasons why the Black model is not an adequate description of market price dynamics. Interest rates, dividend yields, and convenience yields, among other quantities entering the model, are not constant, leading to different sensitivities to the spot price along the forward curve. Nor can the assumption of constant volatility explain volatility surfaces with term structures (different implied volatilities at each tenor) or smiles (different implied volatilities for options of different moneyness). In the realm of interest rate derivatives the Libor Market Model captures the joint dynamics of forward interest rates enough to permit a true forward curve and stochastic volatility, but without reproducing the smile. The competing SABR model reproduces the smile, but without corresponding information about its dynamics. Thus, the Libor Market Model adds another state variable (stochastic volatility) that leaves a certain piece of market reality unexplained, while the SABR model offers a better fit by adding static parameters.

When a model is employed that treats dynamic features of the market as static parameters, successive recalibrations of the model are needed to allow static parameters to adjust. As a result, traders will have to hedge changes in the parameters as if they, too, were state variables. In the Black model, investors should never have to hedge rho or vega (sensitivity to interest rates and volatility, respectively), but they do anyway because changes in model-based values arising from successive recalibrations oblige them to. So while a pricing model should prescribe exactly what risks need to be hedged (and how) by separating state variables from static parameters, they instead lead to ambiguity about hedging because matching market prices from period to period requires recalibrating the model and changing "static" parameters. And as Chib and Ergashev (2009, pp. 1325, 1335–1336) demonstrate for some common interest models, successive recalibrations can result in significant shifts in key parameters, making the risk of a position in a related financial instrument as much a function of the *model risk* as it is a function of *market risk*.

The Statistical Nature of Front-Office Models

As an alternative to the front-office practices sketched above, we could relax the requirement that pricing models must reproduce the structure of market prices *exactly* and admit the possibility of pricing error (Johannes and Polson 2009b). While we might not want to make markets from minute to minute with such a model, relaxing the requirement of an exact fit to the market at all times could afford smoother evolutions for "static" model parameters and a description of the system dynamics in terms of a relatively small set of state variables. The potential gain would be a more stable hedging strategy that is more responsive to market risk than to model risk.

As soon as the possibility of pricing error is admitted (due to market microstructure noise or staleness in pricing, for example), calibrating a pricing model becomes a statistical exercise of searching for parameters that fit a system of prices on many dates, rather than just one date. Accordingly, many different parameter vector values may have more or less probability of being the "correct" values, so an uncertain distribution of parameters becomes possible. By the same token, multiple pricing models can be tried out in parallel, since no one model will capture all of the features of the market at any given time.

It turns out that uncertainties about the parameters in pricing models can be captured by Bayesian techniques in essentially the same way as any statistical model. We will demonstrate an analysis of pricing model uncertainty in Chapter 8 with an online estimation of the Schwartz (1997) commodity forward curve model. The degree of parameter uncertainty captured in such exercises can provide a clue to the expected size of *model risk* hedges. Bayesian model comparisons can also help evaluate whether adding more parameters to a market model channels prior information effectively enough to overcome the loss of parsimony.

In Part Two, we will extend these elements of Bayesian analysis to an online, sequential setting appropriate to time series models of market dynamics. In a dynamic analysis, changes in the uncertainty associated with states and parameters, as well as changes in posterior model probabilities, signal changes in model risk. In other words, sequential Bayesian analysis can furnish real-time evidence of model breakdowns. Quantitative traders will no doubt appreciate the value of being able to spot sudden shifts in the market this way.

The additional information gained from a Bayesian analysis of a pricing model can also inform market making in complex derivatives, particularly when such derivatives are not redundant securities reproducible as a portfolio of simpler instruments. (Since we break the exact link between model and market, it is best to be wary of arbitrage opportunities, albeit without assuming from the outset that the desk will be promptly bankrupted by a surge in demand for a complex or bespoke derivative.) Equipped with better information about the likely cost of hedging the complex derivative over its lifetime, a trading desk may be able to offer the derivative on more competitive terms than others in the marketplace, or offer more competitive margin terms. At the very least, understanding the range in variation of model parameters and their associated hedging cost would be useful to management in understanding the value being produced by financial engineers.

A NOTE ON BACKTESTING

A common device used in model criticism to test the robustness of a model specification is to calibrate a model on data from a given time period, and then to forecast with the model using data from a different time period. Since the training set is usually the more recent of the two, the practice is known as backtesting. Backtesting asks whether today's model with today's parameters would have done a good job of forecasting recent history based on past data. The intention of backtesting is to identify overfitting and structural breaks (changes in parameters) in a chosen model form. Whether the model is overfit or changes in parameters exist, the model forecasts obtained in the backtest will systematically depart from actual results, so that the distribution of errors will have a nonzero mean and/or a different variance out-of-sample than in-sample. Determining whether the problem is overfitting or structural breaks will require further analysis, including reestimating the model over the backtest period (Jorion 2006).

Apart from the limited ability of backtests to disentangle structural breaks (parameter uncertainty) from overfitting (model uncertainty), it is also somewhat unclear what conclusion is to be drawn in the event backtesting shows a discontinuity between historical and current data. If market conditions have changed in the recent past, a successful backtest would be undesirable—indeed, it would ensure that important changes in conditions go unnoticed. On the other hand, unsuccessful backtests may occur for reasons unrelated to changes in market conditions. Excessive errors in forecasts may reflect inadequate accounting for parameter uncertainty; even simulating over individual sampling distributions for model parameters will likely give an incomplete picture.

Backtesting acknowledges the fact that market conditions can change over time, and that changes in market conditions can invalidate model forecasts. Neither of these propositions should be controversial. However, the ability of periodic backtests to catch changes in market conditions or to guarantee that one's model is sufficiently "structural" should be seriously doubted.

Our solution to the impasse introduced by backtesting is to define models that take the ongoing evolution of market conditions for granted, and to seek out diagnostics of model performance that can be reevaluated from day to day. Adaptive models assume variation in parameter and model forms and encompass the special (and extremely limiting) case in which parameters are static (structural) and a single model form is "correct." By contrast, currently accepted approaches merely assume the truth of that limiting case. Online model diagnostics show breakdowns as they happen, without reference to the in-sample/out-of-sample distinction imposed by backtests. Accordingly, we believe adaptive modeling will produce superior results for validation versus the static view imposed by backtesting.

Part Two takes up the construction of adaptive models that can react to new data as they are observed in order to update model-based inferences, while continuing to acknowledge model and parameter uncertainty. We can therefore think of Part Two as the dynamic completion of the static perspective on model risk developed in Part One.

PART

Two

Sequential Learning with Adaptive Statistical Models

CHAPTER 4

Introduction to Sequential Modeling

In the first part of the book, we developed an analysis of how classical statistical methods overlook important dimensions of uncertainty in statistical inference, which lead to errors in estimation and model specification. We undertook that analysis in a static setting in order to make the sources of uncertainty plain with a minimum of complication. Now we begin the work of extending the Bayesian analysis developed previously to a time series setting, allowing us to focus on what is arguably the most important source of model risk: the risk that an adequate description of market phenomena today will not be adequate in the future.

Over the next chapters we develop an approach to time series modeling that is entirely sequential in its orientation, allowing models to adapt themselves continuously to changing market conditions. Developing models that revise and update themselves with each subsequent observation is a necessary response once the assumption of a time-invariant data-generating process is abandoned. We have already argued that it is untenable to assume time-invariant processes for financial data, as well as an abdication of the requisite vigilance for ruptures in market dynamics. Sequential models adapt in response to new information. The more surprising the new information, the more significantly the model adapts. Parameter estimates and their uncertainties will change, models will be assigned more or less posterior probability, and forecasts based on model averages will be revised and reweighted accordingly.

The design of adaptive time series models will require new tactics. Though the models we have examined in the first section of the book can be recast easily in a sequential orientation, we will see that repeated updates to static Bayesian models will reproduce the weaknesses of classical time series methods. As more data are observed, the accumulation of weight in the prior distribution makes the model less sensitive to new data. Bayesian estimates then converge on maximum likelihood estimates. Accordingly, this short introductory chapter addresses some issues associated with the sequential implementation of Bayesian models. A simple probability setting is adopted throughout the chapter, building on the models introduced previously and allowing an uncluttered discussion of the issues before moving into more technically demanding material.

SEQUENTIAL BAYESIAN INFERENCE

In Chapter 1, we characterized the basic Bayesian inference procedure as a transition from a prior distribution to a posterior distribution via the likelihood for the data. Though *prior* and *posterior* are used in a logical sense rather than a temporal sense, there is no reason why the latter interpretation cannot be adopted, particularly when time series data are the object of analysis. Ongoing inference through a sequence of prior and posterior beliefs also conforms well with our everyday experience of continually revising beliefs in light of accumulated information.

The sequential interpretation of Bayes' rule is easily developed in a formal setting. Breaking A apart so that $A = \{A_1, A_2, \dots, A_n\}$ and assuming the observations in A are independent, it is easy to see that

$$\begin{aligned} p(B|A_1) &\propto p(A_1|B)p(B) \\ p(B|A_1, A_2) &\propto p(A_2|B)p(B|A_1) \\ &\vdots \\ p(B|A_1, \dots, A_{n-1}) &\propto p(A_{n-1}|B)p(B|A_1, \dots, A_{n-2}) \\ p(B|A_1, \dots, A_n) &\propto p(A_n|B)p(B|A_1, \dots, A_{n-1}) \end{aligned}$$

At each stage, the posterior probability distribution for B from the previous update becomes the prior probability distribution for the following update. Beliefs about the probability of B are successively refined as each item in A is observed in its turn. If A is a stream of time series data, our interpretation in terms of sequential updating is completely natural. It is just as easy to change the subscripts $i = 1, \dots, n$ to $t = 1, \dots, T$.

Working backward through the chain, however, it can also be seen that the end result is identical to what would have been obtained if we had digested the information in A all at once. Collecting all of the likelihood terms on the right-hand side,

$$p(B|A_1, \dots, A_T) \propto \prod_{t=1}^{T} p(A_t|B) \times p(B)$$

$$p(B|A) \propto p(A|B)p(B)$$

In the absence of modification, our sequential approach leads back to the batch estimation results we have criticized as too rigid and too blithely structural.

Working within the context of the beta-Bernoulli model from Chapter 2 will help to shed more light on the manner in which unmodified sequential inference reproduces the excessive confidence of the maximum-likelihood approach. In Chapter 2, we showed how a posterior estimate of the Bernoulli success probability s could be obtained using the beta distribution, prior hyperparameters, and sufficient statistics. Beginning from a prior distribution B(a,b), we obtained a posterior estimate B(A,B) with $A = a + x$ and $B = b + (n - x)$, and $x = \sum_i x_i$, $x_i = \{0, 1\}$.

Conceiving of Bayesian updating in terms of hyperparameters and sufficient statistics lends itself to sequential implementation of Bayesian inference. Instead of conducting inference using all of $x = \sum_i x_i$ at once, we could break up x into $x = \sum_J x_j$ for some subindex $J \leq n$. Then $A = a + x_1 + \cdots + x_j$, $B = b + (n_1 - x_1) + \cdots + (n_J - x_J)$, and for any intermediate point in the sequence $j = 1, \dots, J$ we can draw a valid inference $B(A_j, B_j)$. Let's check that this is the case. Recall that the likelihood for the Bernoulli trials was $L(x|n,s) = \prod_{i=1}^{n} s^{x_i}(1-s)^{1-x_i}$. Breaking up the sample n into j pieces results in the likelihood

$$L(x|n,s) = \prod_{j=1}^{J} \prod_{i=1}^{n_j} s^{x_{ij}}(1-s)^{1-x_{ij}} = \prod_{i=1}^{n} s^{x_i}(1-s)^{1-x_i}.$$

Here $x_{ij} = 1$ if $x_i = 1$ and i falls into the partition j. At every step through the J subsets of n we can compute sufficient statistics $x_j = \sum_{i=1}^{n_j} x_i$ and n_j, producing J intermediate updates about the hyperparameters of the beta distribution. Clearly in the limit $J = n$, and updates can be made with each observation.

At the end of a sequence of J updates, we will have

$$A = a + \sum_J x_j = a + x$$

$$B = b + \sum_J (n_j - x_j) = b + (n - x)$$

just as when we considered the data$\{x_i\}$in a batch rather than as m online updates in a sequence.

In Chapter 2, we had also characterized $a + b$ and $A + B = a + b + n$ as the effective sample size of the prior and posterior beta distributions. As n grows, so will the effective sample size. Thus, by the time the last observation x_T is being processed, the effective sample size of the prior beta distribution will be $a_{t-1} + b_{t-1} = a + b + (n - 1)$, whereas the effective sample size of the prior when processing x_1 was only $a_0 + b_0$. As a result, later observations will receive progressively less weight relative to the accumulated inference. Likewise, the variance of the prior distribution for s, which is equal to

$$Var(s) = \frac{a_0 b_0}{(a_0 + b_0)^2 (a_0 + b_0 + 1)}$$

reflects increasing confidence in our estimate of s. The denominator of the variance will increase from $(a_0 + b_0)^2(a_0 + b_0 + 1)$ to $(a_0 + b_0 + n - 1)^2(a_0 + b_0 + n)$, whereas the numerator will only increase from $a_0 b_0$ to $a_{t-1} b_{t-1}$, so that overall the variance declines as $1/n$.

A simple example bears out our analysis. One thousand Bernoulli trials were simulated in which the success probability alternates between 0.3 and 0.7 every 100 observations. Thus, we know for sure at the outset that the process generating the data is not a stationary Bernoulli process. If posterior estimates were perfectly adaptive, the mean of the posterior distribution would oscillate back and forth between 0.3 and 0.7. However, in a maximum-likelihood setting, one would expect the model to split the difference and converge on a mean success probability of 0.5. Weighted averages of the success probabilities will swing from 0.3 to $(100(0.3) + 100(0.7))/200 = 0.5$ to $(200(0.3) + 100(0.7))/\ 300 = 0.433$, and so on. Though estimates closer to 0.3 or 0.7 may be possible over the initial observations in the data set, the maximum-likelihood parameter estimate will ultimately converge to 0.5, an equally weighted combination of the two probabilities.

Visualizing the sequence of updates makes it easy to understand the manner in which sequential Bayesian estimates converge on maximum-likelihood estimates. More important, the sequential rendering makes clear how maximum-likelihood estimates produce weighted-average estimates whenever a time period exhibiting changes in the data-generating process is treated as a sample from a time-invariant process.

Figure 4.1 plots the evolution of the posterior distribution when data are viewed sequentially. The graphic is a series of probability distribution profiles, arranged by their position in the sequence of inferences. Moving from the front to the back of the series of profiles represents further progress in the series of inferences. Here, the prior distribution is B(50,50), or $s = 0.5$, with weight equivalent to 100 observations. Over the initial set of observations,

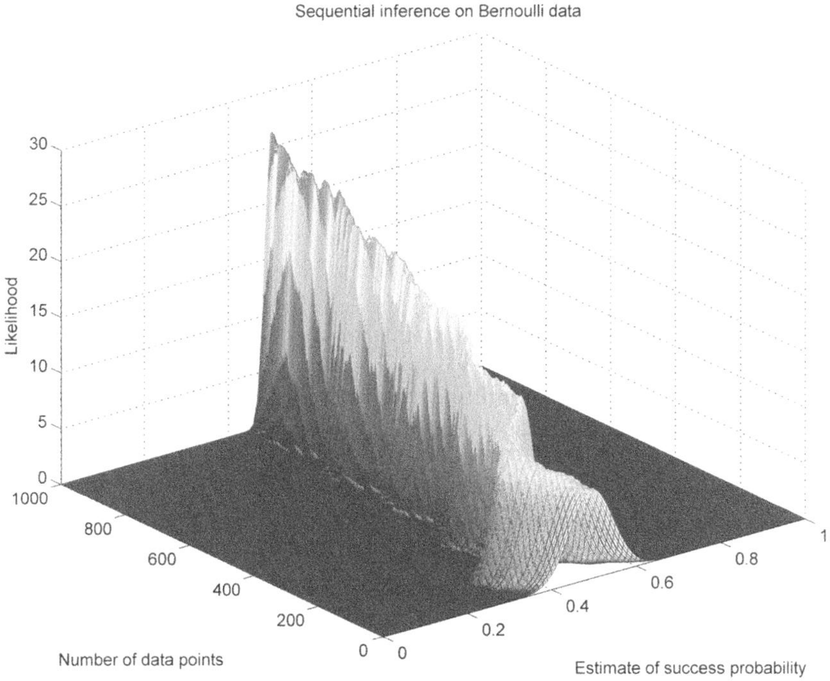

FIGURE 4.1 Sequential Inference on Bernoulli Data with Oscillatory Success Probability

which have a success probability of 0.3, the mode of the posterior distribution drifts toward 0.3, whereas it can be seen to move back toward 0.7 over the next hundred observations. As more data are observed, the oscillations back and forth become less pronounced. The posterior distributions also become more peaked, reflecting the accumulation of weight and increasing confidence in the correctness of the estimate of s. Further, since each posterior distribution becomes the prior distribution for the next observation, the accumulated weight makes the next observation relatively less important. By the time 1000 observations have been observed, the posterior distribution is highly peaked around 0.5, the blended mean of the two success probabilities. Our sequential model has become increasingly sure of an erroneous conclusion.

ACHIEVING ADAPTIVITY VIA DISCOUNTING

In the previous example, it was evident that the final estimate obtained at the end of a sequence of inferences would be identical to the estimate that would be obtained if all of the data were considered at once. As more data were processed, the Bayesian estimates converged on the maximum-likelihood estimates. Thus, whether we work in batches or sequentially, a long time series will lead us to believe that we have reduced parameter uncertainty to a minimum.

Chapter 1 gave several reasons to be suspicious of such a view. The market environment one faces at the end of a long period of time is unlikely to be like the market faced at the outset. As a result, it would be foolish to believe that one has closed in on an "ultimate" answer at the end of a long sequence of estimates.

The mere fact that it is mathematically feasible to update a Bayesian model observation by observation is clearly not enough to ensure that estimates adapt to new market conditions. Some other device is needed to allow parameter estimates to adjust. This device is known as discounting (Harrison 1965, 1967).

Discounting is a subjective intervention in the rules of Bayesian inference that achieves adaptivity by reducing the effective sample size of the posterior and increasing the variance of parameter estimates. Both of these interventions are necessary to prevent convergence on the "ignorant certainty" of the maximum likelihood result. Reducing the effective sample size controls the weight attributed to the prior distribution in successive inferences. Increasing the variance of parameter estimates spreads the prior distribution over more of the parameter space. Thinking of the prior distribution as a collection of hypotheses, the increased variance represents the expectation that outcomes far from the mean will be realized more often than an updating rule based on time-invariance would imply. As a result, data that would normally be regarded as surprising are granted more influence than they would if the variance of the prior distribution were allowed to decline with each observation.

Put somewhat differently, discounting is a way of committing to a maximum permitted level of influence for accumulated prior information in sequential inference. Accordingly, discounting also sets an upper limit for how long any observation may affect inferences. Discounting thereby ensures that distinct segments of a time series are not pooled together uncritically as fungible subsamples of an unchanging data-generation process.

The technique of discounting is crucially important in distinguishing adaptive Bayesian time series inference from classical methods based on prefiltered data. Classical methods currently in wide use combine repeated recalibration of a model with a scheme for repeatedly reweighting the data. Weighting the data with exponentially declining weights or other well-known devices down-weights past observations and can obscure important information in the data. For example, Jaynes (2003, pp. 520–526) describes how obvious cyclicality in a 100-year temperature series was missed over 50 years of analysis due to the uncritical prefiltering of the data. Bayesian discounting methods, on the other hand, create inferences that are more sensitive to current data by *down-weighting the inference*. This is a crucial distinction.

Bayesian methods combined with discounting recognize that the staying power of inferences about the external world is limited. Once an inference is drawn, new data must continue to be consistent with the inference in order for the conclusion to be maintained. Discounting also offers additional flexibility when there is uncertainty about the model specification. By allowing fixed model parameters to drift over a sequence of observations, the discounted version of a model may be regarded as a convenient, locally linear approximation to a nonlinear underlying process.

Discounting in the Beta-Bernoulli Model

Let's return again to our beta-Bernoulli example. The effective sample size $A + B = a + b + n$ also controls the variance of the posterior distribution. If we intervene in the calculation of the effective sample size to keep it from increasing without limit, we will also increase the variance relative to our original benchmark. Suppose we multiply the hyperparameter a by a discount factor $\delta \in [0, 1]$. Consider the successive accumulation of discount factors δ in recursive calculations of the sufficient statistics:

$$
\begin{aligned}
A_1 &= \delta a + x_1 \\
A_2 &= \delta(\delta a + x_1) + x_2 \\
A_3 &= \delta(\delta(\delta a + x_1) + x_2) + x_3 \\
\vdots\ &\ \ \vdots \\
A_t &= \delta^t a + [\delta^{t-1} x_1 + \cdots + \delta x_{t-1}] + x_t
\end{aligned}
$$

As the number of observations t increases without limit, the first term $\delta^t a \to 0$ for any prior hyperparameter a: The original prior hyperparameter will eventually exert no influence over the inference, which is consistent with the notion that information decays over time. In the second part of the sum (in brackets) the total weight of the terms $x_1, \ldots, x_{j-1}$ is $\frac{\delta - \delta^t}{1-\delta}$, which converges to $\frac{\delta}{1-\delta}$ as t increases. Finally the most recent observation x_t enters with a weight of unity. Hence, the overall contribution of the accumulated data to the effective sample size is constant at $\frac{\delta}{1-\delta} + 1$. Analysis of $B_1, \ldots, B_j$ yields a similar result for the prior hyperparameter b and weights applied to the terms $(1 - x_1), \ldots, (1 - x_{j-1})$. Because the same set of weights is added and subtracted by the series of terms $(1 - x_t)$, the hyperparameters b make no additional contribution to the effective sample size, so that when we choose δ we choose an effective sample size $\frac{\delta}{1-\delta} + 1$ for the prior distribution, held constant by repeated application of the discount factor. Values $\delta = 0.98$ and $\delta = 0.99$, for example, correspond to effective sample sizes of 50 and 100, respectively.

Accordingly, we can replace our sufficient statistic updating rules with

$$A = \delta a + x_t$$
$$B = \delta b + (1 - x_t)$$

to obtain a discounted sequential beta-Bernoulli model. By using a constant δ, it is assumed that updates are computed observation by observation. The hyperparameters A and B count successes and failures one by one, while continuously down-weighting the accumulated evidence. We maintain this assumption throughout for simplicity.

Note that at any point in the inference, the mean of the beta distribution is

$$\frac{\delta a_t}{\delta a_t + \delta b_t} = \frac{a_t}{a_t + b_t}$$

while the variance is

$$\frac{\delta^2 a_t b_t}{\delta^2 (a_t + b_t)^2 (\delta a_t + \delta b_t + 1)} = \frac{a_t b_t}{(a_t + b_t)^2 (\delta a_t + \delta b_t + 1)}$$
$$\geq \frac{a_t b_t}{(a_t + b_t)^2 (a_t + b_t + 1)}.$$

The mean is unaffected by discounting, which is desirable, while the denominator of the variance is scaled back, increasing the variance.

Revisiting our simulated example with discounting at each step, we can see that the variance of the beta distribution remains relatively large with successive observations, allowing the estimate to adapt as the frequency of successes rises and falls.

Figure 4.2 analyzes the same data set with a discount factor of $\delta = 0.99$, which implies an effective sample size of 100 observations. Since the prior B(50,50) also is equivalent to 100 observations, the mode of the posterior distribution remains at a constant height as every one of the 1000 observations is processed. The variance of the posterior distribution remains essentially unchanged, while the mean oscillates between 0.3 and 0.7 as desired. Indeed, the discount factor implies $1 - \delta = 1 - 0.99 = 1$ percent of the information is lost with each observation, and about two-thirds ($0.99^{100} \approx 0.63$)

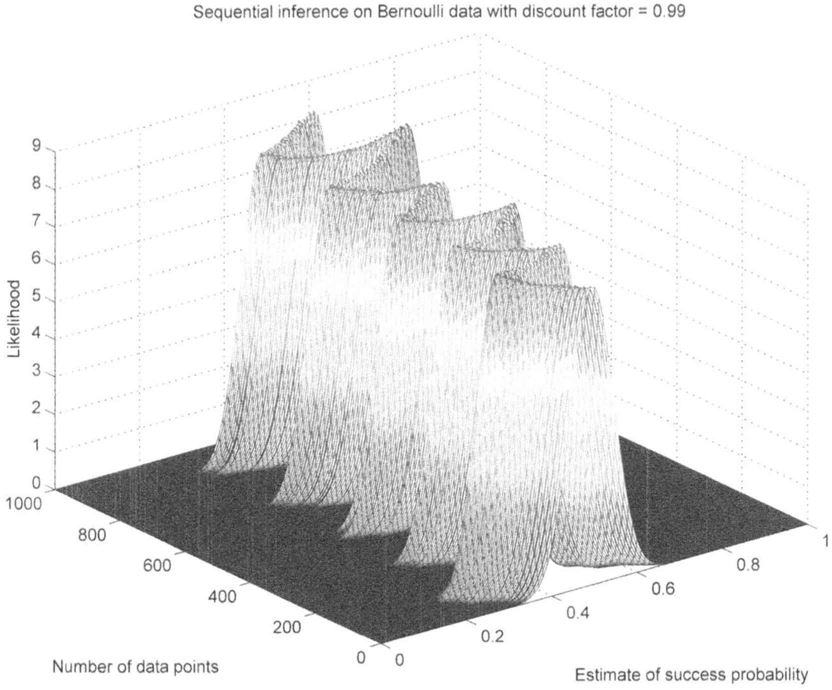

FIGURE 4.2 Sequential Inference on Bernoulli Data with Discount Factor = 0.99

of each hundred-observation segment of the data will be forgotten by the time the next hundred-observation segment is processed.

If we set the discount factor to $\delta = 0.98$, sequential inference follows the pattern traced out by Figure 4.3. With an effective sample size of 50, the long-run height of the posterior distribution is actually lower than the initial prior distribution, which was equivalent to 100 observations. The distributions are both more dispersed and more adaptive. Note that the paths between the poles of 0.3 and 0.7 are not as smooth as before. The inference is actually catching small local runs within the simulated data where there are random increases or decreases in observed successes relative to their theoretical value. Both this extra variability and increased dispersion can be utilized in model comparisons to indicate, in examples where the "correct" rate of information loss is unknown, that one has chosen an excessively large discount factor.

What happens if the underlying success probability actually is constant? Will the discounted model gain confidence that the success probability is constant? Simulating 1000 new observations with $s = 0.5$, Figures 4.4 and 4.5 show the inferences drawn when using discount factors of 0.99 and 0.98.

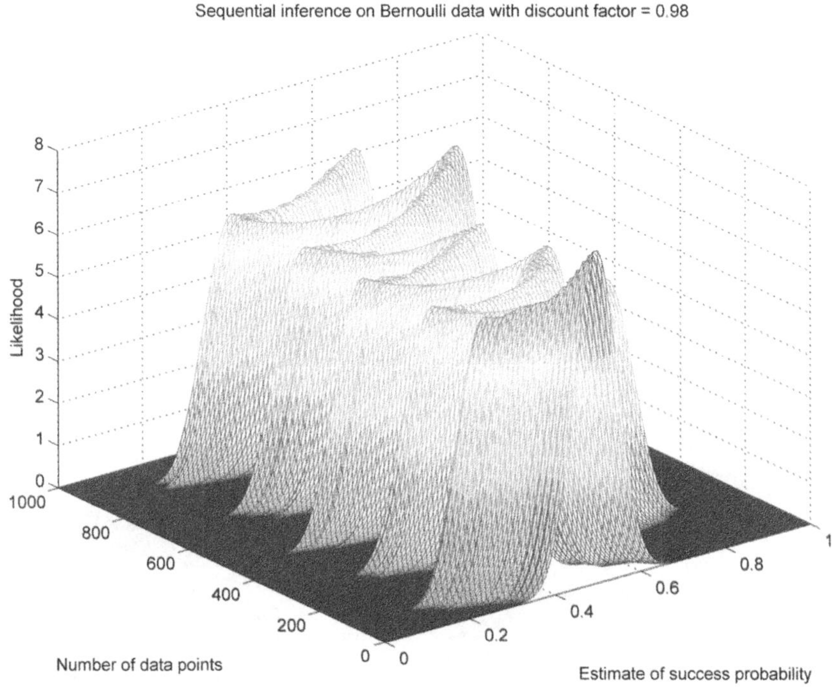

FIGURE 4.3 Sequential Inference on Bernoulli Data with Discount Factor = 0.98

Each of the inferences attains and maintains a maximum level of confidence. Each continues to show variations around the known parameter value of 0.5 because the data are truly random, and local variations around the known success probability occur due to randomness. But even if there were no residual randomness, confidence in the discounted inference would not exceed the level implied by the effective sample size.

This seeming refusal of the model to converge to a definitive conclusion is the price paid for adaptivity. At any instant, if the success probability of the process generating the data were to diverge from 0.5, the model estimates would adapt, regardless of how long $s = 0.5$ had been a good description of the data. Compare this result to the tendency of classical time series to treat all data as sampled from the same process under the assumption of ergodic stationarity. If there is a desire, however, to recognize the possibility of very precise inferences, a model with a very high discount factor (say $\delta = 0.998$) may be included in the set of models under consideration. When such a model is a good description, it will maintain high posterior weight, which will be lost quickly if the success probability deviates from $s = 0.5$ by even a small amount.

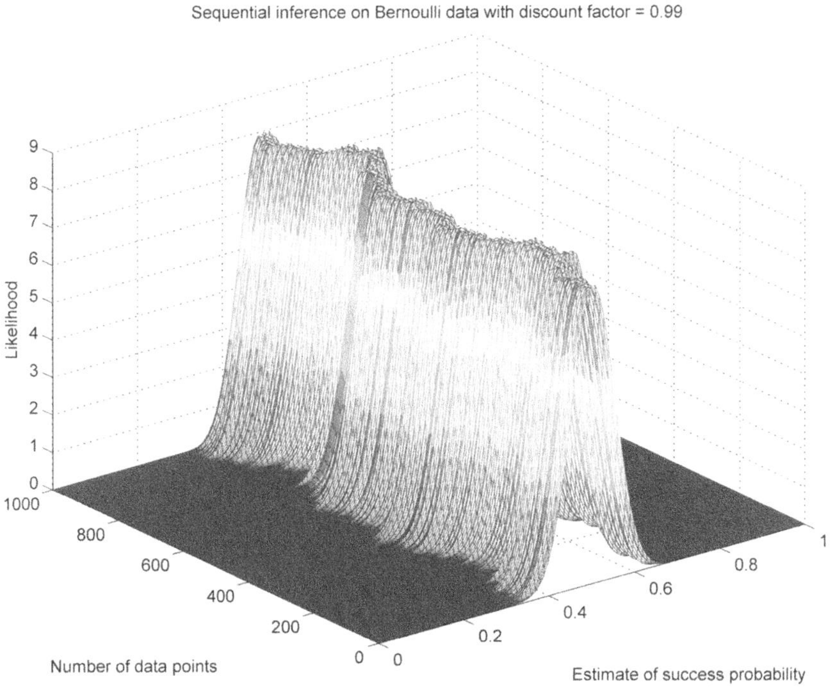

FIGURE 4.4 Sequential Inference on Time-Invariant Bernoulli Process with Discount Factor = 0.99

Discounting in the Linear Regression Model

Discounting can be applied successfully in other models as well. In the normal-inverted gamma model for linear regression, we have two variance terms, $\mathbf{B}_1$ and S_1, the latter associated with the effective sample size term n_1. Discounting can be applied to $\mathbf{B}_1$ or S_1 depending on the kind of adaptivity that is desired: Adaptivity of the coefficients will be achieved by discounting $\mathbf{B}_1$, whereas the standard error of the regression will adapt if S_1 is discounted.

If we choose to adapt $\mathbf{B}_1$ we will have, in place of the usual recursive updates, the observation-by-observation recursions

$$
\begin{aligned}
\mathbf{B}_1^{-1} &= \mathbf{X}'\mathbf{X} + \delta\mathbf{B}_0^{-1} \\
\mathbf{b}_1 &= \mathbf{B}_1(\mathbf{X}'\mathbf{y} + \delta\mathbf{B}_0^{-1}\mathbf{b}_0) \\
n_1 &= n_0 + 1 \\
n_1 S_1 &= n_0 S_0 + (\mathbf{y} - \mathbf{X}\mathbf{b}_1)'\mathbf{y} + \delta(\mathbf{b}_0 - \mathbf{b}_1)'\mathbf{B}_0^{-1}\mathbf{b}_0.
\end{aligned}
$$

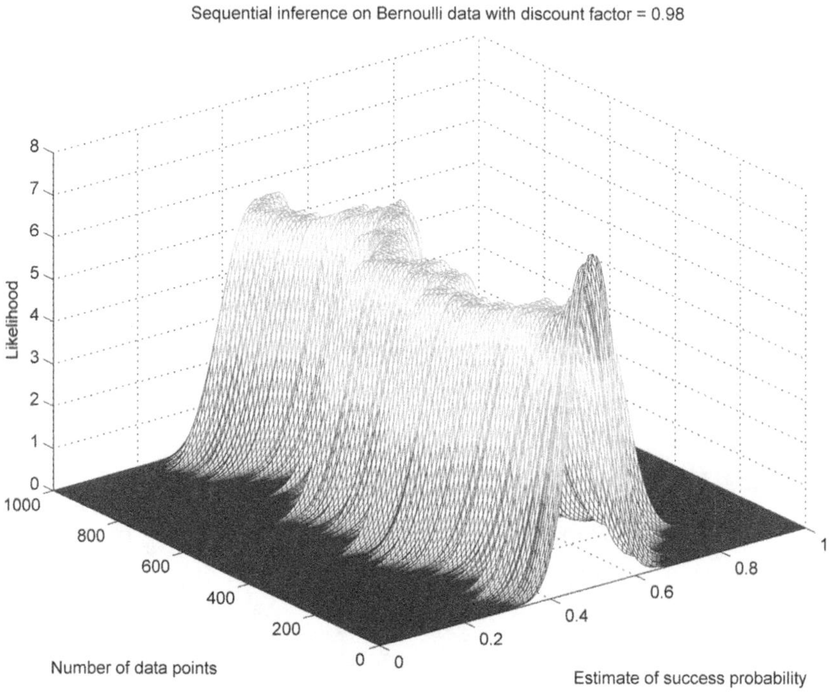

FIGURE 4.5 Sequential Inference on Time-Invariant Bernoulli Process with Discount Factor = 0.98

Discriminating between the discount factors for $\mathbf{B}_1$ and S_1 as δ_B and δ_S, respectively, the recursions become

$$\begin{aligned}
\mathbf{B}_1^{-1} &= \mathbf{X}'\mathbf{X} + \delta_B \mathbf{B}_0^{-1} \\
\mathbf{b}_1 &= \mathbf{B}_1(\mathbf{X}'\mathbf{y} + \delta_B \mathbf{B}_0^{-1}\mathbf{b}_0) \\
n_1 &= \delta_S n_0 + 1 \\
n_1 S_1 &= \delta_S n_0 S_0 + (\mathbf{y} - \mathbf{X}\mathbf{b}_1)'\mathbf{y} + \delta_B(\mathbf{b}_0 - \mathbf{b}_1)'\mathbf{B}_0^{-1}\mathbf{b}_0,
\end{aligned}$$

as can be verified by working through the derivation of the normal linear regression model presented in Chapter 2. The two discount-factor specification allows for evolving coefficients and ARCH-like regression errors. Different rates of persistence for coefficient information and error variances are handled easily by choosing different values for δ_B and δ_S.

To see how discounting the normal regression model plays out in practice, we can examine another simulated data set. One thousand data points are simulated using a cosine function for the intercept and a sine function for the single regression coefficient, both with period 200π as shown in Figure 4.6. We set the prior for the intercept and regression coefficient to 0.1 and −0.1, respectively. If the data were treated as being sampled from a time-invariant process, the intercept and regression coefficient would converge to a mean of zero as more of the data set is processed.

Figures 4.7 and 4.8 reproduce our intuition. Just as in the Bernoulli trial example, the series of undiscounted sequential inferences becomes increasingly sure that the intercept and the beta are equal to zero as more data are processed. Underlying variation in the model parameters is suppressed.

Introducing a discount factor $\delta_B = 0.99$ enforces an effective sample size of 100, preventing accumulated prior weight from dulling the response to

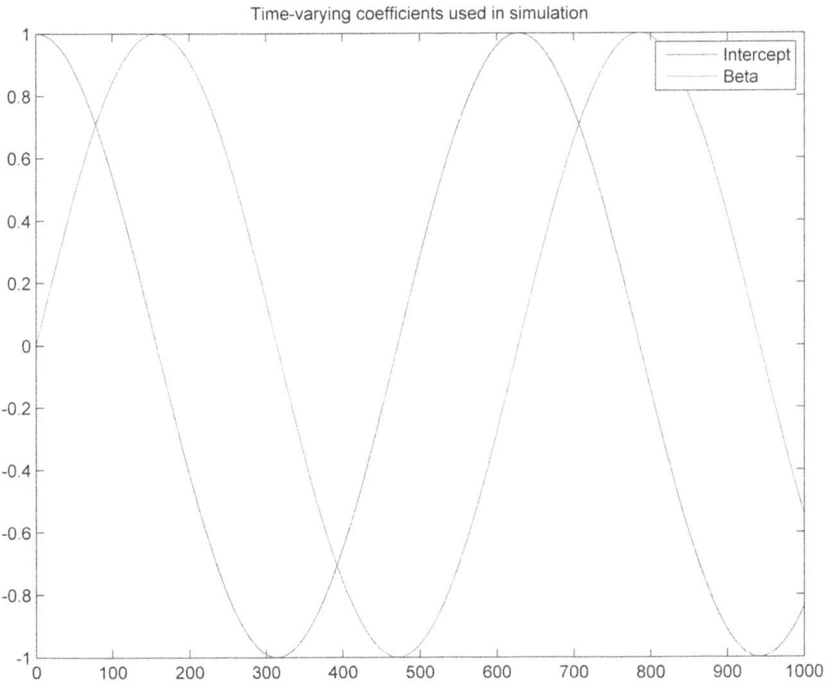

FIGURE 4.6 Time-Varying Coefficients Used to Generate Data for Regression Model

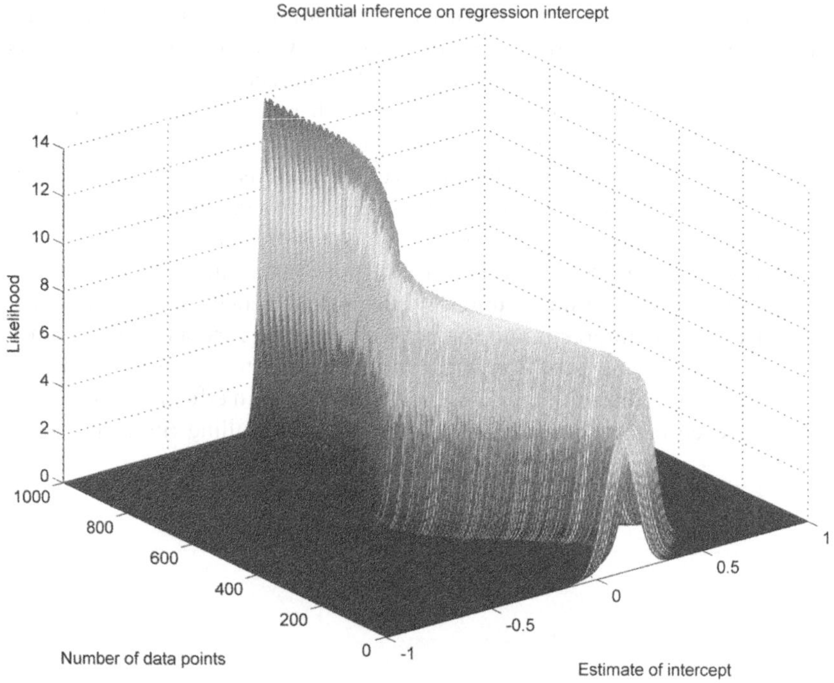

FIGURE 4.7 Sequential Inference on Regression Intercept under Assumption of Time-Invariance

new data. Figures 4.9 and 4.10 show the intercept and regression coefficient tracking their evolutions nicely. Since the prior for the regression coefficient is more at odds with the data than the prior for the intercept, it takes more time to fall into line.

Figure 4.11 shows the evolution of error dispersion estimates when the standard error of the regression is discounted as well with $\delta_S = 0.99$. The regression error is constant in the simulated model, so there are no significant variations in the probability distribution profiles. However, note that there are periods where the likelihood flattens out and the error term widens. These periods correspond to reversals in the regression coefficients. As predictions based on previous estimates of the regression coefficients break down and the new trajectory for those coefficients begins to be learned, the regression error term increases to compensate for the additional uncertainty.

We could also apply different discount factors to the diagonal elements of $\mathbf{B}_1$, for instance, if we believed information on the intercept was being

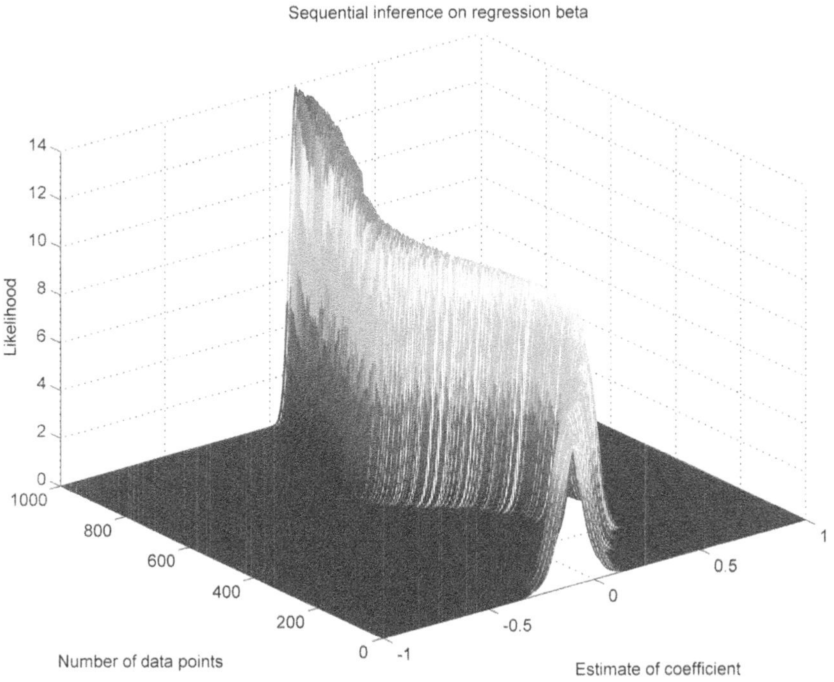

FIGURE 4.8 Sequential Inference on Regression Beta under Assumption of Time-Invariance

lost at a different rate than information on the regression coefficient. The modification of the recursive updates given above to accommodate multiple discount factors is straightforward. Letting $\Delta = diag(\delta_1, \ldots, \delta_K)$ where each δ_i corresponds to one of the k regressors, we obtain

$$
\begin{aligned}
\mathbf{B}_1^{-1} &= \mathbf{X}'\mathbf{X} + \Delta^{1/2}\mathbf{B}_0^{-1}\Delta^{1/2} \\
\mathbf{b}_1 &= \mathbf{B}_1\left(\mathbf{X}'\mathbf{y} + \Delta^{1/2}\mathbf{B}_0^{-1}\Delta^{1/2}\mathbf{b}_0\right) \\
n_1 &= \delta_S n_0 + 1 \\
n_1 S_1 &= \delta_S n_0 S_0 + (\mathbf{y} - \mathbf{X}\mathbf{b}_1)'\mathbf{y} + (\mathbf{b}_0 - \mathbf{b}_1)'\Delta^{1/2}\mathbf{B}_0^{-1}\Delta^{1/2}\mathbf{b}_0.
\end{aligned}
$$

Comparison with the Time-Invariant Case

Both the beta-Bernoulli and linear regression examples help to make the more general point that the parameter estimates obtained in classical time

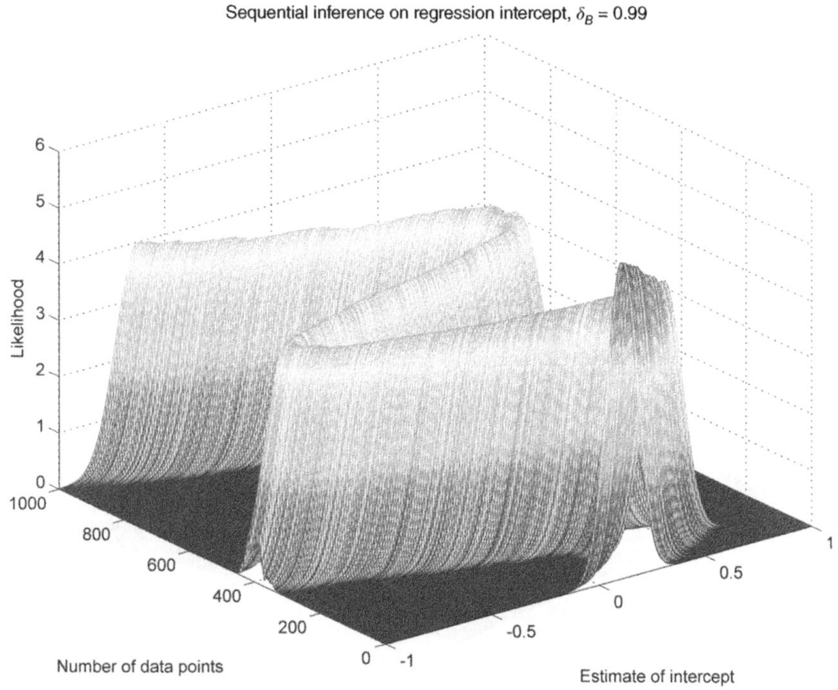

FIGURE 4.9 Sequential Inference on Regression Intercept with Discount Factor = 0.99

series analysis are weighted averages of the true parameter estimates whenever the assumption of a time-invariant underlying process fails to conform to the data. For purposes of illustration, we deliberately constructed situations in which the underlying variation is extreme. However, more subtle variations would also be smoothed over in classical time series. Classical time series estimates will only be correct when the model posited for the data is structural—i.e., when there is no variation in the parameters. Deeming a model to be structural is usually an overly restrictive assumption for financial time series data.

Attempting to correct the deficiency in classical time series by prefiltering the data partially addresses the lack of adaptivity, but it introduces distortions and fails to carry inferences from one data window to the next when models are recalibrated. Discounted Bayesian models carry information from period to period through hyperparameters (or, as we will see, comparable summaries) so that past inferences are not lost through recalibration.

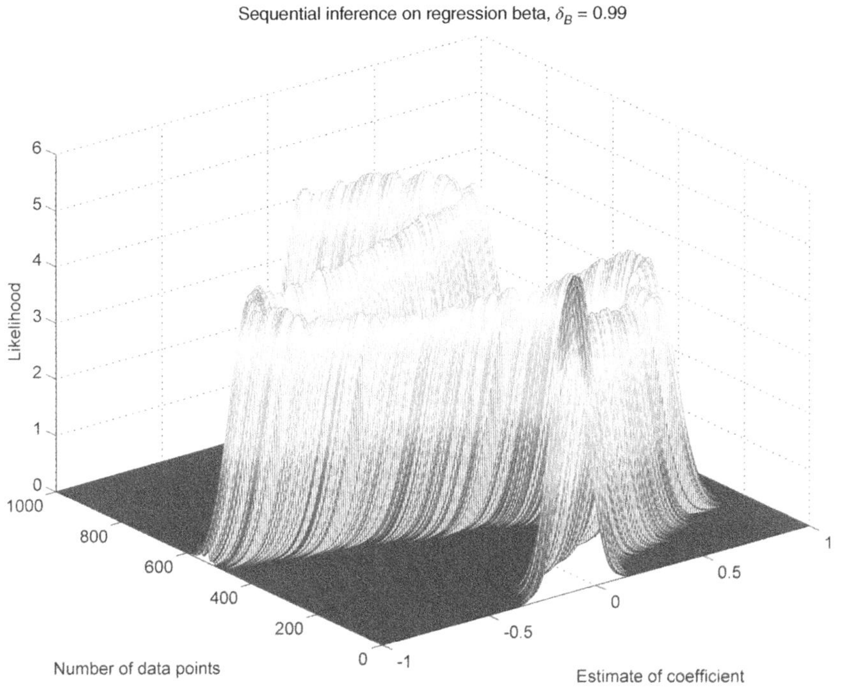

FIGURE 4.10 Sequential Inference on Regression Beta with Discount Factor = 0.99

Discovering discounting schemes for static Bayesian models has the benefit of making them adaptive and preventing convergence with maximum likelihood results. We will see that the same result can be achieved in dynamic models, in a much easier way. Dynamic models will become our preferred approach not only because of their enhanced adaptivity, but also because they encompass most static models of interest.

ACCOUNTING FOR UNCERTAINTY IN SEQUENTIAL MODELS

With the addition of discounting, we can see now that the variance of posterior Bayesian estimates is determined at any time by three factors: the degree of uncertainty associated with the prior probability distribution, the variation present in the data, and the rate at which previous inferences are discounted. One might combine prior uncertainty and discounting as a single source of variance, since the function of discounting is to refresh

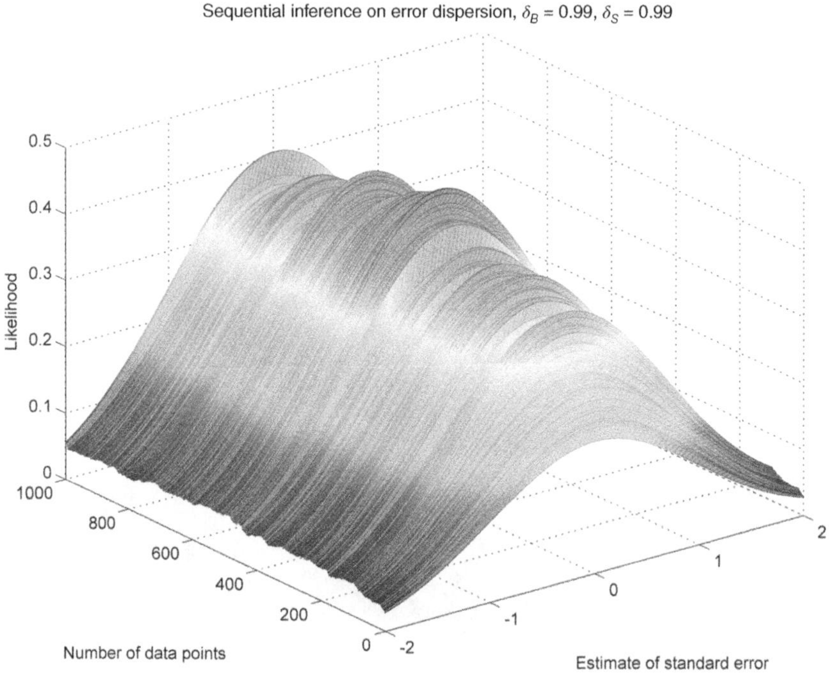

FIGURE 4.11 Sequential Inference on Standard Error of Regression with Discount Factor = 0.99

prior uncertainty in the face of accumulated data. One might also say that Bayesian uncertainty is a combination of data-induced uncertainty and the uncertainty induced by accounting for the fallibility of inferences through information loss.

The distinction drawn above might be associated with the classic Knightian (Knight 1921) distinction between risk and uncertainty, where *risk* captures measurable randomness (data-induced uncertainty) and *uncertainty* recognizes that randomness cannot be definitively measured. In Bayesian inference Knightian uncertainty is acknowledged and approximately quantified by the recognition of information loss. A full appreciation of Knightian uncertainty would capture model uncertainty, too, but it is notable nevertheless that the analysis of discounting undertaken here makes visible and quantifiable one element of generalized risk that has been deemed inaccessible to analysis. In fact, the possibility of making model comparisons between models with different discount factors makes it possible to speak of the degree of uncertainty in a meaningful way.

Classical estimates, on the other hand, treat all variation as quantifiable risk, passing over the possibility of Knightian uncertainty. In our view, classical methods fail to account for a crucially important source of variance in estimates: We cannot be assured that all data are being sampled from the same process, and, as a result, we cannot assume that our inferences are becoming more precise with each passing observation.

The variance of posterior Bayesian estimates is, by construction, likely to exceed the variance of classical estimates in almost all situations. (An important exception is when prior information successfully stands in for sample information, in situations where very limited data are available.) As a result, it would be a mistake to appraise the success of alternative methods by the variance of the estimates produced. Higher discount factors will reduce the variance of estimates, at the expense of adaptivity.

It might be daunting to confront the wide variances associated with adaptive Bayesian parameter estimates, even if it is accepted that they provide an honest accounting of uncertainty in the statistical model at hand. It is almost a reflex to regard a model with lower variances as a better model. Particularly if the precision of forecasts is taken as an index of one's relative advantage in understanding the dynamics of a market, an initial reaction to variances of such magnitude might be to seriously doubt one's ability to operate effectively in the market. But increased precision can be obtained through other channels.

In particular, one reserves the right to intervene with additional relevant prior information that might reduce the overall variance of model estimates (West and Harrison 1997, Chapter 11). Since models are now being updated sequentially, revisions to prior information can be introduced at any time. For a sequence of daily return observations, for example, all forecast quantities for the following day can be computed using the results at the end of a trading day. Before markets open again, one can intervene in the forecasts based on after-hours announcements or additional research undertaken after the market close. Such opportunities for intervention should not be taken lightly. Financial professionals regularly revise their expectations based on new information. Classical methods provide no means to consider such new information because it simply has no meaning in a batch estimation setting.

Bayesian methods seek to reduce parameter uncertainty and forecast variances by providing a channel for the incorporation of meaningful prior information, and encouraging the search for better-specified models, rather than as the foregone conclusion of observing more data. Accordingly, they provide a superior means for understanding and articulating one's comparative advantage in understanding financial markets.

CHAPTER 5

Bayesian Inference in State-Space Time Series Models

The previous chapter took an important first step in constructing adaptive time series models. Within the beta-Bernoulli model and the normal linear regression model, we derived hyperparameter updating rules that could be computed on an observation-by-observation basis. We also introduced discount factors to ensure the accumulated weight of the prior distribution did not drown out new data. The balance achieved thereby between past and present data ensures that we do not arrive at a spuriously precise conclusion.

However, it is possible to improve upon this adaptive but static design in a number of ways. A successful strategy that has been employed for more than 50 years in engineering applications is to specify dynamics for the evolution of model parameters. The parameters are assumed to evolve as states on an underlying state space. More precisely, the parameters are considered to be part of a complete description of the state of the system at any point in time, rather than fixed but unknown constants. Learning about parameters may then be reframed as a problem of filtering unobservable states with the aid of observable data, rather than as a problem of estimation and inference. Filtered state estimates can be improved further by retrospectively smoothing previous estimates with the help of subsequent observations. Our task in this chapter is to understand the formulation of state-space models and the related problems of filtering and smoothing inferences about unobserved states.

A particularly successful strategy for filtering and smoothing state estimates is that developed by Rudolf Kalman in 1960. The strategy, now known as the Kalman filter, is optimal when state-space models are linear and errors are Gaussian. The optimality of the Kalman filter is achieved by the manner in which it enables feedback between the observed data and the evolving states. Feedback captures information on observational forecast errors to adapt state estimates optimally. As a result, the linear-Gaussian state space model can be continuously and immediately adjusted on the basis of its forecasting performance, a property that is simply inaccessible to classical time series methods.

A very fruitful line of research led by Mike West and Jeff Harrison has generalized the Kalman filter to create a class of dynamic linear models (DLMs). In the formulation of West and Harrison (1997), Kalman filter estimates of underlying states can be obtained online as a result of clever choices made in building state-space models from canonical-form components. This modularity in DLM construction allows for the thoughtful handling of trends and seasonality, which are primary concerns in time series modeling, as well as regression components that can now be handled online. We cover the modular construction of DLMs before taking on any questions of inference. Concerns about inference include the filtering and smoothing problems identified earlier, as well as learning forecast and state variances.

By making all inferences conditional on current data and state information, as well as by letting parameters vary in time, the DLM approach permits the analysis of time series to proceed without the assumption of stationary data. In addition, the modular handling of trend and seasonal components sidesteps classical concerns about transforming time series data to arrive at a stationary series, and the loss of information those transformations entail. The DLM approach also makes good use of the discounting techniques already introduced to confer an additional degree of flexibility on the time series analysis. The sequential, conditional Bayesian time series analysis afforded by the DLM makes it the paradigm for models that fully encompass the sources of model risk set out at the beginning of the book.

After showing how DLMs work in a linear, Gaussian setting where many key parameters are already known to the investigator, we will begin in the next chapter to explore the consequences of relaxing certain aspects of the framework. Nonlinear and non-Gaussian modeling possibilities open up with some thoughtful conditioning and transformation of the basic DLM schema. It is also possible to make inferences on unknown DLM parameters with sequential Monte Carlo (SMC) methods, which build on the state-space and DLM methods to which we now turn.

STATE-SPACE MODELS OF TIME SERIES

State-space models seek to describe observed data as a function of (possibly unobserved) states that completely characterize the dynamics of a system (Hamilton 1994; Friedland 2005). Distinguishing between observed and unobserved states is a modeling decision made with the purpose of separating an underlying, maximally "pure" signal from the noisy transmission captured in observed data.

While less familiar to econometricians, state-space modeling has been the basic approach to time series modeling in engineering applications and control system design for over 50 years. State-space models are rich enough to encompass the autoregressive-integrated-moving average (ARIMA) class of models stemming from the research of Box and Jenkins (1970), as well as the vector autoregressions (VARs) that currently dominate multivariate time series modeling (Lütkepohl 2004b). And when they are cast in Bayesian form, state-space models do not require time series data to be stationary, as classical methods do.

Define a system of equations:

$$y_{t+1} = f\left(x_{t+1}, z_{t+1}; \theta^y\right)$$
$$x_{t+1} = g\left(x_t; \theta^x\right)$$

The *observation equation* f describes y_t as a function of unobserved states x_t, other observable states z_{t+1}, and parameters θ^y. Note two shifts in our notation. We use x for unobserved states rather than data, which is now denoted by z_t. Even though x_t will play a parameter-like role in the observation equation, we continue to reserve θ for distributions pertaining to unknown numbers in the model specification. As our concern rests mainly with the interaction between the target series y and the latent states x, we usually suppress z in what follows.

The underlying states develop dynamically according to the *state* or *evolution equation* g, which is a function of past states and parameters. The superscripts on the parameter arguments distinguish parameters in the observation equation (θ^y) from those in the state equation (θ^x). Observations y and states x may be scalars, vectors, or matrices, given conforming definitions of the parameters.

States are typically assumed to follow a Markov process, so that given x_t, the next state x_{t+1} is independent of all other previous states. Further, given x_{t+1}, the dependent variable observations y_{t+1} are conditionally independent of previous states *and* previous observations. These *conditional independence* properties are useful for two reasons. First, they simplify inference by allowing the analysis to proceed using only neighboring states and observations. As a result, state-space models can be analyzed recursively. Second, the conditional independence of the observations means that time series data need not be handled by techniques peculiar to autocorrelated series.

The description of time series in terms of *latent* state variables is the key feature of state-space modeling in finance. For financial applications state-space models are ideal since so many fundamental quantities used to explain asset prices and other financial phenomena are unobservable. Volatility, risk-free interest rates, convenience yields, the equity risk premium, and a variety of risk-neutral parameters, to choose a few examples, are all unobservable quantities that are nevertheless firmly believed to exist and indispensable for analysis in finance. State-space models allow these unobservable quantities to be treated as unobservable, eliminating the choice of proxy variables as a separate source of error.

When conducting inference in state-space models we distinguish between inferences made with data up to a certain point in time, and retrospective inferences made for a certain point in time with the aid of data observed before and after that point in time. For a time series of length T, write y^t to denote all observations seen up to an intermediate point t: $\left(y^t = \{y_i\}_{i=1}^t\right)$ and y^T to denote the entire series, including observations subsequent to the time period of interest. Classical time series methods invariably work with y^T; they cannot conduct inference online.

State-space model inference, by contrast, revolves around two distinct problems: the *filtering problem* of learning states online from y^t and the *smoothing problem* of improving inferences about states at time t retrospectively with the aid of later data in y^T. The scrupulousness about conditioning information described above plays out in both problems. Observations from later in the sample period have no influence on filtered state estimates based on earlier observations, and only a limited influence when information is fed back for smoothing.

We begin with the case where all parameters are known and proceed to the case of unknown parameters. Our exposition at this stage is purely formal to build intuition before undertaking more specific modeling exercises.

The Filtering Problem

Returning to our system

$$y_{t+1} = f\left(x_{t+1}, z_{t+1}; \theta^y\right)$$
$$x_{t+1} = g\left(x_t; \theta^x\right)$$

the filtering problem is concerned with learning the latent states x_{t+1} based on the information contained in y^{t+1}. Put differently, the filtering problem is the problem of making inferences on the conditional probability distribution $p(x_{t+1} \mid y^{t+1})$.

The very possibility of learning about $p(x_{t+1} \mid y^{t+1})$ via solution of the filtering problem is the *sine qua non* of state-space modeling. The distribution $p(x_{t+1} \mid y^{t+1})$ represents the knowledge about the latent variables that is made possible by observing a time series $y^{t+1} = \{y_1, \ldots, y_{t+1}\}$. Without at least an approximation to $p(x_{t+1} \mid y^{t+1})$, no control of the system is afforded by observed data. The more precisely $p(x_{t+1} \mid y^{t+1})$ is known, the more efficiently learning about unobserved states takes place.

From a Bayesian viewpoint, inference on $p(x_{t+1} \mid y^{t+1})$ follows the same schema as any inference problem: One begins with a prior probability distribution $p(x_{t+1} \mid y^t)$, updates on the basis of a likelihood $p(y_{t+1} \mid x_{t+1})$, and obtains a posterior distribution $p(x_{t+1} \mid y^{t+1})$ where $y^{t+1} = \{y^t, y_{t+1}\}$. The analysis cycles from prior to posterior and back again, as in the sequential updating of hyperparameters we relied on previously. Writing $\theta = \{\theta^x, \theta^y\}$ to incorporate all parameters in the model, we have the Bayesian inference problem

$$p\left(x_{t+1} \mid y^{t+1}, \theta\right) \propto p\left(y_{t+1} \mid x_{t+1}, \theta\right) p\left(x_{t+1} \mid x_t, \theta\right).$$

Where inference previously focused on unknown parameters, it now focuses on unknown states. The prior $p(x_{t+1} \mid x_t, \theta)$ is the knowledge available about x_{t+1} before observing y_{t+1} and is generated by the state equation $x_{t+1} = g(x_t; \theta^x)$. For example, if the state equation $g(x_t; \theta^x)$ is $x_{t+1} = x_t + \varepsilon^x_{t+1}$, $\varepsilon^x_{t+1} \sim \mathcal{N}[0, \sigma^2_x]$, then $\theta^x = \sigma^2_x$ and $p(x_{t+1} \mid x_t, \theta^x) \sim \mathcal{N}[x_t, \sigma^2_x]$.

The information available from the prior will be a function of the state of knowledge about x_t and σ^2_x. Whereas the likelihood was previously conditioned only on parameters, it now includes states in the conditioning information set. The likelihood $p(y_{t+1} \mid x_{t+1}, \theta)$ is the forecasting distribution generated by the observation equation $y_{t+1} = f(x_{t+1}; \theta^y)$. So if $f(x_{t+1}; \theta^y) = x_{t+1} + \varepsilon^y_{t+1}$, $\varepsilon^y_{t+1} \sim \mathcal{N}[0, \sigma^2_y]$, then $p(y_{t+1} \mid x_{t+1}, \theta^y) \sim \mathcal{N}[x_{t+1}, \sigma^2_y]$.

Accordingly, we think of obtaining $p(x_{t+1} \mid y^{t+1})$ in a cycle. First, information from x_t and θ^x is used to generate a prior for the state x_{t+1}. Using the prior for x_{t+1} and the parameters θ^y, a forecast of y_{t+1} is generated. The final step toward the posterior for x_{t+1} is a feedback step. The forecast $\widehat{y}_{t+1}$ is compared to the actual y_{t+1} to obtain information about x_{t+1}. Feedback between forecast error and the state equation thus ensures the *adaptivity* of state-space models in solving filtering problems. The problem of feedback is introduced by separating states from other unknown model parameters. Where no states are involved, the inference process reduces to the cycles of hyperparameter updates used in the previous chapter.

The Smoothing Problem

As more information about states, parameters, and processes accumulates, the possibility of retrospectively adjusting previous inferences about latent states arises. Because these changes to previous inferences tend to reduce the variance of inferences on the state space, such retrospective analysis is known as *smoothing*. The essence of smoothing is the shift in conditioning information sets from y^t to y^T. Smoothing allows inferences at any point in the history of the time series to be adjusted on the basis of the entire known time series. We will see that this retrospective adjustment does not amount to a flattening-out of the state profile to a constant long-run average. Smoothing preserves the dynamics specified for the state space, so there is no danger that smoothed estimates will revert to the constant results that would be found by standard time series techniques.

Having already obtained an inference about the state x_t from the filtering process, our prior distribution for x_t is now $p(x_t \mid y^t)$. (We will frequently switch back and forth between versions of the filtering distribution with subscripts t and $t+1$ as a matter of notational convenience. What is important is the relative spacing of the subscripts in each expression.) Since the posterior distribution will take into account the data observed subsequent to y_t, it must be $p(x_t \mid y^T)$. Thus, we are seeking a *smoothing distribution* $p(y_{t+1}, \dots, y_T \mid \cdot) = p(y_s \mid \cdot)$ to update $p(x_t \mid y^t)$ to $p(x_t \mid y^T)$. Characterizing this distribution depends on correctly specifying the conditioning information sets.

Since states are assumed to follow a Markov process, any knowledge that can be gleaned about a state retrospectively is contained entirely in the subsequent state. The availability of all the data suggests working backward from the end of the filtering sequence using a recursive setup based on the joint distribution

$$p(x_t, y_1, \dots, y_t, y_{t+1}, \dots, y_T \mid x_{t+1})$$

in which the distribution of the entire data set and the state of interest x_t is conditioned on the following state x_{t+1}. By the rules of working with joint probability distributions we have

$$\begin{aligned} p(x_t, y_1, \dots, y_t, y_{t+1}, \dots, y_T \mid x_{t+1}) &= p(x_t \mid y_1, \dots, y_T, x_{t+1}) \\ &\quad \times p(y_1, \dots, y_T \mid x_t, x_{t+1}) \\ &= p(x_t \mid x_{t+1}, y^T)\, p(y^T \mid x_t, x_{t+1}) \end{aligned}$$

and

$$\begin{aligned} p(x_t, y_1, \dots, y_t, y_{t+1}, \dots, y_T \mid x_{t+1}) &= p(y_{t+1}, \dots, y_T \mid x_t, x_{t+1}, y_1, \dots, y_t) \\ &\quad \times p(x_t \mid y_1, \dots, y_t, x_{t+1}) \\ &= p(y^s \mid x_t, x_{t+1}, y^t)\, p(x_t \mid x_{t+1}, y^t) \end{aligned}$$

so we arrive at an analogue to Bayes' theorem

$$p(x_t \mid x_{t+1}, y^T) = \frac{p(y^s \mid x_t, x_{t+1}, y^t)\, p(x_t \mid x_{t+1}, y^t)}{p(y^T \mid x_t, x_{t+1})}.$$

Begin with the problematic-looking term

$$\frac{p(y^s \mid x_t, x_{t+1}, y^t)}{p(y^T \mid x_t, x_{t+1})}.$$

Since y_{t+1} is independent of x_t given x_{t+1}, there is no information in $p(y^s \mid x_t, x_{t+1}, y^t)$ that is not in $p(y^T \mid x_t, x_{t+1})$, so the expression results in cancellation. Then we are left with $p(x_t \mid x_{t+1}, y^T) = p(x_t \mid x_{t+1}, y^t)$, an important result.

To obtain $p(x_t \mid y^T)$ and $p(x_t \mid y^t)$ as desired, we will have to take expectations over x_{t+1}. Introduce the distribution of possible values for x_{t+1}, $p(x_{t+1} \mid y^T)$, and integrate over x_{t+1} to find

$$\int p(x_t \mid x_{t+1}, y^T)\, dx_{t+1} = p(x_t \mid y^T) = \int p(x_t \mid x_{t+1}, y^T)\, p(x_{t+1} \mid y^T)\, dx_{t+1}.$$

Then use $p(x_t \mid x_{t+1}, y^T) = p(x_t \mid x_{t+1}, y^t)$ and Bayes' rule to expand the first term under the integral in the final expression above:

$$p(x_t \mid x_{t+1}, y^t) \propto p(x_{t+1} \mid x_t, y^t)\, p(x_t \mid y^t)$$

Substituting under the integral:

$$p(x_t \mid y^T) \propto \int p(x_{t+1} \mid x_t, y^t)\, p(x_t \mid y^t)\, p(x_{t+1} \mid y^T)\, dx_{t+1}.$$

The first two terms under the integral are the prior and the posterior filtering distributions for x_{t+1} and x_t, respectively. The last term in the integral is the smoothed estimate for the subsequent state. If $p(x_T \mid y^T)$ is defined initially, the integral provides a means by which $p(x_t \mid y^T)$ can be found, working backward recursively from T to $t = T-1,\ T-2, \ldots$.

Smoothing raises the interesting possibility that our knowledge of the past may change as new information becomes available. While we know from experience that new information informs and often leads us to revise our view of the past, classical time series methods furnish no means to allow us to do so. When time series are considered in batches, the best one can do with new information is to recalibrate, which does not necessarily reduce the variance of inferences on the past and which may fail to preserve information learned prior to recalibration. There is also no sense in which filtered estimates supply prior information when models are simply recalibrated in batches. Hence, one should not develop the impression that filtering and smoothing together yield the equivalent of a batch-estimated classical time series model.

DYNAMIC LINEAR MODELS

Dynamic linear models (DLMs) are a canonical tool for implementing time series models in state-space form, as fundamental to time series as linear regression is to cross-sectional data analysis. We offer an overview of the DLM framework below which is suitable for a first introduction to the subject. Serious students are well-advised to consult West and Harrison (1997) in its entirety, which pulls together some 30 years' experience in designing, estimating, and forecasting with DLMs, as well as the related explorations in Prado and West (2010).

DLMs encompass and generalize most of the workhorse classical time series models. In particular they allow critical examination of the classical assumption that model parameters must be constant because the model conforms to a stationary data-generating process. This variation in model parameters allows the DLM to be interpreted as an adaptive version of a static model, or as a locally-linear approximation to a nonlinear process. DLMs also allow for the component-wise construction of time series models with separate modeling of trend and seasonal components in individual blocks. Time series may be kept in levels and analyzed without initial modification.

The primary virtue of the DLM is its linear and Gaussian form, which allows the twin state-space problems of filtering and smoothing to be solved with a neat, closed-form set of recursions. In addition, and more important for our purposes, it furnishes a very convenient implementation of the Kalman filter within a Bayesian framework.

General Form

The general form of the DLM is

$$\mathbf{y}_{t+1} = \mathbf{F}_t'\mathbf{x}_{t+1} + \boldsymbol{\nu}_{t+1}$$
$$\mathbf{x}_{t+1} = \mathbf{G}_t\mathbf{x}_t + \boldsymbol{\omega}_{t+1}$$

where $\boldsymbol{\nu}_{t+1} \sim \mathcal{N}_r[\mathbf{0}, \mathbf{V}_t]$ and $\boldsymbol{\omega}_{t+1} \sim \mathcal{N}_n[\mathbf{0}, \mathbf{W}_t]$. Here, $\mathbf{y}_{t+1}$ is an $r \times 1$ vector, $\mathbf{x}_t$ and $\mathbf{x}_{t+1}$ are $n \times 1$ vectors, $\mathbf{F}_t$ (the *observation matrix*) is an $n \times r$ matrix, and $\mathbf{G}_t$ (the *system* or *transition matrix*) is an $n \times n$ matrix. The variances $\mathbf{V}_t$ and $\mathbf{W}_t$ are square matrices of dimension r and n, respectively. In this form, the DLM is fully defined by the ensemble $\{\mathbf{F}_t, \mathbf{G}_t, \mathbf{V}_t, \mathbf{W}_t\}$. (Even more general forms are possible with $\mathbf{Y}_{t+1}$ being matrix-valued; however, as the data in which we are interested for purposes of this book do not occur in matrix form, the most general form we consider is for a vector-valued $\mathbf{y}_{t+1}$.)

As in our general-form state-space model, the DLM includes a state equation describing the evolution of x and an observation equation modeling

y as a function of the state vector. Both equations are linear in the parameter matrices $\mathbf{F}_t$ and $\mathbf{G}_t$, and the error distributions for each equation are multivariate normal (Gaussian). For the development that follows, it is provisionally assumed that $\mathbf{F}_t$ and $\mathbf{G}_t$ are known. Fixing these model parameters in advance may seem to limit the usefulness of DLMs. However, we will see that many possibilities can be realized within this framework. Much of the art of constructing tractable DLMs in fact depends on ensuring that $\mathbf{F}_t$ and $\mathbf{G}_t$ are known a priori. Clever definitions of $\mathbf{F}_t$ and $\mathbf{G}_t$ enable treatment of a variety of problems within the DLM framework, subject to the assumptions of linearity and normality. In fact, both $\mathbf{F}_t$ and $\mathbf{G}_t$ may be built up component-wise to accommodate polynomial trends, seasonality, and regression using other observable time series or lagged values of the variable(s) being modeled. Thus, the key problems in the DLM are specifying $\mathbf{F}_t$ and $\mathbf{G}_t$, learning about the ensemble of latent states $\{\mathbf{x}_t\}_{t=1}^{T}$, and finding the variances $\mathbf{V}_t$ and $\mathbf{W}_t$.

We also assume for simplicity that the observation equation is univariate:

$$y_{t+1} = \mathbf{F}_t' \mathbf{x}_{t+1} + v_{t+1}$$
$$\mathbf{x}_{t+1} = \mathbf{G}_t \mathbf{x}_t + \boldsymbol{\omega}_{t+1}$$

Now $\mathbf{F}_t$ is a $n \times 1$ vector ($r = 1$) and $v_{t+1} \sim \mathcal{N}[0, V_t]$. All of the following results generalize in a straightforward way to the multivariate case, however.

Polynomial Trend Components

The most basic time series model assumes that data evolve according to some kind of trend, which can be assumed without loss of generality to have a polynomial form. Polynomial trends can range in complexity from the one-dimensional, linear case of the local-level model to higher-order trends that might be rationalized as Taylor approximations to more complicated nonlinear trends. A third-order model is generally more than adequate for most applications, capturing the level, rate of increase, and change in the rate of increase for a series.

A pure polynomial trend DLM defines $\mathbf{F}_t = \mathbf{E}_n$ and $\mathbf{G}_t = \mathbf{L}_n$, where n is the order of the approximation. The matrix $\mathbf{E}_n$ is a vector of length n with 1 in the initial position and zeros otherwise: $\begin{bmatrix}1 & 0 & \cdots & 0\end{bmatrix}'$ whereas $\mathbf{L}_n$ is an upper triangular $n \times n$ matrix of ones with zeros in all other positions; for example,

$$\mathbf{L}_3 = \begin{bmatrix} 1 & 1 & 1 \\ 0 & 1 & 1 \\ 0 & 0 & 1 \end{bmatrix}.$$

To see why the above definitions of $\mathbf{F}_t$ and $\mathbf{G}_t$ make sense, write $\mathbf{x}_{t+1} = \left[x_{1,t+1}\ x_{2,t+1}\ x_{3,t+1}\right]'$. Then the system of equations represented by $\mathbf{G}_t = \mathbf{L}_n$ reads

$$\begin{aligned} x_{1,t+1} &= x_{1,t} + x_{2,t} + x_{3,t} + dx_1 \\ x_{2,t+1} &= x_{2,t} + x_{3,t} + dx_2 \\ x_{3,t+1} &= x_{3,t} + dx_3 \end{aligned}$$

in extensive form or

$$\begin{bmatrix} x_{1,t+1} \\ x_{2,t+1} \\ x_{3,t+1} \end{bmatrix} = \begin{bmatrix} 1 & 1 & 1 \\ 0 & 1 & 1 \\ 0 & 0 & 1 \end{bmatrix} \begin{bmatrix} x_{1,t} \\ x_{2,t} \\ x_{3,t} \end{bmatrix} + \begin{bmatrix} dx_1 \\ dx_2 \\ dx_3 \end{bmatrix}$$

in matrix form. The last component $x_{3,t+1}$ starts at $x_{3,0}$ and integrates all of the changes dx_3 from 1 to t, whereas x_2 integrates dx_2 starting at $x_{2,0}$, as well as the integral of dx_3. Since x_1 integrates these components as well as its own history, it is natural to interpret x_2 and x_3 as the discretized first and second derivatives of x_1. With estimates of the states $\mathbf{x}_t$ one can read off levels and rates of change for the observed series y_t. The form of $\mathbf{F}_t = \mathbf{E}_3$ thus becomes clear as well. The row vector $\mathbf{E}_3$ zeroes out all but $x_{1,t+1}$ from the state vector $\mathbf{x}_{t+1}$ because all of the information in $x_{2,t+1}$ and $x_{3,t+1}$ is already captured in $x_{1,t+1}$.

Seasonal Components

It is also typical for time series to exhibit a regular pattern over the course of the year. Standard approaches to time series deal with such seasonal fluctuations through periodic differencing, which changes the interpretation of the time series and leads to a certain awkwardness with higher-frequency data sets. When modeling seasonal commodities like agricultural and energy futures, periodic differencing destroys important information about the level of prices and the shape of the forward curve.

For a time index t, let p be the length of a complete seasonal cycle beginning at t and ending at $t+p-1$. Dividing p into $h = p/2$ harmonics, the seasonal cycle can be analyzed in h Fourier components by defining

$$\mathbf{F}_t = \left[\mathbf{E}_2\ \mathbf{E}_2\ \cdots\ \mathbf{E}_2\right]' \text{ if } p \text{ is odd or}$$

$$\mathbf{F}_t = \left[\mathbf{E}_2\ \mathbf{E}_2\ \cdots\ \mathbf{E}_2\ 1\right]' \text{ if } p \text{ is even}$$

and

$$\mathbf{G}_t = \begin{bmatrix} \mathbf{J}_2(1,\omega) & \mathbf{0} & \cdots & \mathbf{0} \\ \mathbf{0} & \mathbf{J}_2(1,2\omega) & \cdots & \mathbf{0} \\ \vdots & \vdots & \ddots & \vdots \\ \mathbf{0} & \mathbf{0} & \cdots & \mathbf{J}_2(1,h\omega) \end{bmatrix} \quad \text{if } p \text{ is odd or}$$

$$\mathbf{G}_t = \begin{bmatrix} \mathrm{J}_2(1,\omega) & \mathbf{0} & \cdots & \mathbf{0} & 0 \\ \mathbf{0} & \mathrm{J}_2(1,2\omega) & \cdots & \mathbf{0} & 0 \\ \vdots & \vdots & \ddots & \vdots & \vdots \\ \mathbf{0} & \mathbf{0} & \cdots & \mathrm{J}_2(1,h\omega-\omega) & 0 \\ 0 & 0 & \cdots & 0 & -1 \end{bmatrix} \quad \text{if } p \text{ is even.}$$

The Fourier representation becomes clear by letting

$$\mathrm{J}_2^t(\mathrm{r},\omega) = \begin{bmatrix} \cos(r\omega t) & \sin(r\omega t) \\ -\sin(r\omega t) & \cos(r\omega t) \end{bmatrix}$$

where r is the index of the harmonic $r = 1, 2, \ldots, h$, t is the time index for the observation, and $\omega = 2\pi/p$ is the frequency of the fundamental cycle. Then the corresponding state vector will have $p - 1$ components.

Clearly for all time indices that are equivalent mod p, $\mathrm{J}_2^t(\mathrm{r},\omega)$ will be the same for all harmonics r and $\mathbf{G}_t$ will be p-cyclic. Recovering the full p-length seasonal cycle $\mathbf{S}_t$ at any time from the $p-1$ state vector $\mathbf{x}_t$ involves constructing the matrix

$$\underset{p\times(p-1)}{\mathbf{L}_t} = \begin{bmatrix} \mathbf{F}_t' \\ \mathbf{F}_t'\mathbf{G}_t \\ \vdots \\ \mathbf{F}_t'\mathbf{G}_t^{p-1} \end{bmatrix}$$

so that $\mathbf{S}_t = \mathbf{L}_t\mathbf{x}_t$ at any point during the process.

The h pairs (a_r, b_r) that make up $\mathbf{x}_t$ are the Fourier coefficients for each component harmonic $S_r = a_r\cos(r\omega t) + b_r\sin(r\omega t)$. The amplitude and phase of each superposed harmonic can be recovered from a_r and b_r, providing an alternative means of rendering the seasonality over a cycle p. The amplitude is given by the harmonic mean $A_r = (a_r^2 + b_r^2)^{1/2}$ and the phase is $\gamma_r = \tan^{-1}(-b_r/a_r)$. Then $S_r = A_r\cos(r\omega t + \gamma_r)$. Direct calculation of seasonal effects from $\mathbf{x}_t$ is considerably easier than the calculation of $\mathbf{L}_t$, particularly for long cycles or frequently observed data. While the expression for seasonal effects in terms of $\mathbf{F}_t$ and $\mathbf{G}_t$ is too cumbersome for computation, it does help to develop the correct definitions of $\mathbf{F}_t$ and $\mathbf{G}_t$ so that the state estimates we obtain are intelligible.

For longer cycles and/or more frequent data, p can be quite large, making the DLM unwieldy and requiring a long start-up period for the identification of model estimates. In such a case a subset of the h harmonics may be chosen and the unused blocks eliminated from the construction of $\mathbf{F}_t$ and $\mathbf{G}_t$. The definition of $\mathbf{L}_t$ remains the same, with the p multiplications of $\mathbf{G}_t$ from 0 to $p - 1$ ensuring that the seasonality profile still has length p, even though the dimension of $\mathbf{F}_t$, $\mathbf{G}_t$, and $\mathbf{x}_t$ is reduced.

Regression Components

We can also set $\mathbf{f}_t = \mathbf{z}_t = (1, z_{1,t}, \ldots, z_{k,t})$ for each y_t, where z_t is a k-vector of exogenous variables believed to explain variation in y_t. The initial vector of ones can be omitted if a local-level component is also included in the model, or if no intercept is desired. Then, setting $\mathbf{G}_t = \mathbf{I}_{k+1}$ so $\mathbf{x}_t$ is conformable with $\mathbf{z}_t$, we obtain $\mathbf{x}_{t+1} = \mathbf{x}_t + \mathbf{w}_{t+1}$ for each element of the state vector and $y_{t+1} = \mathbf{z}_{t+1}\mathbf{x}_{t+1} + v_{t+1}$ defines the observation equation.

In effect, the DLM becomes a dynamic regression model with time-varying coefficients following a random walk. Random-walk coefficients allow model responses to exogenous variables to adapt over time, either because the "true" relationship is nonlinear or because other phenomena not explicitly captured in the model cause the relationship among the modeled variables to change over time.

The DLM regression encompasses regression with static coefficients as a special case. In the DLM regression model, states and their associated variances play the role of coefficients and sampling distributions in the standard regression model. The close analogy between states and coefficients sheds new light on the handling of coefficients in standard regression models. Not only do coefficients evolve, but the possibility arises that the uncertainty associated with the coefficients can change as well. Hence, tests of hypotheses about regression coefficients defined in analogy with classical tests may reject the significance of a variable at some times, while failing to reject significance at others. When coefficients change, no clear guidance may be gleaned from a process like significance testing on whether certain regressors should be retained or not. (Model comparisons do furnish such information. We discuss the sequential comparison of DLMs at the end of the chapter.)

Building DLMs with Components

Having surveyed the key building blocks in the DLM framework, it is now possible to combine each of the preceding components to achieve models of greater complexity. Combining each of the pieces above is simple:

Build up $\mathbf{F}_t$ columnwise as a partitioned vector, and

Construct $\mathbf{G}_t$ as a block-diagonal matrix.

For example, a model with a second-order polynomial trend, one Fourier-form seasonality component, and two exogenous regressors would have the form

$$\mathbf{F}_t = \left[\mathbf{E}_2\ \mathbf{E}_2\ \mathbf{z}_t\right] = \left[1\ 0\ 1\ 0\ z_{1t}\ z_{2t}\right]$$

$$\mathbf{G}_t = \begin{bmatrix} \mathbf{L}_2 & \mathbf{0} & \mathbf{0} \\ \mathbf{0} & \mathbf{J}_2^t(1,\omega) & \mathbf{0} \\ \mathbf{0} & \mathbf{0} & \mathbf{I}_2 \end{bmatrix} = \begin{bmatrix} \begin{matrix} 1 & 1 \\ 0 & 1 \end{matrix} & \mathbf{0} & \mathbf{0} \\ \mathbf{0} & \begin{matrix} \cos(\omega t) & \sin(\omega t) \\ -\sin(\omega t) & \cos(\omega t) \end{matrix} & \mathbf{0} \\ \mathbf{0} & \mathbf{0} & \begin{matrix} 1 & 0 \\ 0 & 1 \end{matrix} \end{bmatrix}.$$

The vector $\mathbf{F}_t$ is 1×6 and $\mathbf{G}_t$ is 6×6. Extensions to more complex models are straightforward.

Notice that, by construction, both $\mathbf{F}_t$ and $\mathbf{G}_t$ are completely defined for all times t and cycle length p. The only values to be determined are the prior and posterior distributions for $\mathbf{x}_t$ at each time step t, and the observation and system variances **V** and **W**. Prior and posterior distributions for $\mathbf{x}_t$ can be found using a relatively simple set of recursive calculations, while continuing to assume that **V** and **W** are known. Next we will relax the assumptions about **V** and **W** and show how inferences about state and observational variances are made in the DLM framework.

RECURSIVE RELATIONSHIPS IN THE DLM

Having covered the basics of DLM construction, we are now in a position to tackle the problem of making inferences about states by solving the filtering problem and the smoothing problem. We begin with the filtering problem.

Filtering Recursion

Recall the inference problem in filtering as given by Bayes' rule:

$$p\left(x_{t+1} \mid y^{t+1}, \theta\right) \propto p\left(y_{t+1} \mid x_{t+1}, \theta\right) p\left(x_{t+1} \mid x_t, \theta\right).$$

The posterior distribution for x_{t+1} is the proportional to the product of the prior probability distribution for x_{t+1} and the likelihood of observing y_{t+1} conditional on x_{t+1} and θ. The state equation provides an expression for $p(x_{t+1} \mid x_t, \theta)$, and the observational equation defines $p(y_{t+1} \mid x_{t+1}, \theta)$.

The starting point for the filtering problem is a prior distribution of beliefs about the initial state $\mathbf{x}_0$. In the DLM, state distributions are assumed to be Gaussian, so one specifies a best guess for the mean value of the state vector $\mathbf{m}_0$ while the degree of confidence in the initial guess is captured by the variance $\mathbf{C}_0$. The resulting prior distribution for $\mathbf{x}_0$ is $\mathcal{N}_n[\mathbf{m}_0, \mathbf{C}_0]$. It is common to assume that $\mathbf{C}_0$ is diagonal, and it must be symmetric and positive definite.

Using the prior for $\mathbf{x}_0$ we then seek to obtain a prior estimate for $p(\mathbf{x}_{t+1} \mid \mathbf{y}^t)$. Because the state equation is linear and we have assumed a Gaussian distribution for $\mathbf{x}_t$, we know $\mathbf{x}_{t+1}$ will also be Gaussian. Hence, we need to find the mean and variance of the prior distribution for $\mathbf{x}_{t+1}$. Initially, we have $\mathbf{x}_1 \sim \mathcal{N}_r[\mathbf{m}_0, \mathbf{C}_0]$, and in general, we will have $\mathbf{x}_t \sim \mathcal{N}_r[\mathbf{m}_{t-1}, \mathbf{C}_{t-1}]$.

By the definition of the state equation $\mathbf{x}_{t+1} = \mathbf{G}_t\mathbf{x}_t + \boldsymbol{\omega}_{t+1}$ we know that $E[\mathbf{x}_{t+1}] = \mathbf{G}_t\mathbf{m}_{t-1}$. The variance is a function of the prior variance $\mathbf{C}_{t-1}$ and the state equation: $Var[\mathbf{x}_{t+1}] = \mathbf{G}_t\mathbf{C}_{t-1}\mathbf{G}_t' + \mathbf{W}_t$. Putting $\mathbf{a}_t = \mathbf{G}_t\mathbf{m}_{t-1}$ and $\mathbf{R}_t = \mathbf{G}_t\mathbf{C}_{t-1}\mathbf{G}_t' + \mathbf{W}_t$, the prior distribution for $\mathbf{x}_{t+1}$ can be summarized as

$$p\left(\mathbf{x}_{t+1} \mid \mathbf{y}^t\right) \sim \mathcal{N}_r\left[\mathbf{a}_t, \mathbf{R}_t\right].$$

Next we want to come up with a forecast for $\mathbf{y}_{t+1}$, which will be summarized in a distribution $p(\mathbf{y}_{t+1} \mid \mathbf{y}^t)$. The forecast will make use of the prior distribution for $\mathbf{x}_{t+1}$, as well as the elements $\mathbf{F}_t$ and $\mathbf{V}_t$ in the observation equation. The mean of the forecast distribution must be $\mathbf{F}_t'\mathbf{a}_t$, or the observation matrix times the mean of the prior distribution for $\mathbf{x}_{t+1}$. The variance of the forecast distribution is $\mathbf{F}_t'\mathbf{R}_t\mathbf{F}_t + \mathbf{V}_t$ by the same algebra used in finding the variance of the prior state distribution. Putting $\mathbf{f}_t = \mathbf{F}_t'\mathbf{a}_t$ and $\mathbf{Q}_t = \mathbf{F}_t'\mathbf{R}_t\mathbf{F}_t + \mathbf{V}_t$, the forecast distribution can be summarized as

$$p\left(\mathbf{y}_{t+1} \mid \mathbf{y}^t\right) \sim \mathcal{N}_n\left[\mathbf{f}_t, \mathbf{Q}_t\right].$$

Having stated priors for the current state and the current observation, we have arrived at the crucial learning or feedback step, in which we observe $\mathbf{y}_{t+1}$ and use the error $\mathbf{e}_t = \mathbf{y}_{t+1} - \mathbf{f}_t$ to revise our initial views. The goal is to arrive at an expression for the posterior distribution of the state vector

$$p\left(\mathbf{x}_{t+1} \mid \mathbf{y}^{t+1}\right) = p\left(\mathbf{x}_{t+1} \mid \left\{\mathbf{y}^t, \mathbf{y}_{t+1}\right\}\right).$$

Our strategy for finding $p(\mathbf{x}_{t+1} \mid \mathbf{y}^{t+1})$ will be to construct the joint distribution of $p(\mathbf{y}_{t+1} \mid \mathbf{y}^t)$ and $p(\mathbf{x}_{t+1} \mid \mathbf{y}^t)$, and then find $p(\mathbf{x}_{t+1} \mid \mathbf{y}^{t+1})$ by solving for the marginal distribution.

So far, we know that $\mathbf{y}_{t+1} \mid \mathbf{y}^t \sim \mathcal{N}[\mathbf{f}_t, \mathbf{Q}_t]$ and $\mathbf{x}_{t+1} \mid \mathbf{y}^t \sim \mathcal{N}[\mathbf{a}_t, \mathbf{R}_t]$, which implies

$$\begin{matrix}\mathbf{y}_{t+1} \\ \mathbf{x}_{t+1}\end{matrix} \Big| \mathbf{y}^t \sim \mathcal{N}\left[\begin{pmatrix}\mathbf{f}_t \\ \mathbf{a}_t\end{pmatrix}, \begin{pmatrix}\mathbf{Q}_t & \mathbf{V}_{12} \\ \mathbf{V}_{21} & \mathbf{R}_t\end{pmatrix}\right].$$

The off-diagonal covariance components $\mathbf{V}_{12}$ and $\mathbf{V}_{21}$ have not yet been found. Accordingly, we compute $\mathbf{V}_{12} = \text{cov}(\mathbf{y}_{t+1}, \mathbf{x}_{t+1} \mid \mathbf{y}^t)$. By the definition of $\mathbf{y}_{t+1}$ we obtain $\text{cov}(\mathbf{y}_{t+1}, \mathbf{x}_{t+1} \mid \mathbf{y}^t) = \text{cov}(\mathbf{F}_t'\mathbf{x}_{t+1} + \mathbf{v}_{t+1}, \mathbf{x}_{t+1} \mid \mathbf{y}^t)$. Since observational errors are independent of the observations and the states, $\text{cov}(\mathbf{F}_t'\mathbf{x}_{t+1} + \mathbf{v}_{t+1}, \mathbf{x}_{t+1} \mid \mathbf{y}^t) = \mathbf{F}_t'\text{var}(\mathbf{x}_{t+1} \mid \mathbf{y}^t) = \mathbf{F}_t'\mathbf{R}_t$. The last step follows from the prior distribution for the states. Solving for $\mathbf{V}_{12}$ leads immediately to a solution for $\mathbf{V}_{21}$, since $\mathbf{V}_{21} = \mathbf{V}_{12}' = \mathbf{R}_t\mathbf{F}_t$ by the symmetry of $\mathbf{R}_t$. Accordingly, we know that

$$\begin{matrix}\mathbf{y}_{t+1} \\ \mathbf{x}_{t+1}\end{matrix} \Big| \mathbf{y}^t \sim \mathcal{N}\left[\begin{pmatrix}\mathbf{f}_t \\ \mathbf{a}_t\end{pmatrix}, \begin{pmatrix}\mathbf{Q}_t & \mathbf{F}_t'\mathbf{R}_t \\ \mathbf{R}_t\mathbf{F}_t & \mathbf{R}_t\end{pmatrix}\right].$$

Normal distribution theory furnishes a solution for $p(\mathbf{x}_{t+1} \mid \mathbf{y}^{t+1})$ (Poirier 1995, pp. 121–123). Writing $p(\mathbf{x}_{t+1} \mid \mathbf{y}^{t+1}) \sim \mathcal{N}_r[\mathbf{m}_t, \mathbf{C}_t]$, the mean of the distribution is $\mathbf{m}_t = \mathbf{a}_t + \mathbf{R}_t\mathbf{F}_t\mathbf{Q}_t^{-1}(\mathbf{y}_{t-1} - \mathbf{f}_t) = \mathbf{a}_t + \mathbf{R}_t\mathbf{F}_t\mathbf{Q}_t^{-1}\mathbf{e}_t$. Defining $\mathbf{A}_t = \mathbf{R}_t\mathbf{F}_t\mathbf{Q}_t^{-1}$, known as the Kalman gain, we have a compact expression for the mean, with $\mathbf{m}_t = \mathbf{a}_t + \mathbf{A}_t\mathbf{e}_t$. The matrix $\mathbf{A}_t$ is the regression matrix of $\mathbf{x}_{t+1}$ on $\mathbf{y}_{t+1}$ and supplies the feedback rule for $\mathbf{x}_{t+1}$ based on the forecast error $\mathbf{e}_t$. Based on our derivations above, we can see $\mathbf{A}_t = \text{cov}(\mathbf{x}_{t+1}, \mathbf{y}_{t+1} \mid \mathbf{y}^t)\text{var}(\mathbf{y}_{t+1} \mid \mathbf{y}^t)^{-1}$, just as when finding the coefficients in any other linear regression.

The variance $\mathbf{C}_t = \mathbf{R}_t - \mathbf{R}_t\mathbf{F}_t\mathbf{Q}_t^{-1}\mathbf{F}_t'\mathbf{R}_t$ follows from normal distribution theory as well. Substituting in $\mathbf{A}_t$ and multiplying by the identity $\mathbf{Q}_t\mathbf{Q}_t^{-1}$,

$$\mathbf{C}_t = \mathbf{R}_t - \mathbf{A}_t\mathbf{F}_t'\mathbf{R}_t = \mathbf{R}_t - \mathbf{A}_t\mathbf{Q}_t\mathbf{Q}_t^{-1}\mathbf{F}_t'\mathbf{R}_t = \mathbf{R}_t - \mathbf{A}_t\mathbf{Q}_t\mathbf{A}_t'.$$

The derivation of the posterior distribution $p(\mathbf{x}_{t+1} \mid \mathbf{y}^{t+1}) \sim \mathcal{N}_r[\mathbf{m}_t, \mathbf{C}_t]$ is now complete, with $\mathbf{m}_t = \mathbf{a}_t + \mathbf{A}_t\mathbf{e}_t$ and $\mathbf{C}_t = \mathbf{R}_t - \mathbf{A}_t\mathbf{Q}_t\mathbf{A}_t'$. We found that the regression matrix of $\mathbf{x}_{t+1}$ on $\mathbf{y}_{t+1}$ was crucial in obtaining feedback on $\mathbf{x}$ from $\mathbf{e}_t$: The matrix $\mathbf{A}_t$ adjusts the mean of the state vector from its prior value $\mathbf{a}_t$ using information in the forecast errors $\mathbf{e}_t$. It also controls the extent to which the prior state variance is reduced or increased.

To summarize the above:

$$\begin{aligned}\mathbf{x}_t \mid \mathbf{y}^t &\sim \mathcal{N}_r\left[\mathbf{m}_{t-1}, \mathbf{C}_{t-1}\right] \\ \mathbf{x}_{t+1} \mid \mathbf{y}^t &\sim \mathcal{N}_r\left[\mathbf{a}_t, \mathbf{R}_t\right] \\ \mathbf{y}_{t+1} \mid \mathbf{y}^t &\sim \mathcal{N}_n\left[\mathbf{f}_t, \mathbf{Q}_t\right] \\ \mathbf{x}_{t+1} \mid \mathbf{y}^{t+1} &\sim \mathcal{N}_r\left[\mathbf{m}_t, \mathbf{C}_t\right]\end{aligned}$$

with the relationships

$$
\begin{aligned}
\mathbf{a}_t &= \mathbf{G}_t\mathbf{m}_{t-1} \\
\mathbf{R}_t &= \mathbf{G}_t\mathbf{C}_{t-1}\mathbf{G}_t' + \mathbf{W}_t \\
\mathbf{f}_t &= \mathbf{F}_t'\mathbf{a}_t \\
\mathbf{Q}_t &= \mathbf{F}_t'\mathbf{R}_t\mathbf{F}_t + \mathbf{V}_t \\
\mathbf{m}_t &= \mathbf{a}_t + \mathbf{A}_t\mathbf{e}_t \\
\mathbf{C}_t &= \mathbf{R}_t - \mathbf{A}_t\mathbf{Q}_t\mathbf{A}_t'.
\end{aligned}
$$

The process of computing the recursive formulas above for all observations of the series $\mathbf{y}_{t+1}$ with known variances is known as running the Kalman filter (Kalman 1960). As we have seen in the derivation, the Kalman filter recursions depend on the linearity of the observation and system equations, as well as the normality of the error distributions. When these conditions do not obtain, other procedures are necessary for carrying out the filtering calculations.

In general, the variances $\mathbf{V}_t$ and $\mathbf{W}_t$ will not be known in advance. Their estimation is discussed in a later section, along with a discussion of discounting.

Smoothing Recursion

Suppose we have calculated the Kalman filter recursions up to a time T, and would like to obtain improved estimates of the mean and variance of the system equation using information that became available after time t for each of the states $\mathbf{x}_t$. Such a retrospective analysis of a state-space model is known as smoothing. In our initial discussion of the smoothing problem, we had arrived at the following expression for the smoothed distribution of $\mathbf{x}_t$:

$$p(x_t \mid y^T) \propto \int p(x_t \mid y^t)\, p(x_{t+1} \mid x_t, y^t)\, p(x_{t+1} \mid y^T)\, dx_{t+1}.$$

The first two terms under the integral, which resulted from rewriting $p(x_t \mid x_{t+1}, y^t)$ using Bayes' rule, are distributions that are already known from the filtering recursions, conditioned as they are on y^t. Thus, we know

$$
\begin{aligned}
p(\mathbf{x}_t \mid \mathbf{y}^t) &\sim \mathcal{N}_r\left[\mathbf{m}_t, \mathbf{C}_t\right] \\
p(\mathbf{x}_{t+1} \mid \mathbf{y}^t) &\sim \mathcal{N}_r\left[\mathbf{a}_t, \mathbf{R}_t\right].
\end{aligned}
$$

Hence, when computing the filtering recursions, the hyperparameters/sufficient statistics $\{\mathbf{m}_t, \mathbf{C}_t, \mathbf{a}_t, \mathbf{R}_t\}_{t=1}^T$ should be stored for use in the smoothing calculation. To reduce the two terms back to $p(x_t \mid x_{t+1}, y^t)$, we use the same strategy as before with the partitioned normal distribution

$$\begin{matrix} \mathbf{x}_t \\ \mathbf{x}_{t+1} \end{matrix} \mid \mathbf{y}^t \sim \mathcal{N}\left[\begin{pmatrix} \mathbf{m}_t \\ \mathbf{a}_{t+1} \end{pmatrix}, \begin{pmatrix} \mathbf{C}_t & \mathbf{C}_t\mathbf{G}'_{t+1} \\ \mathbf{G}_{t+1}\mathbf{C}_t & \mathbf{R}_{t+1} \end{pmatrix}\right]$$

so that marginalizing yields the distribution we need, $p(x_t \mid x_{t+1}, y^t)$. The covariance term in the upper-right corner of the partitioned variance matrix is found by solving $\text{cov}(\mathbf{x}_t, \mathbf{x}_{t+1} \mid \mathbf{y}^t) = \text{cov}(\mathbf{x}_t, \mathbf{G}_{t+1}\mathbf{x}_t \mid \mathbf{y}^t) = \text{var}(\mathbf{x}_t \mid \mathbf{y}^t)\mathbf{G}'_{t+1} = \mathbf{C}_t\mathbf{G}'_{t+1}$. Relying on the same formulas as before, the mean of the distribution is

$$\begin{aligned} \bar{\mathbf{a}}_t &= \mathbf{m}_t + \mathbf{C}_t\mathbf{G}'_{t+1}\mathbf{R}^{-1}_{t+1}\left(\mathbf{x}_{t+1} - \mathbf{a}_{t+1}\right) \\ &= \mathbf{m}_t + \mathbf{B}_t\left(\mathbf{x}_{t+1} - \mathbf{a}_{t+1}\right) \end{aligned}$$

where the term $\mathbf{B}_t$ is defined as $\mathbf{C}_t\mathbf{G}'_{t+1}\mathbf{R}^{-1}_{t+1}$. The smoothed variance is

$$\begin{aligned} \overline{\mathbf{R}}_t &= \mathbf{C}_t - \mathbf{C}_t\mathbf{G}'_{t+1}\mathbf{R}^{-1}_{t+1}\mathbf{G}_{t+1}\mathbf{C}_t \\ &= \mathbf{C}_t - \mathbf{B}_t\mathbf{R}_{t+1}\mathbf{B}'_t. \end{aligned}$$

With this expression for $p(x_t \mid x_{t+1}, y^t) = p(x_t \mid y^t)\, p(x_{t+1} \mid x_t, y^t)$ it remains to integrate over the distribution $p(x_{t+1} \mid y^T)dx_{t+1}$. The effect of the integration is to replace $\mathbf{x}_{t+1}$ and $\mathbf{R}_{t+1}$ in the expressions above with their smoothed estimates from one time step ahead $\bar{\mathbf{a}}_{t+1}$ and $\overline{\mathbf{R}}_{t+1}$ so that the recursions become

$$\begin{aligned} \bar{\mathbf{a}}_t &= \mathbf{m}_t + \mathbf{B}_t\left(\bar{\mathbf{a}}_{t+1} - \mathbf{a}_{t+1}\right) \\ \overline{\mathbf{R}}_t &= \mathbf{C}_t + \mathbf{B}_t\left[\overline{\mathbf{R}}_{t+1} - \mathbf{R}_{t+1}\right]\mathbf{B}'_t. \end{aligned}$$

The algorithm is run backward for $T = T - 1, \ldots, 1$ and initialized by setting $\bar{\mathbf{a}}_T = \mathbf{m}_T$ and $\overline{\mathbf{R}}_T = \mathbf{C}_T$. The smoothed estimates of $\mathbf{x}_t$ are then distributed $\mathcal{N}[\bar{\mathbf{a}}_t, \overline{\mathbf{R}}_t]$.

To understand the smoothing recursions, it is helpful to compare $\mathbf{B}_t = \mathbf{C}_t\mathbf{G}'_{t+1}\mathbf{R}^{-1}_{t+1}$ to $\mathbf{A}_t = \mathbf{R}_t\mathbf{F}_t\mathbf{Q}^{-1}_t$. The Kalman gain in the filtering recursions worked forward from (a) the *prior* distribution of the states and (b) the errors from online forecasts of the *observation* equation. By contrast, the matrix $\mathbf{B}_t$ in the smoothing recursions works backward from (a) the *posterior* distribution of the states and (b) the errors from online forecasts of the *system* equation. The corrections $\bar{\mathbf{a}}_{t+1} - \mathbf{a}_{t+1}$ summarize the errors of the prior state distribution, just as $\mathbf{e}_t = \mathbf{y}_t - \mathbf{f}_t$ was so important in creating feedback for the filtering problem. We can also write $\mathbf{B}_t = \mathbf{C}_t\mathbf{G}'_{t+1}\mathbf{R}^{-1}_{t+1} = \text{cov}(\mathbf{x}_t, \mathbf{x}_{t+1} \mid \mathbf{y}^t)\text{var}(\mathbf{x}_{t+1} \mid \mathbf{y}^t)^{-1}$, suggesting regression of $\mathbf{x}_t$ on $\mathbf{x}_{t+1}$.

As our concern is the online sequential learning of financial time series, from this point forward we will be focused on the filtering problem exclusively. Further details on smoothing may be found by consulting the references cited in this chapter and the next.

Predictive Distributions and Forecasting

The one-step-ahead forecast distribution was already characterized in the recursions above. Assuming prediction without the benefit of future data, and thus the filtering recursion framework, the one-step-ahead forecast density is given by $\mathcal{N}[\mathbf{f}_t, \mathbf{Q}_t]$. Extending the forecast to several periods ahead requires modification of the quantities $\mathbf{f}_t$ and $\mathbf{Q}_t$, now denoted $f_t(k)$ and $Q_t(k)$, where k is the index of the forecast horizon (West and Harrison 1997, Chapter 4.4). The form is the same:

$$f_t(k) = \mathbf{F}'_{t+k}\mathbf{a}_t(k)$$
$$Q_t(k) = \mathbf{F}'_{t+k}\mathbf{R}_t(k)\mathbf{F}_{t+k} + \mathbf{V}_{t+k}$$

with the exception of the quantities indexed by the forecast horizon k. These can be calculated using the recursions

$$\mathbf{a}_t(k) = \mathbf{G}_{t+k}\mathbf{a}_t(k-1)$$
$$\mathbf{R}_t(k) = \mathbf{G}_{t+k}\mathbf{R}_t(k-1)\mathbf{G}_{t+k}' + \mathbf{W}_{t+k}$$

with $\mathbf{a}_t(0) = \mathbf{m}_t$ and $\mathbf{R}_t(0) = \mathbf{C}_t$. The quantities $\mathbf{a}_t(k)$ and $\mathbf{R}_t(k)$ as defined above parameterize the k-step-ahead forecast distribution for the state vector, analogous to the one-step-ahead forecast given above, $\mathcal{N}[\mathbf{a}_t, \mathbf{R}_t]$. Hence, the recursive definition reflects repeated multiplication by the system matrix as of time $t + k$. Note that the system variance $\mathbf{W}_{t+k}$ is additive with each step rather than multiplicative, and the observational variance is added only once as $\mathbf{V}_{t+k}$. Hence, forecast confidence intervals will expand at a slower rate than is typical for time series forecasts.

When $\mathbf{F}$ and $\mathbf{G}$ are constant, the formulas for $\mathbf{a}_t(k)$ and $\mathbf{R}_t(k)$ simplify to

$$\mathbf{a}_t(k) = \mathbf{G}^k\mathbf{m}_t$$
$$\mathbf{R}_t(k) = \mathbf{G}^k\mathbf{C}_t\mathbf{G}^k + \sum_{i=1}^{k-1}\mathbf{G}^i\mathbf{W}_{t+k-i}\mathbf{G}^i.$$

At this point, with variances $\mathbf{V}_t$ and $\mathbf{W}_t$ assumed known, all forecast distributions will continue to be normal. Once we admit uncertainty in the variances, the forecast distributions become t distributions with degrees of freedom controlled by the variance estimation.

VARIANCE ESTIMATION

So far, we have calculated filtering and smoothing recursions on the simplifying assumptions that both $\mathbf{V}_t$ and $\mathbf{W}_t$ are completely known for all times t. In general, the variances $\mathbf{V}_t$ and $\mathbf{W}_t$ will not be known in advance.

It would be preferable to reduce our problem to estimating a single variance. We can simplify matters by defining the system variance $\mathbf{W}_t$ as a scale multiple of the observational variance $\mathbf{V}_t$ (West and Harrison 1997, Chapter 6.3). In the DLM filtering recursions, recall the estimate of the variance associated with the one-step-ahead state forecast:

$$\mathbf{R}_t = \mathbf{G}_t\mathbf{C}_t\mathbf{G}_t' + \mathbf{W}_t.$$

The matrix $\mathbf{R}_t$ may therefore be viewed as a suitable rescaling of $\mathbf{C}_t$ to account for information lost in the state equation ($\mathbf{W}_t$), due either to system noise or misspecification of the system dynamics. Hence, we can just as easily write

$$\mathbf{R}_t = \frac{1}{\delta}\mathbf{G}_t\mathbf{C}_t\mathbf{G}_t'$$

for the state forecast variance, for $\delta \in [0, 1]$. The entire series of $\mathbf{W}_t$ is identified by the specification of δ, and values of $\mathbf{W}_t$ may be recovered by noting

$$\mathbf{W}_t = \frac{1}{\delta}\mathbf{G}_t\mathbf{C}_t\mathbf{G}_t' - \mathbf{G}_t\mathbf{C}_t\mathbf{G}_t' = \frac{1-\delta}{\delta}\mathbf{G}_t\mathbf{C}_t\mathbf{G}_t'.$$

The number δ is a discount factor like those used in Chapter 4, and reflects information loss at the rate $1 - \delta$. As a proxy for $\mathbf{W}_t$, the discount factor captures the degree to which the system equation fails to represent the system dynamics exactly. Since parameter estimation is accomplished within the system equation in the DLM approach, errors in the system equation allow for ongoing adaptivity in the parameters. If the system dynamics adapt the parameters in a sensible way, values of δ close to 1 will produce good results. Lower values of δ indicate a system specification that is less well matched to the evolution of the data-generating process. The same result achieved by discounting hyperparameters in static Bayesian models can be achieved in dynamic models, in a much easier way.

Recall that the system equation is built by block-diagonal construction of $\mathbf{G}_t$. Information may not be lost at the same rate for all components of the system equation. As a result, different discount factors can be applied to each component of the system, just as we anticipated different discount factors could apply to different parameters in Chapter 4. Choices of δ_i then reflect variation in information persistence among DLM model components. Writing $\Delta = diag(\delta_1, \ldots, \delta_n)$ to collect the individual discount factors, we have $\mathbf{R}_t = \Delta^{-1/2}\mathbf{G}_t\mathbf{C}_t\mathbf{G}_t'\Delta^{-1/2}$ as an expression for the discounted forecast variance.

Now that $\mathbf{W}_t$ has been eliminated from the recursions, our goal in this section is to augment the filtering recursions set out earlier to incorporate inference about volatility.

Univariate Case

For the univariate case with constant variance (or the multivariate case in which the covariance matrix is assumed to be diagonal), $\mathbf{V}$ can be updated based on recursive relationships within the class of inverted-gamma distributions, just as in the error variance of the linear regression model.

The prior for $\mathbf{V}$ has the distribution

$$\mathbf{V}|\mathbf{y}^t \sim IG(n_{t-1}, n_{t-1}S_{t-1})$$

with the hyperparameters n_{t-1} and $n_{t-1}S_{t-1} = d_{t-1}$ representing degrees of freedom and scale, respectively. Updating ϕ occurs by setting

$$\begin{aligned} n_t &= n_{t-1} + 1 \\ d_t &= d_{t-1} + e_t^2/Q_t \\ S_t &= S_{t-1} + \frac{S_{t-1}}{n_t}\left(\frac{e_t^2}{Q_t} - 1\right). \end{aligned}$$

The parameters e and Q are already produced by the filtering recursions, corresponding to the one-dimensional version of the one-step-ahead forecasting error and its variance ($\mathbf{V} = v$, $Q_t = \mathbf{F}_t'\mathbf{R}_t\mathbf{F}_t + v$). At any time, $E[\mathbf{V}|y^{t+1}] = d_t/n_t = S_t$.

Combining inference on $\mathbf{V}_t$ with discounting, we have the following revisions to the filtering recursions:

$$\begin{aligned} \mathbf{R}_t &= \Delta^{-1/2}\mathbf{G}_t\mathbf{C}_{t-1}\mathbf{G}_t'\Delta^{-1/2} \\ Q_t &= \mathbf{F}_t'\mathbf{R}_t\mathbf{F}_t + S_{t-1} \\ n_t &= n_{t-1} + 1 \\ S_t &= S_{t-1} + \frac{S_{t-1}}{n_t}\left(\frac{e_t^2}{Q_t} - 1\right) \\ \mathbf{C}_t &= \frac{S_t}{S_{t-1}}(\mathbf{R}_t - \mathbf{A}_t\mathbf{A}_t'Q_t) \end{aligned}$$

As in other situations, allowing for uncertainty in the variance changes the posterior distributions for the model quantities from normal distributions to T-distributions, with n_{t-1} or n_t degrees of freedom, depending on the position of the algorithm relative to the system variance.

We may also wish to discount the observational variance to allow greater model adaptivity (West and Harrison 1997, Chapter 10.6). In this case, define a discount factor β and a time-varying $\mathbf{V}_t$. Then

$$\begin{aligned} n_t &= \beta n_{t-1} + 1 \\ d_t &= \beta d_{t-1} + S_{t-1}\left(e_t^2/Q_t\right). \end{aligned}$$

Because the observational variance discount factor allows $\mathbf{V}_t$ to evolve over time, it can be thought of as a first basic stochastic volatility model.

Multivariate Case

A more general treatment of $\mathbf{V}_t$ allowing for a full covariance matrix estimate uses inverted Wishart distributions in the place of inverted gamma distributions. Before we can proceed, it helps to restate the multivariate DLM setup to incorporate a multivariate observation series (Prado and West 2010, pp. 266–267). More specifically, we need to find multivariate analogues for the prior hyperparameters S_0, d_0, and n_0, and the sufficient statistics e and Q.

Rewrite the DLM as

$$\begin{aligned} \mathbf{y}'_{t+1} &= \mathbf{F}'_t\mathbf{X}_{t+1} + \mathbf{v}'_{t+1} \\ \mathbf{X}_{t+1} &= \mathbf{G}_t\mathbf{X}_t + \mathbf{\Omega}_{t+1}. \end{aligned}$$

Both $\mathbf{y}_{t+1}$ and $\mathbf{v}_{t+1}$ are q-dimensional vectors, so that the distribution of $\mathbf{v}_{t+1}$ is now multivariate normal, with $\mathbf{v}_{t+1} \sim \mathcal{N}_q[0, v_{t+1}\mathbf{V}_{t+1}]$. Each of the q component series are driven by a p-dimensional state vector, leading to the $p \times q$ state matrix $\mathbf{X}_{t+1}$. $\mathbf{F}_{t+1}$ is the $p \times 1$observation matrix. The system variance is therefore matrix normal with $\mathbf{\Omega}_t \sim \mathcal{N}_{p\times q}[0, \mathbf{W}_{t+1}, \mathbf{V}]$, where the usual variance term $\mathbf{W}_{t+1}$ is now the $p \times p$ left covariance matrix.

Restated in this way, the filtering recursions for the DLM become

$$\begin{aligned} \mathbf{x}_t \mid \mathbf{y}^t &\sim \mathcal{N}_{p\times q}\left[\mathbf{M}_{t-1}, \mathbf{C}_{t-1}, \mathbf{V}_{t-1}\right] \\ \mathbf{x}_{t+1} \mid \mathbf{y}^t &\sim \mathcal{N}_{p\times q}\left[\mathbf{a}_t, \mathbf{R}_t, \mathbf{V}_{t-1}\right] \\ \mathbf{y}_{t+1} \mid \mathbf{y}^t &\sim \mathcal{N}_q\left[\mathbf{f}_t, q_t\mathbf{V}_t\right] \\ \mathbf{x}_{t+1} \mid \mathbf{y}^{t+1} &\sim \mathcal{N}_r\left[\mathbf{m}_t, \mathbf{C}_t, \mathbf{V}_t\right] \end{aligned}$$

with the relationships

$$
\begin{aligned}
\mathrm{a}_t &= \mathrm{G}_t \mathrm{M}_{t-1} \\
\mathrm{R}_t &= \Delta^{-1/2} \mathrm{G}_t \mathrm{C}_{t-1} \mathrm{G}_t' \Delta^{-1/2} \\
\mathrm{f}_t &= \mathrm{a}_t' \mathrm{F}_t \\
q_t &= \mathrm{F}_t' \mathrm{R}_t \mathrm{F}_t + v_t \\
\mathrm{e}_t &= \mathrm{y}_t - \mathrm{f}_t \\
\mathrm{A}_t &= \mathrm{R}_t \mathrm{F}_t / q_t \\
\mathrm{M}_t &= \mathrm{a}_t + \mathrm{A}_t \mathrm{e}_t' \\
\mathrm{C}_t &= \mathrm{R}_t - \mathrm{A}_t \mathrm{A}_t' q_t .
\end{aligned}
$$

As in the univariate case, $\mathbf{W}_t$ is eliminated by the discount factor matrix Δ. Introducing uncertainty about the covariance matrix $\mathbf{V}_t$ can be done with an inverted-Wishart prior with prior hyperparameters (n_0, D_0). Letting $\mathrm{S}_{t-1} = \mathrm{D}_{t-1}/n_{t-1}$, the recursions for the covariance matrix are

$$
\begin{aligned}
n_t &= n_{t-1} + 1 \\
\mathrm{D}_t &= \mathrm{D}_{t-1} + \mathrm{e}_t \mathrm{e}_t' / q_t
\end{aligned}
$$

and the expectation of the covariance matrix at any time is $\mathrm{S}_t = \mathrm{D}_t / n_t$. The undetermined parameter v can be set to unity without loss of generality. No modification of the recursions is necessary because $\mathbf{V}_t$ appears explicitly in all of the distributions. Just as in the univariate case, discount factors can be applied to the multivariate observation variance matrix $\mathbf{V}_t$ to admit time-varying volatility.

SEQUENTIAL MODEL COMPARISON

Having considered the handling of parameter uncertainty in the DLM, we would now like to explore methods to compare multiple DLM specifications to address model uncertainty (West and Harrison 1997, Chapter 12). We maintain our sequential orientation and seek comparisons that can be undertaken observation by observation, to obtain early warnings of a potential model breakdown.

The DLM filtering recursions already supply a ready metric for evaluating the short-term forecasting performance of the model. At each time step

$$
p(y_{t+1} \mid x_t) \sim T_{n_t - 1}\left[\mathrm{f}_t, \mathrm{Q}_t\right]
$$

supplies a predictive likelihood that can be used to evaluate how well the model has anticipated y_{t+1}. When evaluated at y_{t+1}, the model likelihood will be greater or lesser depending on how well the DLM anticipated y_{t+1}.

Now suppose there are multiple DLM specifications available, denoted by M_i, where i indexes the available models. Cumulating over all observations, the likelihood for any individual model is $p(y^{t+1}|x^t, M_i)$. If we begin from a prior probability of the model's validity $p(M_i)$, then by Bayes' rule we have

$$p(M_i \mid y^{t+1}) \propto p(y^{t+1}|x^t, M_i)\, p(M_i)\,.$$

Then for two models M_i and M_j,

$$\frac{p(M_i \mid y^{t+1})}{p(M_j \mid y^{t+1})} = \frac{p(y^{t+1}|x^t, M_i)}{p(y^{t+1}|x^t, M_j)} \cdot \frac{p(M_i \mid y^t)}{p(M_j \mid y^t)}.$$

The outer quantities are the prior and posterior odds ratios for the models, and the inner quantity is the Bayes factor. Bayes factors measure the relative evidence available in support of models M_i and M_j at each time step. They may also be accumulated through time so that

$$\frac{p(M_i \mid y^{t+k+1})}{p(M_j \mid y^{t+k+1})} = \prod_{s=1}^{k} \frac{p(y^{t+s+1}|x^{t+s}, M_i)}{p(y^{t+s+1}|x^{t+s}, M_j)} \times \frac{p(M_i)}{p(M_j)}.$$

The first quantity on the right is the cumulative Bayes factor.

Strictly speaking, an alternative model M_j isn't necessary to measure the relative performance of model M_i on an ongoing basis. Any alternative forecasting system that regularly supplies $p(y_{t+1} \mid x_t)$ can provide a benchmark for evaluation, such as futures prices and implied option volatilities. However, given our desire to entertain multiple candidate models as a control on model risk, we continue to develop criteria to evaluate multiple models.

For larger numbers of models, pairwise evaluation by Bayes factors quickly becomes unwieldy. A straightforward means of obtaining a number of model comparisons is to normalize by

$$\sum_i p(y^{t+1}|x^t, M_i)$$

so that

$$p(M_i \mid y_{t+1}) = \frac{p(y^{t+1}|x^t, M_i)\, p(M_i \mid y_t)}{\sum_i p(y^{t+1}|x^t, M_i)\, p(M_i \mid y_t)}.$$

The same caveats about the completeness of the model space apply.

Within the conceptual framework of state-space time series models, the DLM provides a Bayesian forecasting approach that is sensitive to parameter uncertainty and model uncertainty, without an underlying assumption of ergodic stationarity. The ability of all model parameters to adjust, along with the conditional independence of observations given the current state estimate, divorces the DLM from the assumption that the future must always look like the past. Accordingly, the DLM furnishes a first solution to the problem of developing a modeling approach that recognizes and measures the components of model risk that are inaccessible under classical statistical approaches.

Not all state-space models will work within the linear, Gaussian framework of the DLM. Nor will it always be possible to specify the state and observation matrices of the DLM a priori. In the next chapter, we pursue a more general approach to state-space time series modeling based on stochastic simulation known as sequential Monte Carlo inference.

CHAPTER 6

Sequential Monte Carlo Inference

In the last chapter, we introduced the class of dynamic linear models (DLMs), with which it became possible to undertake learning about latent states and error variances with a set of closed-form expressions, while accommodating parameter and model uncertainty in a conditional framework. These methods relied on the linearity of the underlying state-space model, as well as the assumption that error variances were normally distributed. Though good approximations may be obtained under these conditions, there are a number of situations—particularly situations involving financial data and models—in which those foundational assumptions will prove restrictive. In particular, the class of DLMs defined the state space in a way that all parameters in the equations except the error variance were known a priori. It is often the case that we would like to estimate unknown parameters in the state equations as well.

Sequential Monte Carlo (SMC) methods offer tractable solutions for both of these situations in state-space time series models. Using SMC methods, one can estimate states in nonlinear, non-Gaussian models. As with DLMs, state learning with SMC may be undertaken online, solving the filtering problem, or retrospectively, solving the smoothing problem. In addition, one can expand the set of unknown quantities targeted for inference to include both states and parameters, allowing filtered and smoothed parameter estimates to be obtained for the model equations.

The important subclass of SMC methods examined here is the class of *particle filters*. The notion of the particle filter relies on discrete approximations to probability distributions, or *particle sets*. The particle set approximation allows us to work with virtually any probability distribution of known or unknown form. Then, in contrast to batch Monte Carlo methods that update a series of conditional distributions (perhaps via their hyperparameters), particle filter methods make point wise updates to the particle set. The particle filter updates evaluate the candidate particle set with a fitness criterion, which leads to the selection of particles more likely to have generated the observed data.

In settings where state and parameter learning are of interest, the particle filter methodology considers the joint distribution of states and parameters. The masses tracked in the particle set are extended vectors including the state and unknown parameters. Alternative methods for state and parameter learning with particle filters are distinguished by how they define the extended vectors of the particle set, and their treatment of the resulting joint distribution.

Particle filter methods also provide for sequential model evaluation and comparison. As before, consideration of multiple candidate models may be employed as a search for the "best" candidate model or as a means of developing mixture models. In the latter case, more tractable distributions like Gaussians can be combined in location and scale mixtures to approximate skewed, fat-tailed, and multimodal distributions.

Particle filters thus furnish an extremely general methodology for state and parameter learning. In most cases the only requirements to use a particular filter successfully are the ability to simulate draws from the state equation and the ability to evaluate the likelihood function for the observation equation—requirements that can be met in many practical situations. Accordingly, *particle filter methods represent a completion of the goal set out in the beginning of the book: online estimation of a wide class of time series models within a Bayesian framework that does justice to discontinuous data-generation processes and parameter and model uncertainty.*

This chapter begins by generalizing the DLM framework in a way that makes the DLM linear and Gaussian conditional on a larger set of unknown parameters. The resulting conditional DLM model can be estimated by a Gibbs-sampler-like technique known as forward-filtering backward-sampling (FFBS). Though FFBS requires batch estimation and can become highly inefficient as an algorithm, it is a helpful first model for building intuition about the estimation of dynamic state-space models.

Our discussion of SMC methods begins by introducing the notion of a particle set in a simple state-space setting with known parameters and unknown states. This simple example allows us to introduce the bootstrap filter and the auxiliary particle filter while explaining the technical challenges of particle set degeneracy. We then proceed to the problem of joint state and parameter learning. The Liu-West (2001) filter and the particle-learning method of Carvalho, Johannes, Lopes, and Polson (2010) are treated in detail. Though many methods for joint parameter and state learning have been put forward, these two are preferred for their efficiency and flexibility. We recommend using particle learning when inference based on hyperparameters and sufficient statistics for the states and parameters is possible, and the Liu-West filter otherwise.

NONLINEAR AND NON-NORMAL MODELS

In canvassing methods to break free of the linear/Gaussian framework of the DLM, one elegant strategy involves specifying a nonlinear or non-Gaussian model that is linear and Gaussian conditional on another quantity. For example, it is possible to approximate distributions of almost any form via mixtures of Gaussian distributions. If the DLM specification were conditioned on a latent variable λ with a multinomial likelihood, each conditional DLM would be linear and Gaussian, though the combination weighted by λ would be non-Gaussian.

Similarly, the DLM filtering and smoothing recursions were conditioned on knowledge of $\mathbf{F}_t$ and $\mathbf{G}_t$ for all periods. Were $\mathbf{F}_t$ and $\mathbf{G}_t$ allowed to be unknown and uncertain, the DLM would be able to accommodate a certain amount of nonlinearity.

Gibbs Sampling

Both situations suggest estimation of nonlinear, non-Gaussian time series models via a kind of Gibbs sampling scheme. In a Gibbs sampler, one seeks a sampling scheme for each conditional component of a more complicated joint distribution. Cycling through the component sampling schemes yields a sample for the joint distribution in a computationally efficient way.

To understand the concern about computational efficiency, consider the generation of random samples as the dimension of the parameter space expands. In one-dimensional space, it is possible that 1000 draws provides a good approximation to the distribution of interest with low Monte Carlo error. However, if we begin to work in two dimensions, one would need $N = 1000^2 = 1{,}000{,}000$ draws to ensure the same coverage. The number of necessary draws quickly spirals out of control for larger dimensions, a phenomenon known as the *curse of dimensionality*.

Thus, when faced with parameter spaces of high dimension, we would like to devise a sampling scheme that confronts the curse of dimensionality. The key insight in developing sampling schemes is the Clifford-Hammersley theorem, which states that any multivariate probability distribution is completely characterized by its full conditional distributions (Johannes and Polson 2009a, pp. 1002–1003). If j indexes dimensions and $-j$ refers to all dimensions other than j, $p(x_1, \ldots, x_j, \ldots, x_D \mid y)$ is fully determined by the product of $p(x_j \mid y, x_{-j})$ for all j. The Clifford-Hammersley theorem implies that if we can sample the full conditional distributions, we have obtained a sample from the joint distribution that is not subject to the curse of dimensionality. If we would need 1000^D draws to sample $p(x_1, \ldots, x_D \mid y)$ directly, we would only need D × 1000 draws to sample every $p(x_j \mid y, x_{-j})$.

Gibbs sampling schemes are designed to cycle through each $p(x_j \mid y, x_{-j})$ while progressively updating information in the conditioning sets of each sampled dimension. Hence, on each cycle i of N cycles, a four-dimensional Gibbs sampler would loop through the following draws:

$$x_1^{(i)} \sim p\left(x_1 \mid y, x_2, x_3, x_4\right)$$

$$x_2^{(i)} \sim p\left(x_2 \mid y, x_1^{(i)}, x_3, x_4\right)$$

$$x_3^{(i)} \sim p\left(x_3 \mid y, x_1^{(i)}, x_2^{(i)}, x_4\right)$$

$$x_4^{(i)} \sim p\left(x_4 \mid y, x_1^{(i)}, x_2^{(i)}, x_3^{(i)}\right)$$

Upon returning to the beginning of the cycle, each component of the joint distribution will have undergone an update, which allows the Gibbs sampler Markov chain to converge to the joint distribution on repetition.

Gibbs sampling is particularly effective when conjugate family representations can be found for the components $p(x_j \mid y, x_{-j})$. For instance, we could have created a Gibbs sampler to perform inference in the linear regression model without reference to the closed-form formulas given in Chapter 2. Formally, breaking $p(\beta, \sigma^2)$ into $p(\beta \mid \sigma^2) \sim \mathcal{N}[\mu_0, \sigma_0^2]$ and $p(\sigma^2 \mid \beta) \sim \mathcal{IG}[n_0, n_0 S_0]$, the Gibbs sampler would cycle through draws of $p(\beta \mid s^{2^{(i)}}, y) = b^{(i)}$ and $p(\sigma^2 \mid \beta, y) = s^{2(i)}$. When no distributional forms suggest themselves for the components, a variety of Metropolis-Hastings methods may be used to explore that region of the parameter space with the use of a proposal density. We will have more to say about proposal densities when we discuss importance sampling later in the chapter.

Markov Chain Monte Carlo (MCMC) methods based on Gibbs sampling and Metropolis-Hastings methods are an extensive subject in their own right, and account for much of the rapid development of Bayesian statistics since the early 1990s. We touch on them only in passing here, referring the reader to Gamerman and Lopes (2006) and Johannes and Polson (forthcoming) for comprehensive treatments of MCMC methods.

Forward-Filtering Backward-Sampling

Conditioning on the latent variable λ and writing the states and DLM parameters as a single block $\mathbf{D} = \left\{\mathbf{x}_t, \mathbf{m}_t, \mathbf{C}_t, \mathbf{a}_t, \mathbf{R}_t, \mathbf{f}_t, \mathbf{Q}_t, n_t, S_t\right\}_{t=1}^{T}$, a Gibbs sampler can be employed to search for the joint distribution of $\{\mathbf{D}, \lambda, \mathbf{F}, \mathbf{G} \mid y\}$ in a nonlinear, non-Gaussian conditional DLM. We abuse notation somewhat by having λ stand in for the parameters that govern its distribution. From the DLM theory developed thus far, we already know how to evaluate $\mathbf{D} \mid y, \lambda, \mathbf{F}, \mathbf{G}$ using the filtering and smoothing recursions. To implement non-Gaussian distributions, we need to sample the parameters governing $\lambda \mid y, \mathbf{D}, \mathbf{F}, \mathbf{G}$, which will have a beta or Dirichlet distribution if λ takes on a binomial or multinomial set of values, possibly indexing a set of possible regimes. Then, conditional on λ, we would sample $\mathbf{F}, \mathbf{G} \mid y, \mathbf{D}, \lambda$ (separately or jointly) from an appropriate distribution.

The key step in implementing the Gibbs sampling scheme sketched above is evidently the sampling scheme for $\mathbf{D} \mid y, \lambda, \mathbf{F}, \mathbf{G}$. An approach simultaneously proposed by Carter and Kohn (1994) and Frühwirth-Schnatter (1994) for sampling $\{\mathbf{x}_t\}_{t=1}^{T} \sim \mathbf{D} \mid y, \lambda, \mathbf{F}, \mathbf{G}$ is known as the forward-filtering backward-sampling (FFBS) algorithm. On each iteration of the FFBS algorithm, one obtains a sample of the states $\{\mathbf{x}_1, \ldots, \mathbf{x}_T\}^{(i)}$. In the context of a Gibbs sampler, the draws $\{\mathbf{x}_1, \ldots, \mathbf{x}_T\}^{(i)}$ can be introduced into the conditioning information sets for the other sampler blocks in place of the stand-in notation $\mathbf{D}$.

The FFBS algorithm uses the DLM filtering equations to find $\mathcal{N}[\mathbf{m}_T, \mathbf{C}_T]$ given the data, an initial guess for $\mathbf{m}_0$ and $\mathbf{C}_0$, and the elements λ, $\mathbf{F}$, and $\mathbf{G}$. The algorithm begins by sampling $\mathbf{x}_T^{(i)} \sim \mathcal{N}[\mathbf{m}_T, \mathbf{C}_T]$. Working backward through the smoothing recursions, the other states are sampled from the distributions $\mathcal{N}[\mathbf{h}_t, \mathbf{H}_t]$ defined as:

$$
\begin{aligned}
\mathbf{h}_t &= \mathbf{m}_t + \mathbf{B}_t \left[\mathbf{x}_{t+1}^{(i)} - \mathbf{a}_{t+1}\right] \\
\mathbf{H}_t &= \mathbf{C}_t + \mathbf{B}_t \mathbf{R}_{t+1} \mathbf{B}_t' \\
\mathbf{B}_t &= \mathbf{C}_t \mathbf{G}_{t+1}' \mathbf{R}_{t+1}^{-1}.
\end{aligned}
$$

These are exactly the same as the Kalman smoothing recursions, with the replacement of a known $\mathbf{x}_{t+1}$ by a draw $\mathbf{x}_{t+1}^{(i)}$. The quantities $\mathbf{C}_t$ and $\mathbf{R}_t$ are calculated in the filtering stage as before. The system matrix $\mathbf{G}_t$ may be fixed by definition or treated as an additional unknown quantity to be sampled. Once a draw of $\mathbf{x}_T^{(i)}$ has been obtained, samples of $\mathbf{x}_{T-1}^{(i)}, \ldots, \mathbf{x}_1^{(i)}$ are obtained to complete the draw of states for one iteration of the algorithm. Finding $\mathcal{N}[\mathbf{m}_T, \mathbf{C}_T]$ conditional on λ, $\mathbf{F}$, and $\mathbf{G}$ constitutes the *forward-filtering* component, whereas the smoothing equations permit *backward sampling* of the states.

To summarize:

Sample states $\mathbf{D} = \{\mathbf{x}_1, \ldots, \mathbf{x}_T\}^{(i)}$ conditional on y, λ, $\mathbf{F}$, and $\mathbf{G}$:

Run the DLM filtering recursions forward to time T.

Sample $\mathbf{x}_T^{(i)}$ from $\mathcal{N}[\mathbf{m}_\mathrm{T}, \mathbf{C}_\mathrm{T}]$.

Sample $\mathbf{x}_{T-1}^{(i)}, \ldots, \mathbf{x}_1^{(i)}$ backward using the modified DLM smoothing recursions.

Then, depending on the nature of the model, complete the Gibbs sampling scheme using the following components:

Sample $\lambda \mid y$, **D**, **F**, **G** from a discrete probability distribution.

Sample **F** $\mid y$, **D**, λ, **G** if **F** is not fixed by the definition of the DLM.

Sample **G** $\mid y$, **D**, λ, **F** if **G** is not fixed by the definition of the DLM.

Certain weaknesses of FFBS are apparent. It is a batch method that operates on the entire time series at once. For very long time series, the sampling scheme will be drawing a sample from a very high-dimensional joint distribution for the states, so the curse of dimensionality may apply even with full conditionals available. If **F** and **G** are treated as unknowns, the problem compounds. Nevertheless, FFBS makes certain problems with Bayesian time series inference evident in a straightforward way, while also showing the usefulness of the DLM as scaffolding for a simulation scheme. Both the DLM and FFBS will supply important intuition as we develop SMC methods next.

STATE LEARNING WITH PARTICLE FILTERS

In place of the Markov Chain Monte Carlo (MCMC) batch sampling approach of FFBS, we seek to implement a sequential Monte Carlo (SMC) approach for inference in a nonlinear non-Gaussian state-space framework. By working sequentially, the time series can be analyzed an observation at a time as a series of marginal distributions, rather than as a joint distribution over a long period. In addition to the gains in computational efficiency, one might expect that the state space will be more thoroughly sampled at each time step in an SMC scheme than when it is approached as one link in a chain of samples.

We begin again within our simple state-space model setting. Define the observation and system equations as

$$y_{t+1} = f(x_{t+1}, \theta^y)$$
$$x_{t+1} = g(x_t, \theta^x).$$

The notation distinguishes elements of the parameter set $\theta = \{\theta^y, \theta^x\}$ according to their position in the state equation g or the observation equation f.

As a first basic example, let $\theta^y = \sigma_y^2$ and $\theta^x = \sigma_x^2$, and define the model as

$$y_{t+1} = x_{t+1} + \varepsilon_{t+1}^y$$
$$x_{t+1} = x_t + \varepsilon_{t+1}^x$$

with $\varepsilon_{t+1}^y \sim \mathcal{N}[0, \sigma_y^2]$ and $\varepsilon_{t+1}^x \sim \mathcal{N}[0, \sigma_x^2]$. Neither linearity nor normality is necessary for what follows, but further complicating the model at this point would only distract from understanding the simulation scheme. We will assume that we know σ_y^2 and σ_x^2 but do not know the time series of states x_t, $t = 1, \ldots, T$. The inference problem consists of finding states only. The initial state distribution may be uniform over the most likely region of the state space or a distribution of a particular form motivated by the problem at hand. Instead of a parametric distribution, we define this prior distribution as a *particle set*, or a random histogram over a region of the state space.

The Particle Set

The particle set is intended to be a discrete approximation to a continuous probability distribution. To reduce Monte Carlo error, the set is given a large size N. Denote the particle set for x_t as

$$\left\{x_t^{(i)}\right\}_{i=1}^N$$

to represent N candidate draws of x_t, indexed by the superscript i.

Associated with each $x_t^{(i)}$ will be a probability weight denoted $w_t^{(i)}$. At the outset we will have $w_t^{(i)} = \frac{1}{N}$ for all $x_t^{(i)}$. A key challenge will be to update these probabilities in light of the likelihood that the candidate $x_t^{(i)}$ could have generated the observed data. To distinguish the updated particle sets from the candidates with $w_t^{(i)} = \frac{1}{N}$, we will notate the update as $r : i \to k(i)$ so that we have $\left\{x_t^{k(i)}\right\}_{i=1}^N$ and $\left\{w_t^{k(i)}\right\}_{i=1}^N$ after updating. The operation $r : i \to k(i)$, which updates the probabilities of the candidate state particles, is the relevant *filtering* operation in the context of sequential inference.

A First Particle Filter: The Bootstrap Filter

With a candidate initial particle set $\left\{x_0^{(i)}\right\}_{i=1}^N$ in hand, perhaps an obvious first attempt at the filtering problem sketched above would proceed via the following algorithm:

Prior $p(x_{t+1} \mid x_t)$. Simulate the next step in the state equation $\left\{x_1^{(i)}\right\}_{i=1}^N$ by evaluating $x_1^{(i)} = x_0^{(i)} + \varepsilon_1^{x(i)}$ for each member of the initial candidate set $\left\{x_0^{(i)}\right\}_{i=1}^N$ and N draws of $\varepsilon_1^x \sim \mathcal{N}[0, \sigma_x^2]$.

Forecast $p(y_{t+1} \mid x_{t+1})$. Set $y_1^{(i)} = x_1^{(i)}$ based on the observation equation, for each $x_1^{(i)}$. The result is a prior distribution for y_1.

Posterior $p(x_{t+1} \mid y_{t+1})$*: Part 1*. Evaluate the likelihood $y_1 - y_1^{(i)} \sim \mathcal{N}[0, \sigma_y^2]$ for each $y_1^{(i)}$ and define the result as $k(i)$. This gives us $r : i \to k(i)$. Normalize $k(i)$ by defining $k(i)' = k(i)/\sum_{i=1}^N k(i)$.

Posterior $p(x_{t+1} \mid y_{t+1})$*: Part 2*. Draw a new sample $\left\{x_1^{k(i)'}\right\}_{k(i)'=1}^N$ in which each of the candidates $\left\{x_1^{(i)}\right\}_{i=1}^N$ has probability $k(i)'$ of being drawn.

Repeat the cycle by generating $x_2^{(i)} = x_1^{k(i)'} + \varepsilon_2^{x(i)}$, evaluating $\mathcal{N}[y_2 \mid x_2^{(i)}, \sigma_y^2]$, finding $k(i)'$, and drawing $\left\{x_2^{k(i)'}\right\}_{k(i)'=1}^N$.

This first proposed solution to the particle-filtering problem is known as the *bootstrap filter* (Gordon, Salmond, and Smith 1993). Within the bounds of the bootstrap filter, we can see elements that are common to all particle filters, as well as several virtues.

The first step conducted with the candidate state draws is known as *propagation* of the state equation. The propagation step involves a simulation of $p(x_{t+1} \mid x_t, \theta^x)$, which in this case we have defined to be $\mathcal{N}[x_t, \sigma_x^2]$. We can write the particle approximation obtained from propagation as $p^N(x_{t+1} \mid x_t, \theta^x)$.

In the following two steps, we resample $p^N(x_{t+1} \mid x_t, \theta^x)$ by applying a fitness criterion to each of the draws created in the propagation step. This provides our all-important approximation to $p^N(x_{t+1} \mid x_t, \theta^x, y^{t+1})$. The efficiency and reliability of learning from one time step to the next turns on the quality of this approximation. In the bootstrap filter, fitness is evaluated using the likelihood function. If $x_{t+1}^{(i)}$ is a perfect forecast, y_{t+1} will be at the mode of $\mathcal{N}[x_{t+1}, \sigma_y^2]$ and will have the highest probability among the N draws. The fitness information is then summarized in $k(i)'$, the normalized version of $k(i)$. The set $k(i)'$ is constructed so that $\sum_{i=1}^N k(i)' \equiv 1$ and $k(i)' \geq 0$ for all i, so the $k(i)'$ properly serve as probabilities. Finally, we draw a sample $\left\{x_{t+1}^{k(i)'}\right\}_{k(i)'=1}^N$, where each $x_{t+1}^{(i)}$ has probability $k(i)'$ of being drawn.

Though the previous discussion is broken into distinct steps—evaluating likelihoods, normalizing, and drawing a new sample—the resampling process may be understood as a single functional step. More precisely, resampling may be conceived as drawing from a multinomial distribution where buckets 1 through N each have probability $k(i)'$, then using those draws as indices for resampling the propagated states. Many statistical software packages have a sampling command that will draw from $x_{t+1}^{(i)}$ using the unnormalized $k(i)$, eliminating the normalization step.

The bootstrap filter provides both a means of refreshing candidate draws and winnowing the field of candidates based on their adequacy to the data. It relies only on the ability to simulate from the state equation, and to evaluate the likelihood for the observation equation.

The Auxiliary Particle Filter

The bootstrap filter has certain weaknesses, however. In particular, the propagation step at the beginning of the algorithm does not attempt to evaluate which candidate states are most likely to generate priors in high-probability regions for y_{t+1} (Pitt and Shepherd 1999).

To see the weakness in the bootstrap filter, consider a case where there is a sudden jump in y so that y_{t+1}, y_{t+2}, and y_{t+3} are each significantly above y_t, y_{t+1}, and y_{t+2}, respectively. Each of the forecasts $p(y_{t+j} \mid x_{t+j})$ will be in the left tail of the likelihood, more so when the jumps in y are larger. Those forecasted values that are closer to y_{t+1} will have a higher probability of being resampled, but the resulting set $p^N(x_{t+1} \mid x_t, \theta^x, y^t)$ will contain many candidate draws for x_{t+1}, which, when propagated to x_{t+2}, will be nowhere near y_{t+2}. With each successive jump, the variance of the importance weights will increase and the filter's ability to correct itself diminishes, perhaps to the point where there are no more particles in the high-likelihood region of $p(y_{t+1} \mid x_{t+1})$. It would be nice to reorient the search for x_{t+1}, rather than continuing to search over states that did the best job of forming a poor expectation for y_{t+1}.

A second weakness of the bootstrap filter comes from the resampling step. As the filtering algorithm proceeds, we hope to consistently obtain large numbers of states in the particle set with high values of $k(i)'$. However, in the limit we end up with a reduced set of high-probability $x_{t+1}^{(i)}$ clustered around the mode. At each propagation step noise will be added to these $x_{t+1}^{(i)}$ via $\{\varepsilon_{t+1}^{x(i)}\}$, so the algorithm won't necessarily stop. However, the filter will stop exploring the state space because future draws will remain in the neighborhood of these few $x_{t+1}^{(i)}$. This weakness in the resampling step is known as sample impoverishment or particle degeneracy.

It turns out that solving the propagation problem contributes to solving the particle degeneracy problem as well. Using y_{t+1} to improve the search for x_{t+1} is called *adapting* the filter. Since we had an explicit expression for $p(x_{t+1} \mid y^{t+1})$ in the Kalman filter, it is said to be fully adapted. An adapted particle filter takes advantage of the information in the new observation to propagate states that will have higher likelihoods. Hence, we need a way to get information about $p(y_{t+1} \mid x_{t+1})$ for use in the propagation step, preferably without actually propagating a particle set $\{x_{t+1}^{(i)}\}$, although that is a default option.

Based on the form of the state equation, one can define a best guess about x_{t+1} conditional on x_t (and possibly y_{t+1}) as $\alpha(x_t)$. In other words, $\alpha(x_t)$ provides a summary of $p(x_{t+1} \mid x_t)$. Ideally, $\alpha(x_t)$ would be an analytically known mean or mode of $p(x_{t+1} \mid x_t)$. However, analytical formulas are not necessary to develop a reasonable definition for $\alpha(x_t)$; its function is simply to point toward the x_{t+1} that will most likely be associated with each $x_t^{(i)}$.

The auxiliary particle filter begins by sampling an auxiliary index variable k with weights proportional to $p(y_{t+1} \mid \alpha(x_t^{(i)}))$ rather than $p(y_{t+1} \mid x_{t+1}^{(i)})$. The random index variable then carries information about the relative importance of different particles $x_t^{(i)}$ while also enabling a random sample $x_{t+1}^{(i)}$ to be obtained from the most important previous states.

From this point on, the auxiliary particle filter operates like the bootstrap filter with importance resampling based on the predictive likelihood. To summarize the algorithm:

Generate a summary $\alpha(x_t^{(i)})$ of $p(x_{t+1} \mid x_t)$ for each $x_t^{(i)}$.

Evaluate the observation equation likelihood to obtain $p(y_{t+1} \mid \alpha(x_t^{k(i)}))$.

Sample an index k with importance weights $w_k^{(i)} \propto p(y_{t+1} \mid \alpha(x_t^{(i)}))$.

Propagate $x_t^{k(i)}$ to $x_{t+1}^{(i)}$.

Calculate $y_t^{(i)}$ for each $x_t^{(i)}$.

Evaluate the observation equation likelihood to obtain $p\left(y_{t+1} \mid x_{t+1}^{(i)}\right) p\left(x_{t+1}^{(i)} \mid x_t^{k(i)}\right)$.

Resample $x_{t+1}^{k(i)}$ from $x_{t+1}^{(i)}$ with weights $w_x^{(i)} \propto \dfrac{p\left(y_{t+1} \mid x_{t+1}^{(i)}\right) p\left(x_{t+1}^{(i)} \mid x_t^{k(i)}\right)}{p(y_{t+1} \mid \alpha(x_t^{k(i)}))}$.

JOINT LEARNING OF PARAMETERS AND STATES

Up to this point, we have achieved samples $p^N(x_{t+1} \mid y_{t+1})$ by propagating states and resampling based on a fitness criterion. By these samples we obtain an approximation to $p(x_{t+1} \mid y_{t+1})$. Learning states and parameters jointly raises the question of sampling from $p(x_{t+1}, \theta \mid y_{t+1})$, the joint posterior distribution of states and parameters. Our estimates for states will depend on the parameter samples, and parameter estimates will depend on the choice of states.

The first step in joint learning involves augmenting the components of the particle set. We append a parameter vector of length K_θ to the K_x-element state vector to obtain a collection of K-dimensional particles, with $K = K_\theta + K_x$. The resulting multidimensional particle set becomes our approximation to the joint distribution of x_t and θ. The curse of dimensionality applies: All else equal, Monte Carlo error will increase exponentially with the dimension K. Hence, we approach the sampling of the joint distribution as in other Monte Carlo settings by breaking it into approximations for the full conditional distributions. Operationally, this means first updating the state information in a block, followed by updates to the parameter information.

An approach that further mitigates the curse of dimensionality when sampling from $p(x_{t+1}, \theta \mid y_{t+1})$ involves the use of low-dimensional sufficient statistics for x_t and/or θ. In a linear-Gaussian setting, for instance, sufficient statistics will be available for the state vector ($\mathbf{m}_t$ and $\mathbf{C}_t$) as well as for the parameters (using the normal-inverse gamma formulation for linear regressions introduced in Chapter 2). One can just as well randomize over these sufficient statistics as over the parameters themselves. In fact, randomizing over the sufficient statistics offers two benefits. The collection of candidate sufficient statistics can be viewed as generating a mixture distribution that more closely approximates nonstandard distributions for the parameters and states. In addition, one can draw samples of states and/or parameters from the distributions parameterized by the available sufficient statistics. This adjustment to the resampling process helps to combat the problem of particle degeneracy.

Distinguishing sufficient statistics for states and/or parameters requires some knowledge—conjectured or otherwise—about the joint distribution of states and parameters, so methods based on sufficient statistics are not the most general available. The particle filter of Liu and West proceeds without knowledge of the joint distribution via a kernel approximation using a mixture of multivariate normal distributions. Though generally less computationally efficient than the particle-learning approach we advocate for the case where sufficient statistics are available, the Liu-West filter supplies a tractable, flexible solution for a variety of inference problems. We begin with this method and then proceed to develop the particle-learning approach via the Storvik filter, a first attempt to incorporate sufficient statistics in the inference problem.

Introducing parameters into the particle set involves committing to a distinction between quantities that are *fixed* and quantities that vary over time. The estimation methods discussed here are designed to confine evolution to the latent states. Parameter drift is avoided. In the Liu-West filter, the discount factor is used not to enable ongoing adaptation, but to ensure that no information is lost in parameter learning. If one wishes to reintroduce parameter drift, it must be done through different means.

The reappearance of fixed parameters does not imply the collapse of our enterprise. Recovering latent state dynamics that describe the evolution of asset prices and volatilities, among other things, allows quantities that are generally regarded as fixed to be treated as variable. The online orientation of our analysis is not rendered ineffectual, either. New corrective information may be reintroduced in the prior information set at any point in time—and indeed the convergence seen in the parameter-learning state space algorithm directly reflects the absence of any productive interventions of that sort. Finally, flexibility can be reintroduced in other forms. Rather than indexing models by discount factors, they could be indexed by the point in time at which learning begins. Alternatively, as mentioned, parameter drift can be artificially reintroduced.

The Liu-West Filter

Joint inference on states and parameters begins by augmenting the particle set from $\{x_t^{(i)}\}_{i=1}^N$ to $\{(x_t, \theta)^{(i)}\}_{i=1}^N$, increasing its dimension from K_x to $K = K_x + K_\theta$, as above. To fight the curse of dimensionality, we will sample the K_x-dimensional vector x_t conditional on θ, and the K_θ-dimensional vector conditional on x_t. Practically speaking, this breaks the propagation operation into two steps.

Since we have already considered how to sample $p(x_{t+1} \mid x_t, \theta^x, y_t)$, we turn to the problem of sampling $p(\theta \mid x_{t+1}, x_t, y_{t+1})$. In the Liu-West filter, the conditional distribution for θ is approximated by a mixture of multivariate normal distributions (Liu and West 2001). The components of the mixture thus have the form

$$\mathcal{N}\left[m_t^{(i)}, h^2 V_t\right]$$

where

$$m_t^{(i)} = a\theta_t^{(i)} + (1-a)\bar{\theta}_t$$

$$V_t = \frac{1}{N}\sum_{i=1}^{N}\left(\theta_t^{(i)} - \bar{\theta}_t\right)\left(\theta_t^{(i)} - \bar{\theta}_t\right)'$$

and

$$\bar{\theta}_t \equiv \frac{1}{N}\sum_{i=1}^{N}\theta_t^{(i)}.$$

Here we abuse notation somewhat—neither θ nor m nor V is time-varying, but we use θ_t, m_t, and V_t to denote the state of knowledge about θ and V as of time step t. The h^2 term multiplying the parameter covariance matrix V ensures that information about the parameter vector is not lost in successive time steps. Accordingly, $h^2 V$ represents an evolution variance term with no parameter drift. Both a and h^2 are calculated from the discount factor δ, with $a = \frac{3\delta-1}{2\delta}$ and $h^2 = 1 - a^2$. For typical discount factor values, h^2 will be quite small, on the order of 0.01 to 0.10, so eliminating h^2 would create more information loss than would ever be introduced through discounting in a DLM or static regression setting. However, it is worthwhile to note that smaller values of δ will imply higher values of h^2, more variation in subsequent parameter draws, and a longer path to convergence in the parameter estimates. The discount factor is thus less a statement about information loss than a statement about the period of time needed to learn the fixed parameters of the model.

With this treatment of the marginal parameter distribution in hand, we can augment the auxiliary particle filter algorithm to obtain the Liu-West filter algorithm:

- Evaluate the observation equation likelihood to obtain $p(y_{t+1} \mid x_t^{(i)}, \alpha(x_t^{(i)}), m_t^{(i)})$. The values $m_t^{(i)}$ play an auxiliary variable role for the parameters similar to the role $\alpha(x_t)$ plays for the state evolution.
- Resample $\{(x_t, \theta_t)^{(k_1(i))}\}$ from $\{(x_t, \theta_t)^{(i)}\}$ with adapted weights $w_t^{(i)} \propto p(y_{t+1} \mid x_t^{(i)}, \alpha(x_t^{(i)}), m_t^{(i)})$.
- Propagate $\{\theta_t^{(k_1(i))}\}$ to $\{\theta_{t+1}^{(i)}\}$ by drawing from the mixture components $\mathcal{N}[m_t^{(i)}, h^2 V_t^{(i)}]$.
- Propagate $\{x_t^{(k_1(i))}\}$ to $\{x_{t+1}^{(i)}\}$ via $p(x_{t+1} \mid x_t^{(k(i))}, \theta_{t+1}^{(i)})$.
- Evaluate the observation equation likelihood to obtain $p(y_{t+1} \mid (x_{t+1}, \theta_{t+1})^{(i)})$.
- Resample $\{(x_{t+1}, \theta_{t+1})^{k_2(i)}\}$ from $\{(x_{t+1}, \theta_{t+1})^{(i)}\}$ with adapted weights $w_t^{(i)} \propto p(y_{t+1} \mid (x_{t+1}, \theta_{t+1})^{(i)}) / p(y_{t+1} \mid x_t^{(k_1(i))}, \alpha(x_t^{(k_1(i))}), m^{(k_1(i))})$.

The two resampling steps are notable and show the twofold impact of the new data observed. The new observation reweights draws before the state and parameter draws are updated, and again after the updates occur. Thus, only "good" particles are propagated, and the result is further cleaned up after propagation.

As with the bootstrap and auxiliary particle filters, the only technical requirements of the Liu-West filter are the ability to simulate new states from the evolution equation and the ability to compute the likelihood of new observations conditional on parameter and state estimates. These conditions will obtain whenever the conditional means of the state-space model equations are well-defined and the error distributions have a known form.

Even the last condition may be relaxed somewhat if multiple candidate models are employed and the results averaged.

Improving Efficiency with Sufficient Statistics

Given a sample of a fixed size, its ability to approximate a continuous probability distribution diminishes as the dimension of the distribution increases. Sufficient statistics allow a sample of the same size to work harder, increasing the effective sample size in a particle filter. Just as the variance of a sample mean will always be less than the variance of the sample itself, the variance of a sample of sufficient statistics will be less than a sample of parameter values of equal size. And because sufficient statistics "encode" more information than individual parameter draws, parameter samples may be recovered from them without loss of fidelity.

The first attempt to embed sufficient statistics in a particle-filtering framework for parameter learning was made by Storvik (2002). His filter proceeds as follows:

- Propagate $\{x_t^{(i)}\}$ to $\{x_{t+1}^{(i)}\}$ via $p(x_{t+1} \mid x_t^{(i)}, \theta_t^{(i)}, y_{t+1})$.
- Evaluate the observation equation likelihood to obtain $p(y_{t+1} \mid x_{t+1}^{(i)}, \theta_t^{(i)})$ $p(x_{t+1} \mid x_t^{(i)}, \theta_t^{(i)})$.
- Resample $\{(x_{t+1}, s_t)^{k(i)}\}$ from $\{(x_{t+1}, s_t)^{(i)}\}$ with weights $w_{t+1}^{(i)} \propto \frac{p\left(y_{t+1} \mid x_{t+1}^{(i)}, \theta_t^{(i)}\right) p\left(x_{t+1} \mid x_t^{(i)}, \theta_t^{(i)}\right)}{p\left(x_{t+1} \mid x_t^{(i)}, \theta_t^{(i)}, y_{t+1}\right)}$.
- Propagate $\{s_t^{k(i)}\}$ to $\{s_{t+1}^{(i)}\}$ using $s_{t+1}^{k(i)} = S(s_t^{(i)}, x_{t+1}^{k(i)}, y_{t+1})$.
- Sample $\{\theta_{t+1}^{(i)}\}$ from $p(\theta \mid s_{t+1}^{(i)})$.

The absence of an initial resampling step, as in the bootstrap filter, leads to particle degeneracy, which is why we prefer the particle-learning and Liu-West filters. However, we observe a couple of critical items. Sufficient statistics allow us to focus on (x_t, s_t) rather than (x_t, θ). When low-dimensional sufficient statistics are available a significant gain in efficiency can be obtained. The parameter update is replaced with the sufficient statistic update $s_{t+1}^{(i)} = S(s_t^{k(i)}, x_{t+1}^{k(i)}, y_{t+1})$. Such updates are just like the movement from (a,b) to (A,B) in the beta-Bernoulli example or from $\{\mathbf{b}_0, \mathbf{B}_0, n_0, n_0 S_0\}$ to $\{\mathbf{b}_1, \mathbf{B}_1, n_1, n_1 S_1\}$ in the normal linear regression example. In fact, what we are now calling sufficient statistics we previously called hyperparameters. Then, when values are needed for θ, a sample for θ is recovered from the sufficient statistics. Because the sufficient statistic updates are deterministic and the draws of $\{\theta_{t+1}^{(i)}\}$ are random, a second resampling step is no longer needed after the parameter information is propagated.

Particle Learning

Particle learning (Carvalho, Johannes, Lopes, and Polson 2010) adds an initial resampling step to the Storvik filter scheme, resulting in a better-adapted filter. Further, in the cases where the underlying state-space models may be cast in the conditional DLM form, the sufficient statistic structure can be exploited for state learning as well as parameter learning. Of course, where a conditional DLM form is not available, states may be handled as particle sets.

The particle-learning algorithm may be thought of as a Gibbs sampling scheme cycling through the joint distribution of states, sufficient statistics, and parameters $p(x_t, s_t, \theta)$ one time step at a time. Working with the particle approximation $p^N(x_t, s_t, \theta)$, the algorithm begins by resampling from the particle set using the likelihood for y_{t+1}. The propagation steps move through the (x_t, s_t, θ) block by updating each quantity in turn. States x_t are propagated, updating rules for s_t are applied, and new values of θ are sampled conditional on the sufficient statistics.

The handling of sufficient statistics and parameters is key to combating particle degeneracy. It is probably also the component of the algorithm that is least obvious. To understand the sufficient statistic updating rule, recall the example from Chapter 2 in which updates to the beta-binomial distribution were made via the hyperparameters a and b. For batch runs the new hyperparameters were obtained as $A = a + x$ and $B = b + (n - x)$. The quantities n and $x = \sum_i x_i$ were sufficient statistics for the data since no other information about the data was needed in order to develop the posterior. Within the same example in Chapter 4 we broke up the observation of the data $\{x_i\}$ in order to implement the posterior updates sequentially. When each observation triggers an update, the hyperparameter a is incremented by 1 whenever a success is observed $(x_i = 1)$ and b is incremented by 1 in the event of a failure $(x_i = 0$ and $n - x_i = 1)$.

Propagating sufficient statistics in the particle filter works the same way. The components of the sufficient statistic vector are initialized at $t = 0$ with a chosen set of hyperparameters—in the beta-Bernoulli example, these are a and b. At each time step thereafter, sufficient statistic updates are made using the $x_{t+1}^{(i)}$, cumulating the results of previous time steps along with the prior hyperparameter values. The authors of the particle filter methodology summarize the updates as

$$s_{t+1} = S(x_t, s_t, \theta),$$

highlighting the recursive quality of the updates as well as the conditioning of incremental sufficient statistics on candidate states and parameters.

The last step in the particle filter updating cycle draws a new set of parameters $\{\theta^{(i)}\}$ using the distribution $p(\theta \mid s_t)$. In our simple example, this would mean simulating data from a beta distribution B(A, B), where $s_t = \{A, B\}$. Refreshing $\{\theta^{(i)}\}$ from sufficient statistics produces useful variation in $\{\theta^{(i)}\}$, which cannot be achieved by resampling alone. Indeed, there will be N distributions $p(\theta \mid s_t^{(i)})$ to sample from, preserving uncertainty in the parameter-learning process and ensuring that the particle set does not degenerate into a singularity.

Finally, note that the sufficient statistic vector may be partitioned into s_t^x and s_t^θ in situations where a conjugate structure is available for the states and the parameters. With two sets of statistics, updating is done in two cycles:

$$s_{t+1}^\theta = S(x_t, s_t^x, s_t^\theta, \theta)$$
$$s_{t+1}^x = K(x_t, s_t^x, s_t^\theta, \theta).$$

The first cycle updates sufficient statistics for the parameters, as before, while the second cycle updates sufficient statistics for the states (the K stands for the Kalman filter). Then, in addition to sampling $p(\theta \mid s_t^{\theta(i)})$ to obtain new parameter draws, samples may be drawn from $p(x_t \mid s_t^{x(i)})$ to further update information about the states.

Thus, we can summarize the particle-learning algorithm as follows:

- Evaluate the observation equation likelihood $p(y_{t+1} \mid (x_t, s_t, \theta)^{(i)})$.
- Resample $\{(x_t, s_t, \theta)^{k(i)}\}$ from $\{(x_t, s_t, \theta)^{(i)}\}$ with weights $w_t^{(i)} \propto p(y_{t+1} \mid (x_t, s_t, \theta)^{(i)})$.
- Propagate $\{x_t^{k(i)}\}$ to $\{x_{t+1}^{(i)}\}$ via $p(x_{t+1} \mid (x_t, s_t, \theta)^{k(i)}, y_{t+1})$.
- Propagate $\{s_t^{k(i)}\}$ to $\{s_{t+1}^{(i)}\}$ via $s_{t+1}^{(i)} = S(s_t^{k(i)}, x_{t+1}^{(i)}, \theta^{(i)}, y_{t+1})$.
- Sample $\{\theta^{(i)}\}$ from $p(\theta \mid s_t^{(i)})$.

SEQUENTIAL MODEL COMPARISON

As in other model comparison settings, the marginal likelihood for each model is the key quantity for pairwise model comparisons. Recall that the marginal likelihood is obtained by integrating the likelihood over the prior distribution for the parameters:

$$p(y \mid M_i) = \int_\theta p(y \mid \theta_i, M_i) p(\theta_i \mid M_i).$$

In state-space models with parameter learning, one has to integrate over the states as well:

$$p(y_{t+1} \mid M_i) = \int_{x_{t+1}} \int_{\theta} p(y_{t+1} \mid \theta_i, x_{t+1}, M_i) p(x_{t+1} \mid x_t, \theta_i, M_i) p(\theta_i \mid M_i).$$

A discrete approximation is available as

$$p(y_{t+1} \mid M_i) = \frac{1}{N} \sum_{N} p^N(y_{t+1} \mid \theta_i, x_{t+1}, M_i).$$

In the course of running any of the particle filters above, the likelihood for any model $p^N(y_{t+1} \mid \theta_i, x_{t+1}, M_i)$ will have been evaluated for N simulations of $p(\theta^{(i)} \mid M_i)$ and $p(x_{t+1}^{(i)} \mid x_t, \theta^{(i)}, M_i)$ in order to formulate importance weights for resampling. If these likelihood evaluations are saved and averaged, the marginal likelihood for any model may be found immediately, without any additional computation. As with general models (Chapter 3) and the DLM (Chapter 5), the accumulated evidence for and against models will depend on products of marginal likelihoods. Using the natural log function, these are easily converted to cumulative sums.

Computation of marginal likelihoods will reward parsimony in the state-space model specification just as they reward parsimony in parameterization. Higher-dimensional state-space specifications will spread probability mass more thinly over $p(x_{t+1}^{(i)} \mid x_t, \theta^{(i)}, M_i)$. It is also likely that the number of unknown parameters will expand accordingly, introducing another penalty via $p(\theta^{(i)} \mid M_i)$. At the same time, a more complex state-space model can be supported when the structure allows more targeted introduction of prior information via the parameters.

In addition to varying the state equation, alternative likelihoods for the data may be entertained, a comparison not readily accomplished via other means. A Student T-distribution, a robust likelihood like the check-exponential, or a power-law distribution might provide a better description of model residuals than the normal distribution; the Weibull might be more appropriate than the gamma; and so on. In this way, one of the more arbitrary choices routinely made in statistical modeling can be subjected to scrutiny in a framework that rewards parsimony.

In this second part of the book we have achieved a significant goal: We now have a toolkit to estimate dynamic, adaptive time series models in an online, sequential, and Bayesian framework that does justice to both parameter and model uncertainty.

The next two sections of the book examine the practical consequences of adopting a sequential learning perspective with uncertainty in financial markets. The first of these sections (Part Three) applies sequential models to some workhorse problems in financial risk management. We seek to benchmark these new models against widely used non-Bayesian methods, while also showing how the new modeling perspective enables one to examine assumptions that are essentially inscrutable when orthodox techniques are employed.

The next section, and the last of the book (Part Four), considers general questions of risk governance raised once model risk is placed at the forefront of one's concerns. Risk management at the enterprise level will have to be reoriented to acknowledge the need for multiple models, the usefulness of prior knowledge, and the ineluctable subjectivity of risk. We also maintain that risk governance ought to be integrated more fully into the strategic management of the firm. Efforts to regulate risk taking and ensure risk management competence by a variety of government and quasi-governmental bodies can also benefit from change, not only to better fulfill regulatory mandates but also to foster competition in financial markets and mitigate systemic risk.

PART

Three

Sequential Models of Financial Risk

CHAPTER 7

Volatility Modeling

Perhaps the two most basic problems of risk management are the estimation of single-asset return volatilities and covariance matrices for the returns of asset portfolios. However, it is well known that maximum-likelihood estimates and other estimates widely used by practitioners are subject to nontrivial estimation error and lack responsiveness to changing market conditions, and as a result their forecasting performance is generally unsatisfactory.

With volatility modeling, as with other aspects of our modeling enterprise, our goals are twofold. First, we seek methods that will furnish maximally responsive online estimates for changing market conditions. All estimates should be computable based on information available at the present date, without creating undue prejudice concerning their reliability in forecasting. Second, we seek to expose *degrees of freedom* where alternative decisions can be made concerning the form of the model. Volatility is not simply 'out there' to be found for every asset, and, depending on a variety of other modeling choices, the form and value given to volatility can vary significantly. We shall see this again in Chapter 8 when the volatility of oil futures prices is decomposed into spot price volatility, convenience yield volatility, and interest rate volatility.

Reexamining the fundamentals of volatility and covariance matrix estimation with Bayesian methods thus entails comparing the forecasting performance of online Bayesian models to that of industry-standard models, while exposing multiple approaches to each problem. Along the way, we will make some observations about fat-tailed asset return distributions and breakdowns in diversification, two topics that have commanded the close attention of risk managers in recent years. We will also make some critical comments concerning some lines of research initiated to solve such problems.

SINGLE-ASSET VOLATILITY

It has often been noticed by risk managers and academics alike that the unconditional distribution of asset returns is non-normal in several ways. First, unconditional asset returns are more peaked and have fatter tails than the normal distribution, meaning extreme observations occur empirically more often than a normal model would predict. Second, unconditional asset returns exhibit skewness or asymmetry. Skewness reflects shifts in the business cycle where trends in asset returns shift from positive to negative, as well as the tendency of downward moves to be more extreme than upward moves, due to the concurrent effect of deleveraging.

As models of unconditional asset returns based on the normal distribution are clearly inadequate, risk practitioners have taken two broad approaches to better reproduce the empirical distributions of asset returns. On the one hand, researchers have investigated the usefulness of distributions with more parameters than the normal. The additional parameters provide more flexibility for capturing skewness and fat tails in the return series, albeit in a static setting that says nothing about *when* skewness and extreme returns are realized. (See Malevergne and Sornette [2005] for an example of this direction of research.) On the other hand, researchers have explored whether conditioning information might be introduced so that *conditional* asset returns are normally distributed. Rather than attempting to parameterize a normal model with static parameters, it may be possible to update the mean and variance so that, conditional on these time-varying parameters, asset returns are once again normal.

In this section, I will use the discussion of Allen, Boudoukh, and Saunders (2004, Chapter 2) as a point of departure. (Dowd 1998, pp. 94–98, and Hull 2005, Chapter 19, provide broadly similar treatments.) The authors present a thoughtful and thorough discussion of industry-standard practices for volatility estimation from a non-Bayesian point of view. As a benchmark data set, I model the returns of the S&P 500 over the period 2000 to 2013.

Classical Models with Conditional Volatility

By shifting the focus from the distribution of unconditional asset returns to the distribution of conditional returns, it becomes clear that the first important choice to be made concerns selection of a relevant information set. If the goal is to forecast volatility conditional on a particular information set, more recent data will likely be more useful for forecasting than data from the more distant past.

Rolling-Window-Based Methods Assuming the normality of continuously compounded financial asset returns, finding the volatility of a single financial return series $\{y_t\}_{t=1}^{T}$ begins with the simple estimator

$$\hat{\sigma}_y = \sqrt{\sum_{t=1}^{T}(y_t^2) \Big/ (T-1)}.$$

This "elementary" calculation assumes the return series has a normal distribution and a known mean of zero. The resulting estimator for the variance is unbiased due to the $T - 1$ term in the denominator. The longer the return series, the less important the degrees-of-freedom correction is.

In the classical view, the standard-deviation estimator is also subject to sampling or statistical error. Because $\hat{\sigma}_y^2$ is defined as a sum of squared normal random variables, it has a chi-squared distribution with one degree of freedom. In the classical analysis, uncertainty in the variance estimate can be found by reading off critical values of the *chi-squared* distribution, which becomes highly peaked for large values of T. More data therefore imply less uncertainty about $\hat{\sigma}_y^2$.

A basic approach to obtain more adaptive estimates of $\hat{\sigma}_y$ is to restrict volatility estimates to a fixed window of recent return history. The analyst selects a fixed window length K and reestimates volatility $\hat{\sigma}_{yt} | \{y_s\}_{s=t-K+1}^{t}$ at each date using only the most recent K observations. For shorter window lengths, the analyst faces a trade-off between estimation error and responsiveness. As Allen, Boudoukh, and Saunders observe (p. 39), "This discussion seems to present an argument that longer observational windows reduce statistical error. However on the other side of the coin is that small window lengths provide an estimator that is more adaptable to changing market conditions."

Estimates of conditional volatility based on the rolling standard-deviation estimator are presented in Figure 7.1. The return series for the S&P 500 appears on top, with the lower three panels showing results for three choices of window length. Notice that for the shortest window length of 30 days, the estimates are more volatile, with greater day-to-day changes and more pronounced peaks. The longest window length, 100 days, has a smoother profile. The decay of the standard-deviation estimates from their peaks is slower, suggesting measurements of increased risk will persist with a longer window length.

An evident problem in the rolling standard-deviation estimator is that past observations within the window are given the same weight as current

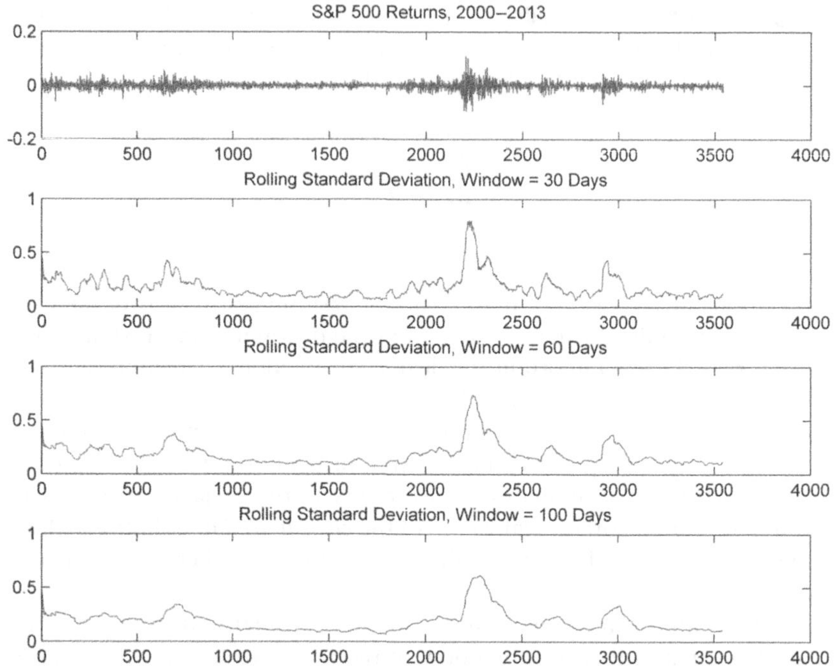

FIGURE 7.1 Rolling Standard-Deviation Estimates of S&P 500 Volatility for Three Choices of Window Length

observations within the window, leading to an estimate of the conditional volatility that is probably too smooth. Since changes in the volatility of financial time series are commonplace, a first extension employed by practitioners is to put more weight on current observations, while down-weighting past observations. The exponentially weighted moving-average (EWMA) filter incorporated in an early version of the popular RiskMetrics system created a smooth decay profile for data weights (Mina and Xiao 2001, p. 15).

Given a weighting term λ, assume all observations are multiplied by λ from when they enter the rolling window until the end of the window is reached. Using the algebra of infinite series, the sum of the weights over the length of the window will be

$$\frac{1}{(1-\lambda)}.$$

The K observations in the window will have resulting normalized weights

$$(1-\lambda), \lambda(1-\lambda), \lambda^2(1-\lambda), \ldots, \lambda^{K-1}(1-\lambda)$$

which differ from unity by a small factor $\lambda^K/(1-\lambda)$. For most values of λ this normalization correction for the window length K is minor. Hence, an explicit choice of a rolling window K is not necessary and the effective data window is controlled by λ in a manner similar to the discount factors introduced in Chapter 4.

The EWMA filter makes volatility calculations recursive, which is a big advantage. Replacing the aggregate weighting term with the approximate normalization above, it is evident that

$$\hat{\sigma}_t^2 = \lambda\hat{\sigma}_{t-1}^2 + (1-\lambda)y_t^2$$

so it is extremely computationally easy to refresh volatility estimates. RiskMetrics incorporates a variety of values for λ based on the nature of the return series, but conventional wisdom suggests a value of $\lambda = 0.94$ is a good modeling choice (Fleming, Kirby, and Ostdiek 2001).

Figure 7.2 compares EWMA volatility estimates for three choices of λ. Larger values of λ lead to a larger effective window length and smoother

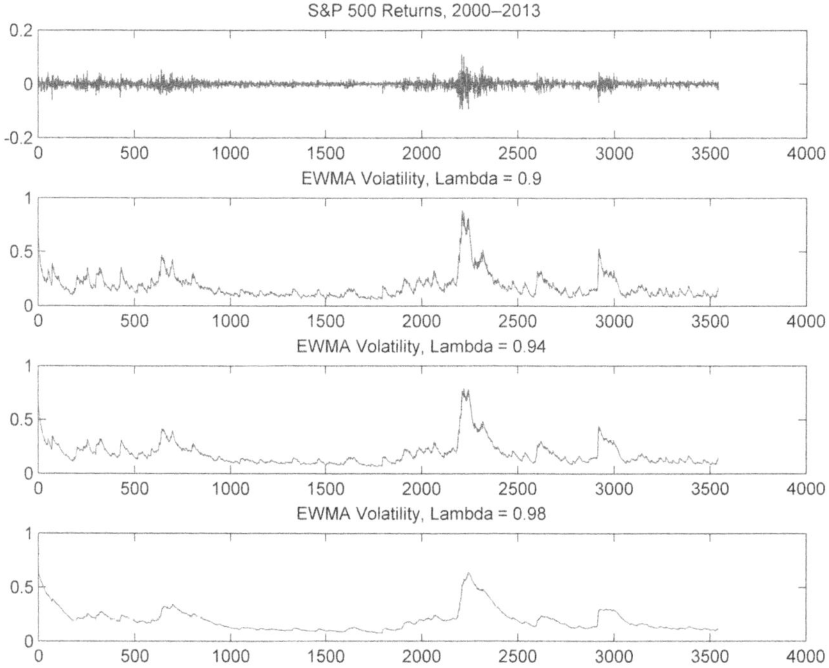

FIGURE 7.2 Exponentially Weighted Moving-Average Estimates of S&P 500 Volatility for Three Choices of Lambda

volatility estimates. Note especially the differences in peaks during the crisis period of 2008. Volatility estimates range from approximately 90 percent for $\lambda = 0.90$ to somewhat more than 60 percent for $\lambda = 0.98$.

Allen, Boudoukh, and Saunders (2004, pp. 51–54) also discuss a density-based estimator that conditions returns on a set of covariates. Given covariates corresponding to the present date, the density estimator reweights historical data according to how closely the historical covariates match the current covariates. Unsurprisingly, this approach is superior to the rolling-window based approaches because it relies on conditioning information beyond the history of the series being modeled. For this reason, it is not strictly comparable to the other techniques and we do not pursue this method in our discussion.

GARCH Models The class of generalized autoregressive conditional heteroskedasticity (GARCH) models has become a workhorse approach for modeling stochastic volatility (Bollerslev, Engle, and Nelson 1994). GARCH models describe the evolution of a time series variance as a function of its past values and innovations:

$$\sigma_t^2 = \alpha + \sum_{p=1}^{P} \beta_p \sigma_{t-p}^2 + \sum_{q=1}^{Q} \gamma_q \varepsilon_{t-q}^2.$$

The model is similar in spirit to the autoregressive moving-average (ARMA) class of models popularized by Box and Jenkins, and suffers from the same ambiguities involved in selecting the order P and Q for the model. As a result, the GARCH(1,1) model serves as a kind of industry standard.

GARCH models are popular in part because they do a good job of reproducing the clusters of volatility regularly observed in plots of financial time series. This property of GARCH models is evident in Figure 7.3. As with the rolling standard-deviation estimates in Figure 7.1, the GARCH(1,1) estimates are obtained with three different window lengths. The graphs plot the one-step-ahead forecast given the previous K days of data.

In principle, once α, β, and γ are calibrated, estimates could be updated for the GARCH model recursively, much like in the EWMA formulation. In fact, the EWMA is a special case of the GARCH(1,1) model, with $\alpha = 0, \beta = \lambda$, and $\gamma = (1 - \lambda)$. However, the forecasting performance of GARCH models is known to deteriorate quickly out-of-sample. In order to adapt the GARCH parameters and improve estimates, new batch recalibrations of the parameters will be needed. Indeed, the estimates in Figure 7.3 were obtained by recalibrating daily. Allen, Boudoukh, and Saunders correctly remark, "As new information arrives, the econometrician updates the parameters

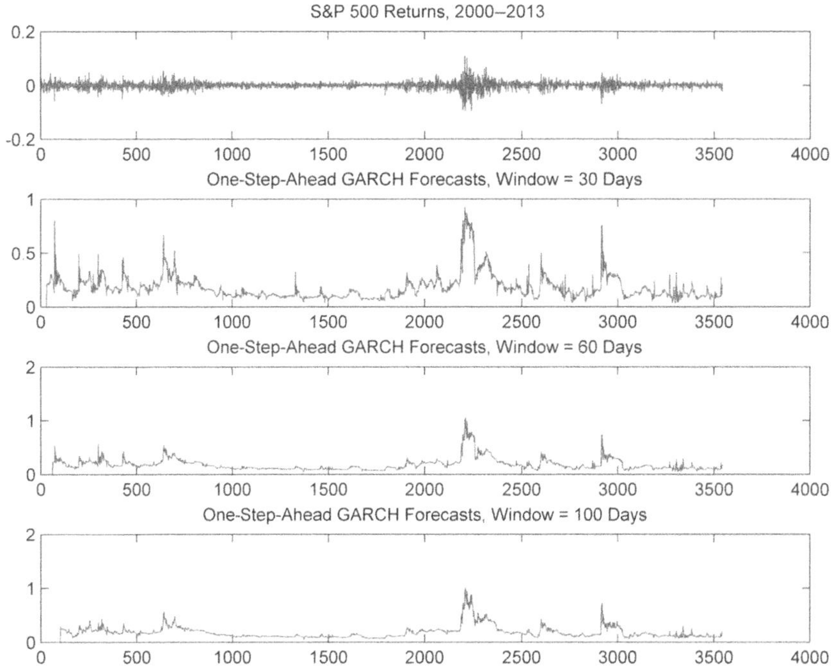

FIGURE 7.3 GARCH(1,1) Estimates of S&P 500 Volatility for Three Choices of Window Length

of the model to fit the new data. Estimating parameters repeatedly creates variations in the model itself, some of which are true to the change in the economic environment, and some simply due to sampling variation.... This can create model risk" (p. 47).

The extent to which reestimation creates model risk can be seen in Figure 7.4, which plots the evolution of the parameters β and γ over the duration of the return series. The upper panel plots the fitted estimates for γ, the persistence of the previous shock, for each of the three window lengths, whereas the lower panel plots β, the persistence of the volatility. Significant shifts in coefficient estimates occur from one day to the next, supporting our suspicion that forecasts from a calibrated GARCH(1,1) model are very likely to break down over periods of more than a few days. The figure also offers a compelling illustration of why recalibrating a classical time series model is not equivalent to online estimation. The sharp changes in coefficient estimates are evidence of information in the data not being carried effectively from one period to the next.

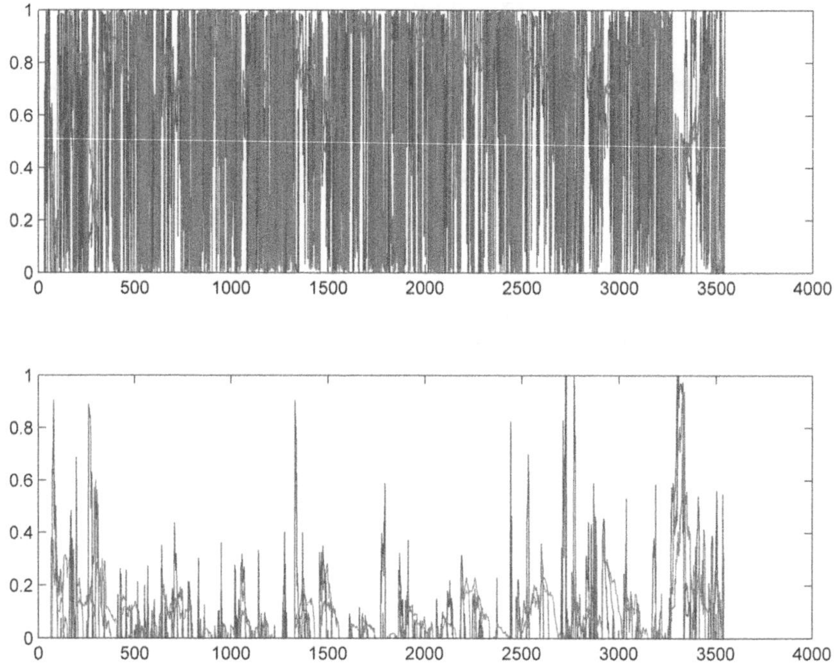

FIGURE 7.4 GARCH(1,1) Model Parameters: Daily Recalibration of S&P 500 Volatility Model

Bayesian Models

Though we classed the EWMA volatility estimate with classical models like the rolling standard deviation and GARCH, it can be shown that the EWMA estimate is equivalent to a discounted estimate obtained from a Bayesian inverted-gamma model.

The EWMA filter estimate calculation resembles the recursive calculation of the error variance in the normal linear regression model. In the regression model the error variance was parameterized by an inverted-gamma distribution $IG[n_0, n_0 S_0]$, with the expectation of the variance equal to S_0. Introducing a discount factor into the linear regression recursions yielded adaptive estimates

$$n_1 = \delta_S n_0 + 1$$

$$n_1 S_1 = \delta_s n_0 S_0 + (\mathbf{y} - \mathbf{X}\mathbf{b}_1)'\mathbf{y} + (\mathbf{b}_0 - \mathbf{b}_1)'\Delta^{1/2}\mathbf{B}_0^{-1}\Delta^{1/2}\mathbf{b}_0$$

Setting the regression components to zero, the recursions become

$$n_t = \delta_S n_{t-1} + 1$$

$$n_t S_t = \delta_S n_{t-1} S_{t-1} + y_t^2.$$

Thus, if we consider the recursive updates to S_t, the expectation of the error variance, we have $S_t = aS_{t-1} + by_t^2$, where $a = \delta_S(n_{t-1}/n_t)$ and $b = 1/n_t$. With $\delta_S = 1$ we have $b \approx 1 - a$, so setting $b = 1 - \lambda$ makes the expectation of the inverted-gamma distribution approximately equal to the result of the EWMA filter. However, it should be noted that the value yielded by the EWMA filter is only an expectation, and that the full distribution of the estimate for $\hat{\sigma}_y^2$ is inverted-gamma with $(\lambda/(1 - \lambda)) + 1$ degrees of freedom. Rather than using a discount factor, the EWMA sets the effective sample size directly through the choice of λ.

In the analysis above, we just as easily could have proceeded without zeroing out the regression model of the mean. In their analysis of conditional return distributions, Allen, Boudoukh, and Saunders curtail any discussion of modeling the conditional *mean* of the return series, arguing that doing so would be "based on the implausible assumption that market participants know, or can predict in advance, future changes in asset prices" (p. 27). However, allowing the mean to take on nonzero values does not necessarily assume predictability of asset returns; rather, it allows for the possibility that while the average forecast mean return is zero, individual mean returns can take on nonzero values. The resulting random walk around the zero mean may be equally effective in capturing variation in the conditional return distribution as assuming a mean that is identically zero.

Volatility Modeling with the DLM Thus, as a first heterodox approach to modeling the conditional return distribution we estimate a local-level DLM in which the mean of the return series follows a random walk. Instead of transforming the data as in the EWMA, the local-level DLM is made more responsive to recent history by discounting the state variance.

Somewhat surprisingly, the time-varying mean in the local-level DLM absorbs most of the variation in the S&P 500 return series, with little remaining variation left to be handled by the observational variance. The results shown in Figure 7.5 are combined in the bottom panel so that $\sigma_t^{DLM} = \sqrt{x_t^2 + \sigma_y^2}$, where x_t, is the one-step-ahead forecast of the time-varying mean and σ_y^2 is the observational variance. Once the mean and variance are combined, σ_t^{DLM} displays a profile very much like the other time-varying volatility estimates.

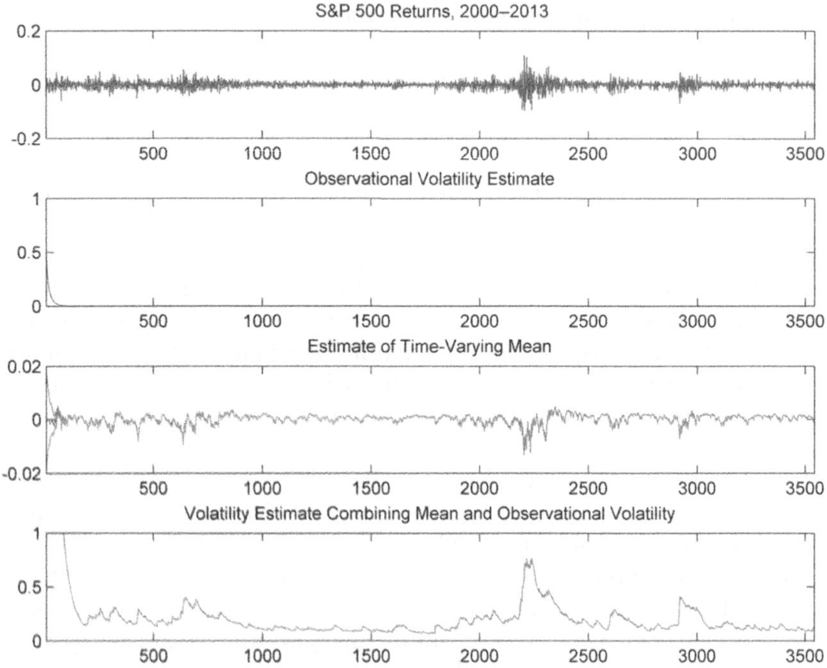

FIGURE 7.5 S&P 500 Volatility Estimates from a Local-Level DLM with Discount Factor = 0.95

Whether there is useful information in the mean depends on whether a trading strategy can be devised using the mean that improves over a simple buy-and-hold strategy. Some experimentation using easy rules based on the sign of the one-step-ahead forecast mean did not yield results over the long run. However, some of the largest increases in volatility are driven by a sharply lower conditional mean, consistent with the leverage effect identified by Black (1976a). If one would have shorted the market during these episodes where the conditional mean turned sharply negative, prolonged periods of loss could have been avoided. However, the gains from avoiding the downturn are subsequently lost in the recovery period, and difficulties selling short under such negative market conditions may make a short-selling strategy infeasible.

State-Space Models of Stochastic Volatility The basic structure of the GARCH stochastic volatility model can be reformulated as a state-space time series model (Lopes and Polson 2010). The observation equation assumes log returns are normal with mean zero and an unknown, time-varying variance

$$y \sim \mathcal{N}[0, \exp(x_t/2)].$$

The log-variance evolves according to an autoregressive process on the state space:

$$x_{t+1} = \alpha + \beta x_t + \varepsilon^x_{t+1}$$

$$\varepsilon^x_{t+1} \sim \mathcal{N}[0, \tau^2].$$

Inference focuses on the sequence of volatility states $\{x_t\}$ and the unknown parameters $\theta = \{\alpha, \beta, \tau^2\}$. Unlike the GARCH model, the state-space stochastic volatility model is not recalibrated from day to day but updated sequentially. As a result, we expect greater stability in the parameter estimates.

Since we can simulate easily from the state equation and evaluate the likelihood for the observation equation, we can use the Liu-West filter to estimate parameters and states. (See the demonstration and code in Lopes and Tsay 2011.) Prior information can also be crafted to encourage local stationarity of the estimates and incorporate ideas about the persistence of volatility states. Figure 7.6 shows how the Liu-West filter converges on an estimate for the persistence of volatility states of roughly 0.986. The volatility of volatility (τ^2) wanders in a limited range of 33 percent to 35 percent. Finally, in the bottom panel it is possible to put a 95 percent probability band around the central volatility estimate, showing the skewness of the volatility distribution. The probability mass to the upside is clearly much greater than the mass to the downside.

Note that in the Liu-West filter, the volatility state estimate is the only factor contributing to the adaptivity of the model. The volatility state steps up at the time of the Lehman bankruptcy in September 2008 and during episodes of the European sovereign debt and banking crises afterward. The Liu-West filter aims to arrive at fixed parameter estimates, so the variations in β and τ^2 should only be interpreted as the particular manner in which those estimates converge for this data set.

Comparison

To compare the Bayesian estimators with orthodox estimators, we conduct two analyses. The first examines the performance of the estimators in capturing the tails of the conditional return distribution. For each estimator, we compute the 1-day VaR at a 95 percent confidence level. Over 13 years, or approximately 3500 observations, we would expect about 175 exceptions, or days where returns are worse than the 1-day 95 percent VaR. Regulators monitor VaR exceptions for evidence of an inadequate model.

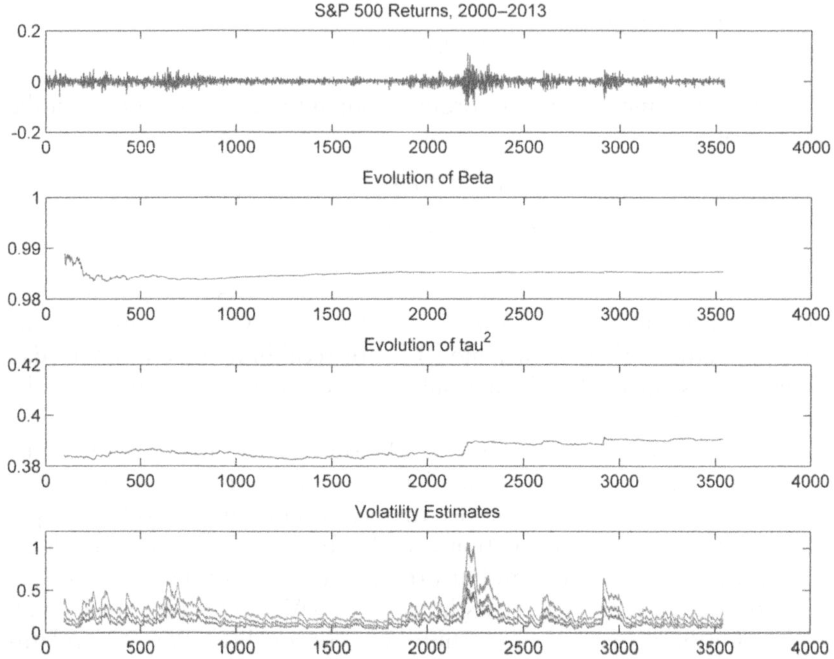

FIGURE 7.6 S&P 500 Volatility Estimates from a State-Space Volatility Model: Liu-West Filter with Discount Factor = 0.95

The count of VaR exceptions for each of the estimators is presented in Table 7.1. All of the conventional methods produce more exceptions than theory would suggest. Using Jorion's (2006, Chapter 6.2.1) approach to modeling exceptions as binomial data, many of the exception counts are outside of a 95 percent confidence bound for the theoretical number of exceptions.

Somewhat paradoxically, the less-adaptive varieties of the rolling standard deviation and EWMA methods are the only ones that give satisfactory performance in the tails. It appears that the more adaptive conventional methods lag sharp moves into the tails of the distribution. All of the Bayesian methods, on the other hand, deliver satisfactory performance in capturing the tails of the distribution.

As a second comparison, we compute posterior model probabilities by evaluating the predictive likelihoods of each model. In contrast to the analysis of tail behavior above, evaluating predictive likelihoods will give a measure of models' overall performance, as better matching in normal markets will be rewarded in addition to strong performance in abnormal markets. Sets of comparisons were obtained by comparing subgroups of models with

TABLE 7.1 Exception Counts for 95% 1-Day VaR Calculated with Each Volatility Model

Model	Parameter	Exceptions
Rolling standard deviation	30 days	222
Rolling standard deviation	60 days	219
Rolling standard deviation	100 days	202
EWMA	Lambda = 0.90	216
EWMA	Lambda = 0.94	203
EWMA	Lambda = 0.98	181
GARCH(1,1)	30 days	256
GARCH(1,1)	60 days	228
GARCH(1,1)	100 days	204
DLM		173
LW filter		199
Theoretical count		177
Theoretical lower bound	95%	152
Theoretical upper bound	95%	203

Data source: S&P 500 return data from Bloomberg, author's calculations.

the state-space stochastic volatility model, which a comparison of all models showed to be superior. Breaking the comparison into subgroups makes it easier to track the relative merits of models, without making claims about the models' ability to span all possible outcomes.

Figures 7.7 to 7.10 show the state-space stochastic volatility model outperforms the rolling standard-deviation, EWMA, and GARCH methods. Within the universe of Bayesian models, the stochastic volatility model outperforms the DLM once its prior information advantage is overcome. Comparing within classes of models, we can also see that more adaptive models display better overall performance, as in the previous analysis, which focused on tail behavior. The 30-day rolling standard deviation proves better than longer-window counterparts, as does the EWMA with $\lambda = 0.90$ in the early part of the sample. Some interesting switches in model rank are seen in the EWMA comparison, as EWMA with $\lambda = 0.90$ initially outperforms. Later EWMA with $\lambda = 0.94$ gains some credibility.

Already in a simple modeling situation, the benefits of a Bayesian approach are evident. Data may be analyzed online, rather than in batches, eliminating arbitrary decisions about the "right amount" of history for calibration or the choice of a data-weighting scheme. Model uncertainty is captured through state and parameter uncertainty and the ability to entertain alternative distributional forms and likelihoods simultaneously. When using the techniques on actual financial market data, Bayesian methods proved more responsive than traditional methods. It is clear that the batch

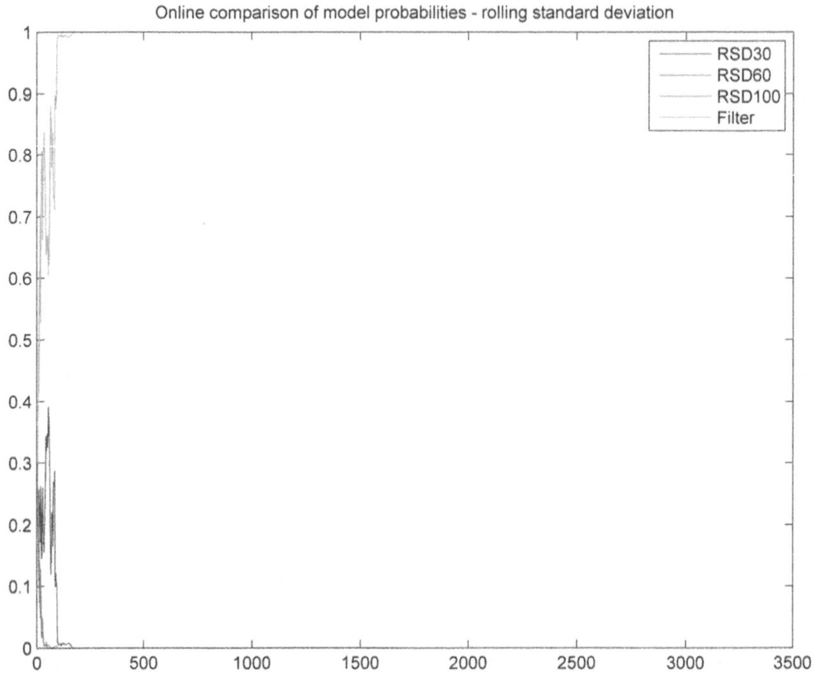

FIGURE 7.7 Posterior Model Probabilities: State-Space Volatility Model versus Rolling Standard-Deviation Models

estimation requirements for traditional volatility models smooth changes in the data considerably and fail to reproduce extremes. Recalibration also amplified estimation error and highlighted an important element of model risk in traditional volatility modeling.

VOLATILITY FOR MULTIPLE ASSETS

Estimating time-varying multivariate volatilities holds the promise of responding to changes in correlations for portfolios of assets and systems of underlying risk factors. Advances on this front have the potential to improve asset allocation decisions, identify breakdowns in diversification, and generally to improve our understanding of the dependency structure for aggregates of asset values.

EWMA and Inverted-Wishart Estimates

Time variation in multivariate volatility is conventionally captured in a manner similar to univariate volatility. Using the same EWMA schema as before

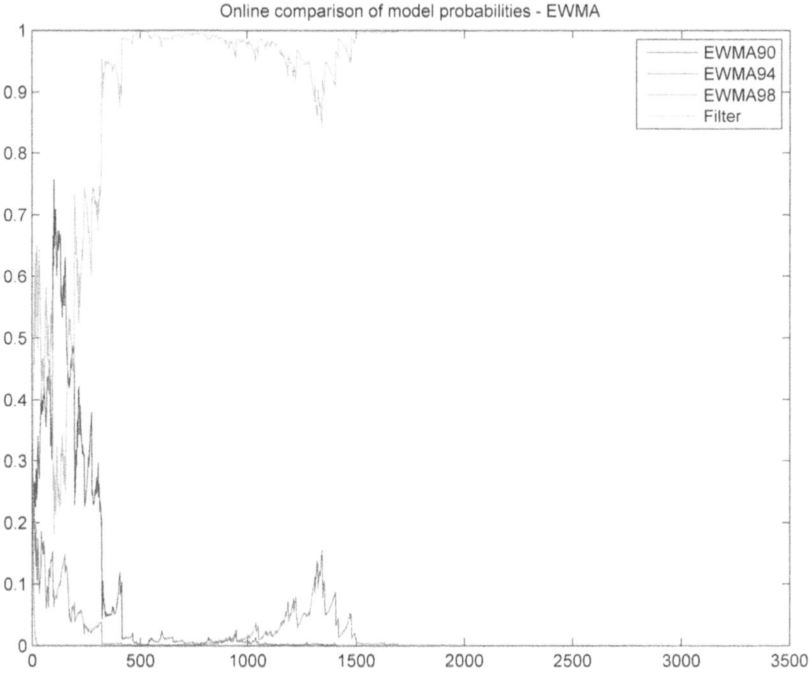

FIGURE 7.8 Posterior Model Probabilities: State-Space Volatility Model versus Rolling EWMA Models

and replacing the asset return y_t^2 with the outer product $\mathbf{y}_t\mathbf{y}_t'$, we obtain the estimator

$$\mathbf{\Sigma}_t = \lambda \cdot \mathbf{\Sigma}_{t-1} + (1-\lambda) \cdot \mathbf{y}_t\mathbf{y}_t'$$

as an exponentially weighted moving-average estimate of the covariance matrix. As in the univariate case, the EWMA estimate has a structure analogous to a Bayesian estimator based on an inverted-Wishart prior, which we now demonstrate.

The likelihood for a set of observations y_t for time indices $t = 1, \ldots, T$ conditional on a known mean of zero and a covariance matrix $\sum$ is

$$\begin{aligned} p(\mathbf{y}_1, \ldots, \mathbf{y}_T|\mathbf{\Sigma}) &\propto \prod_{t=1}^{T} |\mathbf{\Sigma}|^{-1/2} \exp\left\{-\frac{1}{2}\mathbf{y}_t'\mathbf{\Sigma}^{-1}\mathbf{y}_t\right\} \\ &\propto |\mathbf{\Sigma}|^{-n/2} \exp\left\{-\frac{1}{2}\sum_{t=1}^{T} \mathbf{y}_t'\mathbf{\Sigma}^{-1}\mathbf{y}_t\right\} \end{aligned}$$

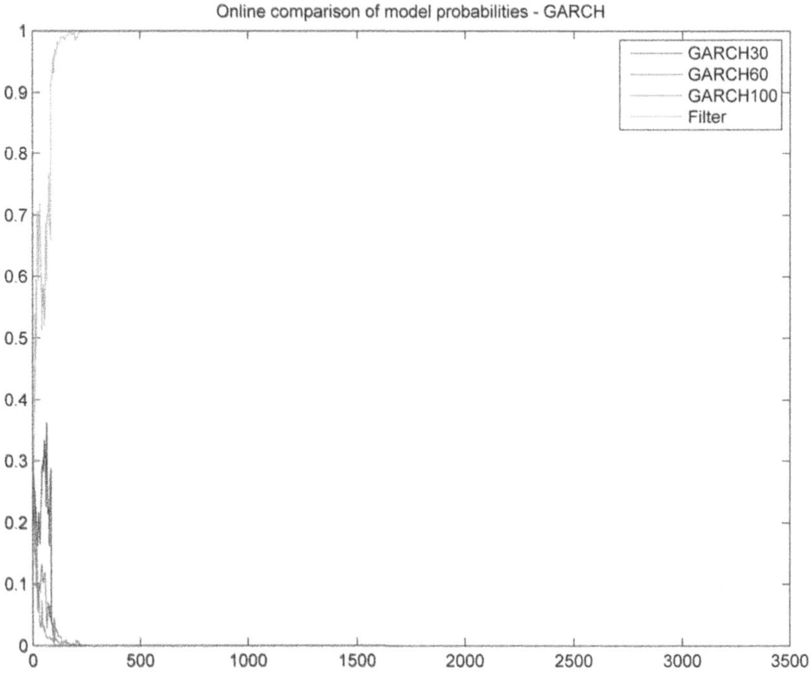

FIGURE 7.9 Posterior Model Probabilities: State-Space Volatility Model versus GARCH Models

$$\propto |\boldsymbol{\Sigma}|^{-n/2} \exp\left\{-\frac{1}{2}\sum_{t=1}^{T} \mathrm{tr}\left(\mathrm{y}_t \mathrm{y}_t' \boldsymbol{\Sigma}^{-1}\right)\right\}$$

$$\propto |\boldsymbol{\Sigma}|^{-n/2} \mathrm{etr}\left\{-\frac{1}{2}\mathrm{S}\boldsymbol{\Sigma}^{-1}\right\}.$$

The trace operator is denoted tr and in conjunction with the exponential becomes etr. The final step follows by putting

$$\mathrm{S} = \sum \mathrm{y}_t \mathrm{y}_t',$$

which shows that the information in the data is captured in the outer product of the observations, which are vectors of arbitrary dimension m.

The inverted-Wishart family of distributions furnishes a conjugate prior family for this likelihood. For hyperparameters υ_0 and V_0, the inverted Wishart prior is defined as

$$p(\boldsymbol{\Sigma}|\upsilon_0, \mathrm{V}_0) \propto |\boldsymbol{\Sigma}|^{-(\upsilon_0+m+1)/2} \mathrm{etr}\left\{-\frac{1}{2}\mathrm{V}_0\boldsymbol{\Sigma}^{-1}\right\}.$$

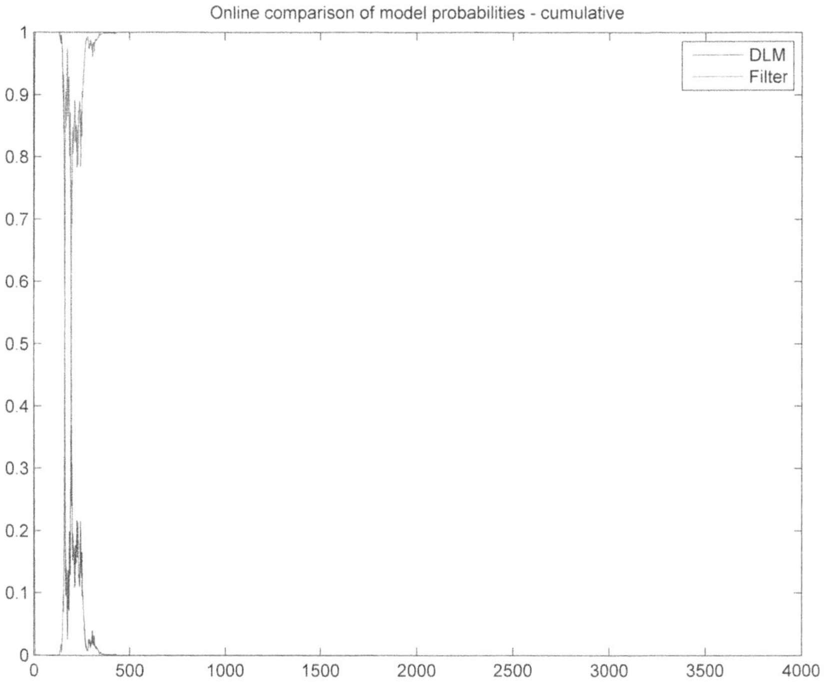

FIGURE 7.10 Posterior Model Probabilities: State-Space Volatility Model versus DLM

The posterior follows immediately:

$$\begin{aligned} p(\boldsymbol{\Sigma}|\mathbf{y}_1,\ldots,\mathbf{y}_T) &\propto p(\mathbf{y}_1,\ldots,\mathbf{y}_T|\boldsymbol{\Sigma})p(\boldsymbol{\Sigma}) \\ &\propto |\Sigma|^{-n/2}\,\mathrm{etr}\left\{-\frac{1}{2}\mathbf{S}\boldsymbol{\Sigma}^{-1}\right\}\times|\boldsymbol{\Sigma}|^{-(\nu_0+m+1)/2}\,\mathrm{etr}\left\{-\frac{1}{2}\mathbf{V}_0\Sigma^{-1}\right\} \\ &\propto |\boldsymbol{\Sigma}|^{-(\nu_0+n+m+1)/2}\,\mathrm{etr}\left\{-\frac{1}{2}\left(\mathbf{V}_0+\mathbf{S}\right)\boldsymbol{\Sigma}^{-1}\right\}. \end{aligned}$$

Thus, via sufficient statistics n and S, an inverted-Wishart distribution with hyperparameters $(\nu_0, \mathbf{V}_0)$ gets updated to an inverted-Wishart distribution with hyperparameters $(\nu_0 + n, \mathbf{V}_0 + \mathbf{S})$. The relationship suggests the interpretation of the prior hyperparameter ν_0 as a data-equivalent number of observations and $\mathbf{V}_0$ as an initial estimate of the covariance matrix (Rossi, Allenby, and McCulloch 2005, pp. 28–30). Putting $\nu_0 = \lambda/(1-\lambda)$, $\mathbf{V}_0 = \boldsymbol{\Sigma}_{t-1}$, $n = 1$, and $\mathbf{S} = \mathbf{y}_t\mathbf{y}_t'$ reconciles the EWMA estimator with the inverted-Wishart model.

Decompositions of the Covariance Matrix

For a collection of N assets, the covariance matrix has N^2 parameters, of which $\frac{1}{2}N(N+1)$ are unique. Because the number of parameters to be estimated grows with the square of the number of assets, it is productive to consider ways in which additional structure may be imposed on the covariance matrix in order to reduce the number of parameters estimated. A first decomposition of the covariance matrix writes the covariance of assets as σ_i^2 when $i = j$ and $\sigma_i \sigma_j \rho_{ij}$ when $i \neq j$. Then, defining $\mathbf{D} = diag(\sigma_1, \ldots, \sigma_N)$ and

$$\mathbf{R} = \begin{bmatrix} 1 & \rho_{12} & \cdots & \rho_{1,N-1} & \rho_{1,N} \\ \rho_{21} & 1 & & \rho_{2,N-1} & \rho_{2,N} \\ \vdots & & \ddots & & \vdots \\ \rho_{N-1,1} & \rho_{N-1,2} & & 1 & \rho_{N-1,N} \\ \rho_{N,1} & \rho_{N,2} & \cdots & \rho_{N,N-1} & 1 \end{bmatrix}$$

with $\rho_{ij} = \rho_{ji}$, we have the decomposition $\mathbf{\Sigma} = \mathbf{DRD}$. This representation of the covariance matrix has the intuitive appeal of resolving covariances into easily understood standard-deviation and correlation coefficient components. Although it does not reduce the number of parameters to be estimated, prior knowledge about individual asset volatilities and correlations may be brought to bear in a useful way.

A second decomposition of the covariance matrix posits an underlying factor structure for the assets. Consider the CAPM, for example. The return of any asset r_i is equal to

$$r_{i,t} = \alpha_i + \beta_i r_{M,t} + \varepsilon_t$$

where $r_{M,t}$ is the return on the market risk factor. Then the variance of r_i is

$$\sigma_i^2 = \text{var}(r_{i,t}) = \text{var}(\alpha_i + \beta_i r_{M,t} + \varepsilon_t) = \beta_i^2 \sigma_M^2 + \sigma_{\varepsilon i}^2$$

and the covariance of returns for two assets is

$$\begin{aligned} \text{cov}(r_i, r_j) &= \text{cov}(\alpha_i + \beta_i r_{M,t} + \varepsilon_{it}, \alpha_j + \beta_j r_{M,t} + \varepsilon_{jt}) \\ &= \beta_i \beta_j \sigma_M^2 + \text{cov}(\varepsilon_i, \varepsilon_j). \end{aligned}$$

These expressions suggest the separation of multivariate volatilities into systematic and idiosyncratic components, with

$$\mathbf{\Sigma} = \boldsymbol{\beta}\boldsymbol{\beta}' \sigma_M^2 + \boldsymbol{\varepsilon}\boldsymbol{\varepsilon}'$$

where $\boldsymbol{\varepsilon\varepsilon}'$ is a square matrix with $\sigma_{\varepsilon i}^2$ on the diagonal and $\text{cov}(\varepsilon_i, \varepsilon_j) = \text{cov}(\varepsilon_j, \varepsilon_i)$ off the diagonals. When market betas are relatively high, the portion of the asset volatilities and covariances accounted for by market volatility will be greater.

For multiple orthogonal factors indexed by k, the decomposition can be carried further to yield

$$\boldsymbol{\Sigma} = \sum_k \left(\boldsymbol{\beta}_k \boldsymbol{\beta}_k' \sigma_k^2\right) + \boldsymbol{\varepsilon\varepsilon}'.$$

Time-Varying Correlations

Attaching time subscripts to $\boldsymbol{\Sigma}$ entails making choices about which components of the decompositions are permitted to vary in time. Building on progress made in modeling time-varying volatilities by GARCH methods, Robert Engle (2009) and his coauthors have applied GARCH techniques to time-varying covariance matrices. Engle's dynamic conditional correlations (DCC) method makes use of the decomposition

$$\boldsymbol{\Sigma}_t = \mathbf{D}_t \mathbf{R}_t \mathbf{D}_t$$

where each of the elements of $\mathbf{D}_t$ is modeled by GARCH. Similarly Engle's Factor DCC approach applies GARCH models to factor and idiosyncratic volatilities. Time-varying correlations and factor betas are recovered by means of the GARCH estimates in DCC and Factor DCC, respectively.

The key weakness of Engle's DCC and Factor DCC methods is the need to preestimate the component GARCH models, which creates an in-sample/out-of-sample divide and leaves the determination of the key parameters of interest (correlations and factor betas) to a second stage in which errors from the first stage are lost. In Engle's approach for obtaining DCC estimates, component series are first "de-GARCHed" to obtain i.i.d. residual series. Quasi-correlations are estimated from the de-GARCHed time series, and then rescaled in a third stage to achieve a valid correlation matrix (Engle 2009, p. 43). Factor DCC and other variations on the same theme likewise involve first-stage GARCH models of individual asset and factor volatilities, from which time-varying factor betas are recovered by dividing time-varying covariances by time-varying variances.

We saw in the previous section that parameter estimates for GARCH models can shift discontinuously as models are recalibrated to new data. Such structural breaks in parameters cast doubt on the ability of GARCH models estimated on historical data to provide useful forecasts of the future. In our view, DCC and Factor DCC fail to cross the in-sample/out-of-sample divide in a convincing way. Engle's (2009, pp. 111–117) own results show only modest gains in efficiency when used to form portfolios, and only in certain experiments.

In contrast to Engle's methods, one can attempt online estimates of factor stochastic volatility using the multivariate DLM. The time-varying covariance matrix is estimated as

$$\mathbf{\Sigma}_t = \sum_k \left(\boldsymbol{\beta}_{k,t} \boldsymbol{\beta}'_{k,t} \sigma^2_{k,t} \right) + \mathbf{V}$$

so that the systematic components of volatility are time-varying, whereas the idiosyncratic volatility is static. Time-varying betas are obtained as state estimates using the dynamic regression model. Choosing a lower discount factor in the DLM estimation can allow $\mathbf{V}$ to vary slowly as well.

However, leaving $\mathbf{V}$ fixed in this specification posits that increases in correlations occur because of time-varying factor volatilities or time-variation in the loadings of assets on different risk factors. Increases in either

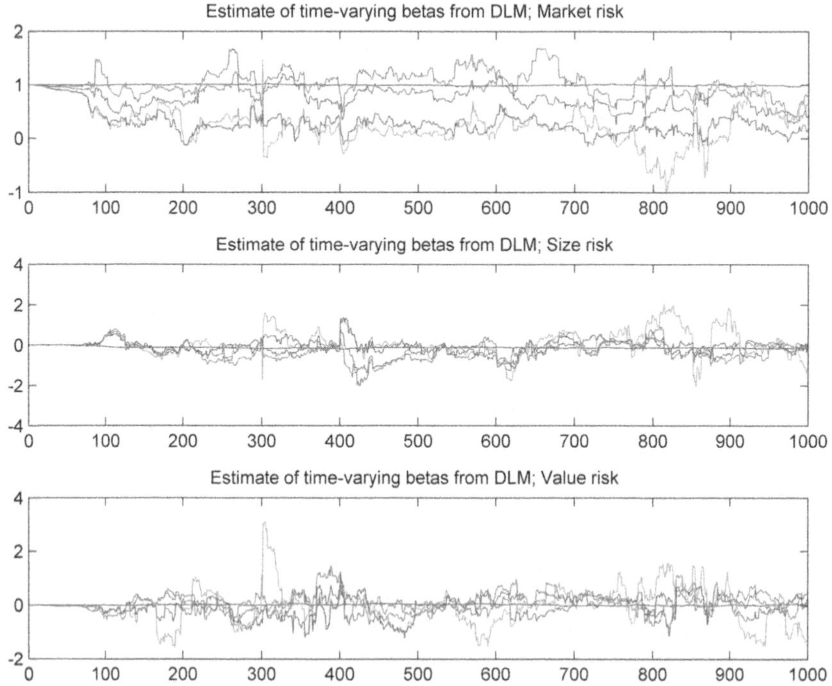

FIGURE 7.11 Loadings of Major Stock Market Indices on Market, Size, and Value Factors

component will tend to push correlations toward 1, which is consistent with experience in periods of market stress.

To resolve systematic volatility into factors, I use the three Fama-French factors from Ken French's website (Fama and French 1996). The series modeled are aggregate stock indices from the United States, Europe, United Kingdom, Japan, and Australia. To benchmark the factor stochastic volatility estimates, I compute EWMA estimates of the covariance matrix, with $\lambda = 0.95$. The discount factor for the DLM is set to the same value. In each case, I recover time-varying correlations from the covariance matrix using the $\mathbf{\Sigma}_t = \mathbf{D}_t\mathbf{R}_t\mathbf{D}_t$ decomposition. Estimates cover the period from January 2010 to December 2013.

Changes in the weights on each of the factors are presented in Figure 7.11, starting from priors of $\beta_{MKT} = 1$ and $\beta_{SMB} = \beta_{HML} = 0$ for all indices. Whereas the US aggregate index (the S&P 500) tracks the prior parameter values closely, there is a great deal of variation among the other major stock markets. The Japanese and Australian indices have market betas very close to 0, with the Japanese market beta turning negative in certain periods. The UK index displays a market beta that is significantly

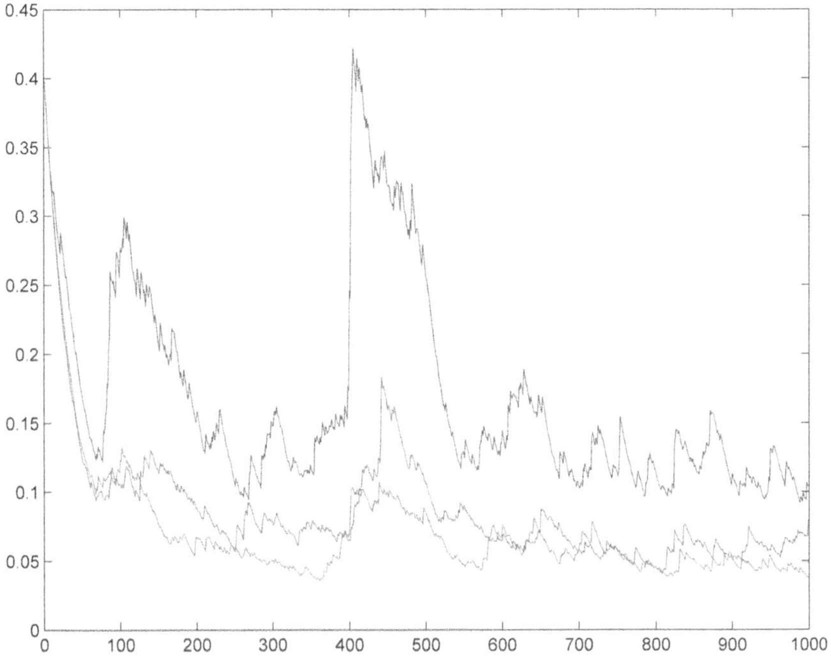

FIGURE 7.12 Evolution of Market, Size, and Value Factor Volatilities

less than 1, whereas the EU index often has a market beta in excess of 1. Japanese stocks at times weigh heavily on the size (SMB) and value (HML) factors, shown in the second and third panels of the figure, respectively. European and Australian stocks show long periods of negative weight on size and value, respectively. The dispersion in the values of the various factor betas and heterogeneity in their distribution across the factors in each major market suggest opportunities for diversification from holding equities in multiple countries.

Figure 7.12 shows EWMA estimates for volatilities of each of the factors. Some clustering in volatility across the factors suggests that the factors may not be completely orthogonal, as assumed. The decision to rely on EWMA volatility estimates is based on a desire to isolate the relative ability of the time-varying factor stochastic volatility model to articulate correlations against the EWMA covariance matrix estimate. Representing correlations in terms of factors introduces multiple degrees of freedom into the estimation of correlations: Each of the factor volatilities and each of the factor betas serves to articulate the structure of correlations between each of

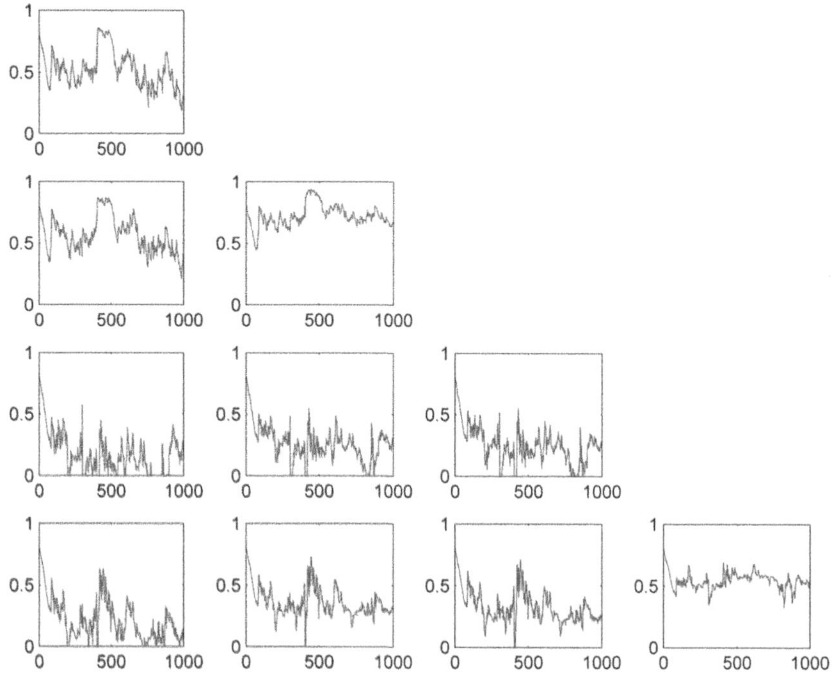

FIGURE 7.13 Implied Correlations from Factor Stochastic Volatility Model, Discount Factor = 0.95

the indices, whereas the EWMA covariance matrix estimate has only a single parameter. In effect, the idiosyncratic volatility matrix **V** would approximate the EWMA covariance matrix estimate if the three factors and factor betas provided no further information about the dependency structure.

Differences in the correlations obtained from each model are plotted in Figures 7.13 to 7.15. Following the initial start-up period, there continue to be meaningful differences between the correlations obtained from each model of the covariance matrix. The EWMA model tends to find higher correlations between United States, United Kingdom, and European stocks than the factor model (top three cells). The correlation between Japanese and Australian stocks (bottom right-hand cell) fluctuates significantly in the EWMA model, but remains steady at roughly 0.5 in the factor model. Other correlations between Japanese and Australian indices (second-to-last and last rows, respectively) and other major markets are consistently low in both models, though gaps continue to open up between the two sets of estimates. The heterogeneity in correlation estimates will have important implications for asset allocation among the major market indices.

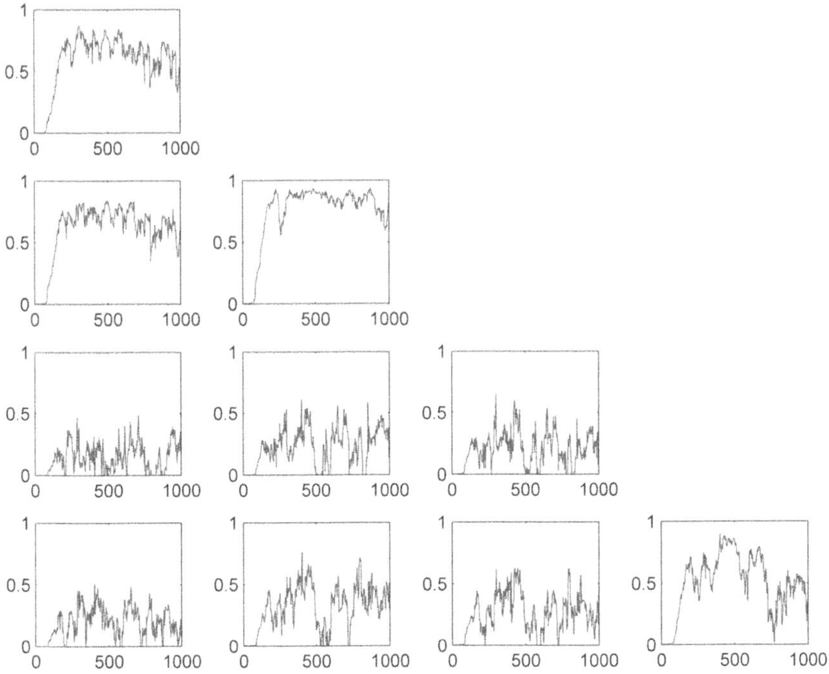

FIGURE 7.14 Implied Correlations from EWMA Stochastic Volatility Model, Lambda = 0.95

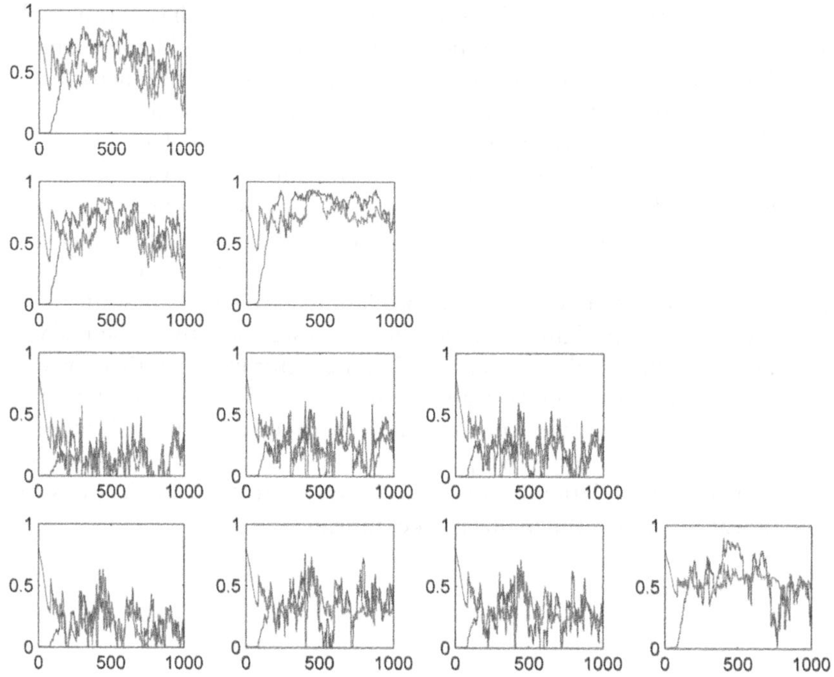

FIGURE 7.15 Comparison of Implied Correlations from Both Models

We have thus shown that online estimates of covariance matrices can be obtained in a straightforward way using Bayesian methods, with a gain in information relative to the reduced-form methods currently in production as the industry standard. While more study is merited to draw out the relative strengths of the methods demonstrated here versus DCC and Factor DCC, we find the relatively modest technical demands of the DLM approach encouraging, as well as its ability to furnish time-varying online forecasts without preestimation.

Many other methods for modeling multivariate stochastic volatility by Bayesian means have been proposed, relying on the decompositions presented here, as well as the Cholesky decomposition of a symmetric positive definite matrix. Carvalho, Johannes, Lopes, and Polson (2010, p. 95) present a version of the factor DLM that may be used to estimate factor stochastic volatility without identifying the factors, as we have done here using the three Fama-French factors. Time variation in the parameters is modeled using a Markov switching process. Additional approaches are surveyed in Lopes and Polson (2010, Section 2).

CHAPTER 8

Asset-Pricing Models and Hedging

One of the great achievements of modern finance is the analytical derivation of arbitrage-free or equilibrium prices for a variety of financial instruments, including bonds, futures, options, and other derivatives. Beginning from relatively simple primitives about the dynamics of underlying assets and economic fundamentals, pricing formulas can be developed for a variety of instruments, often in closed form.

The prices obtained from equilibrium and arbitrage-free models assume that parameters governing the underlying asset and economic factor dynamics are already known, and that state variables are identifiable without error from available data. The inverse problem of recovering the parameters and state variables that generate observed prices is more difficult. In some cases, the asset price formula may be inverted to solve for an unknown parameter, as with implied volatility in the Black-Scholes-Merton analysis. Other situations allow for static optimization by minimizing the squared differences between model-implied and observed values for a selected data history. However, in instances where inverted formulas give conflicting answers, or when analytical solutions are not available, recovering the parameters governing asset price dynamics becomes an econometric problem. These problems have pushed mainstream econometrics to its limits, relying on simulated and feasible estimators where maximum-likelihood and GMM methods break down (see Singleton [2006] for a number of related investigations).

As an alternative to mainstream methods, dynamic asset pricing models can be estimated in state-space form, employing the sequential Monte Carlo (SMC) methods developed previously. For a class of problems generally regarded as intractable by many practitioners, online Bayesian estimates of latent parameters driving asset price dynamics can be obtained. In contrast to current practice, the state variables or factors need not be identified with an observable series, eliminating a possible source of specification error and enabling tests of commonly employed proxies. Further, the methods lend themselves to sequential model comparisons, allowing practitioners to consider multiple models simultaneously and to gain further insight into the evolution of price dynamics. As in Chapter 3, our approach here is based on the fundamental insight of Johannes and Polson (2009b), with SMC methods replacing the MCMC methods employed in that paper.

The interest of dynamic asset-pricing models for risk management is twofold. First, the ability to obtain useful hedging ratios is often predicated on a calibrated asset-pricing model. Reducing price dynamics to those of a low-dimensional state vector enables parsimonious hedging strategies, while the introduction of parameter and model uncertainty via Bayesian analysis will shed light on uncertainties related to hedging. Second, obtaining explicit estimates of parameters under the physical and risk-neutral measures allows market prices of risk to be recovered. Better information about the market price of risk enables better decision making about the business mix in market-making and trading operations. An improved understanding of asset price dynamics also contributes to one of the ancillary goals of the book—namely, identifying one's comparative advantage in pricing, hedging, and speculating in the markets being modeled.

DERIVATIVE PRICING IN THE SCHWARTZ MODEL

The focus of this chapter is an in-depth exploration of the Schwartz (1997) model of the stochastic behavior of commodity futures prices. Schwartz's analysis provides an excellent starting point for our investigation of dynamic asset-pricing models. Closed-form pricing equations for commodity derivatives are derived from factor dynamics specified in continuous time. The factor dynamics are then discretized and recast in a state-space time series model form, which Schwartz uses to calibrate his model via a batch-estimated version of the Kalman filter. The specification is also sufficiently parsimonious that the underlying risk-neutral and physical process parameters can be recovered from linear model estimates.

Nevertheless, we go beyond Schwartz in a few important ways. Whereas Schwartz uses the Kalman filter to batch-estimate the best-fit parameters for the state-space model over the entire time period considered, we aim to estimate models online, remaining mindful of conditioning information sets and parameter uncertainty. In addition, we expand the specification of the underlying factor dynamics to simplify the estimation, dispense with preestimating certain components of the model, and extend the models, albeit in simple ways.

State Dynamics

Standard no-arbitrage pricing arguments for futures pricing rely on a cash-and-carry argument: The futures price should be equal to the cost of financing an inventory of the underlying commodity until the delivery date. Hence, the futures price is a function of the spot price of the commodity, the rate on borrowed money available to commodity traders, and the flow of services enjoyed by a commodity merchandiser or producer by virtue of having a stock of the commodity on hand (net of maintenance costs, insurance, and other upkeep). The latter quantity is known as the convenience yield that, in conjunction with the money interest rate, determines the "own rate of interest" for the commodity (Culp 2004, pp. 173–211).

In the event that all of the above quantities are known and constant, the relationship between spot and futures prices is given by

$$F(t, T) = S(t)\exp((r - \delta)(T - t))$$

where the current date is t, the futures delivery date is T, $S(t)$ is the spot price, r is the risk-free rate, and δ is the convenience yield. Because the own interest rate is constant, the dynamics of the futures price are completely determined by the dynamics of the spot price and the passage of time.

Describing Futures Prices as a Function of Latent Factors While futures prices are readily observable by design, spot commodity prices and convenience yields generally are not. (In fact, as a residual quantity, the convenience yield is a phenomenon economists have struggled to explain in a satisfactory way. The justification given above rationalizes convenience yield through an argument about an individual firm, which does not explain why it would exist in the aggregate for market prices.) Indeed, in most markets where futures trading is well developed, trading in futures far surpasses spot trading in the physical commodity. Spot prices may not be widely quoted or well supported by transactional activity. Delivery lags created by the logistics of physical delivery through pipelines, tankers, or rail transport can make the notion of spot trading elusive. Even where reasonably reliable spot prices are available, high-frequency econometric studies have found that changes in futures prices tend to lead changes in spot prices, suggesting that spot market price discovery is driven by the futures market. Accordingly, it may be advantageous to treat the spot price of a commodity as if it were latent (unobservable), and to test subsequently whether, given suitable initial conditions, the filtered spot price factor corresponds to any observable price series.

As the more volatile component of a commodity's own interest rate, the convenience yield connects spot price dynamics to futures price dynamics and is, consequently, a quantity of great interest. It can be backed out of futures prices from day to day as a constant, but convenience yields are not constant, in fact. Their role in facilitating the reallocation of inventories in time suggests that movements in convenience yields will be sharp but rapidly mean-reverting. Further, the differences in the volatilities of spot and futures prices imply that convenience yields must have their own dynamics; if convenience yields were constant, volatilities would be equal all along the futures curve, as pointed out previously. Accordingly, convenience yields are also prime candidates for inclusion as a latent state variable.

Finally, interest-rate processes can be incorporated via one of a number of interest rate factor models. Schwartz chooses a one-factor Vasicek model for interest rates, in which short-term interest rates exhibit reversion to a long-run mean. As a result, the futures market model also furnishes a simple introduction to modeling fixed income price dynamics. Though practitioners typically identify the single factor of the Vasicek model with a particular short-term interest rate, we treat the interest rate as a latent factor when estimating the three-factor version of the Schwartz model. Though much less information about the interest-rate process is furnished by a futures curve than, say, the yield curve, adding the interest rate to the state vector and estimating its process alongside the other state variable processes allows us to dispense with preestimation.

Continuous- and Discrete-Time Factor Dynamics The Schwartz model starts from a one-factor specification of underlying factor dynamics. If $X_t = \log(S_t)$ is the logarithm of the spot price, one can describe the spot price process with a mean-reverting model:

$$dX = \kappa(\alpha - X)dt + \sigma_1 dZ_1$$

Because X is taken to be lognormally distributed, its expected mean is $\alpha = \mu - \frac{1}{2}\sigma_1^2$, with the speed of reversion to the mean controlled by κ. We expect κ to be positive so that low values of X create upward drift, and vice versa.

In what follows, we will repeatedly have to find the discrete-time version of the specified factor dynamics. To translate the continuous-time specification, write differential terms like dX as $X_t - X_{t-1}$ and replace any values of X on the right-hand side with lagged values X_{t-1}. Then replace dt with the discrete time step Δt, and replace the Brownian motion term $\sigma_1 dZ_1$ with an error term $\varepsilon_t^x \sim \mathcal{N}[0, \sigma_1^2]$. From the above equation we therefore obtain

$$\begin{aligned} X_t - X_{t-1} &= \kappa\alpha\Delta t - \kappa\Delta t X_{t-1} + \varepsilon_t^x \\ X_t &= \kappa\alpha\Delta t + (1 - \kappa\Delta t)X_{t-1} + \varepsilon_t^x. \end{aligned}$$

Expanding the model to incorporate the convenience yield as a second factor, we can allow the convenience yield to influence the drift term of the spot price dynamics. From the cash-and-carry relation given previously we expect the drift of the log spot price to be $(r - \delta)dt$. Under the risk-neutral measure we must have $\mu - \frac{1}{2}\sigma_1^2 = r$ for a lognormal variable, so that the drift is $\left(\mu - \frac{1}{2}\sigma_1^2 - \delta\right) dt$. Now when we introduce the convenience yield as a state variable, both spot prices and current convenience yields will be a function of the lagged convenience yield.

Convenience yields are assumed to follow a mean reverting process

$$d\delta = (\kappa(a - \delta) - \lambda)dt + \sigma_2 dZ_2$$

where the market price of convenience yield risk λ arises because changes in the convenience yield cannot be hedged directly in a specific market. To limit the number of free parameters Schwartz defines $\hat{\alpha} = \alpha - \frac{\lambda}{\kappa}$ so that

$$d\delta = \kappa(\hat{a} - \delta)dt + \sigma_2 dZ_2.$$

In discrete time, the dynamics of the convenience yield are

$$\begin{aligned} \delta_t - \delta_{t-1} &= \kappa\hat{\alpha}\Delta t - \kappa\Delta t\delta_{t-1} + \varepsilon_t^\delta \\ \delta_t &= \kappa\hat{\alpha}\Delta t + (1 - \kappa\Delta t)\delta_{t-1} + \varepsilon_t^\delta. \end{aligned}$$

The reformulated spot price dynamics become

$$\begin{aligned} X_t - X_{t-1} &= \left(r - \frac{1}{2}\sigma_1^2 - \delta_{t-1}\right) \Delta t + \varepsilon_t^x \\ X_t &= \left(r - \frac{1}{2}\sigma_1^2\right) \Delta t + X_{t-1} - \Delta t\delta_{t-1} + \varepsilon_t^x. \end{aligned}$$

Accordingly, the system equation for the joint dynamics of the spot price and the convenience yield can be expressed in matrix form as

$$\begin{bmatrix} X_t \\ \delta_t \end{bmatrix} = \begin{bmatrix} \left(r - \frac{1}{2}\sigma_1^2\right) \Delta t \\ \kappa\hat{\alpha}\Delta t \end{bmatrix} + \begin{bmatrix} 1 & -\Delta t \\ 0 & 1 - \kappa\Delta t \end{bmatrix} \begin{bmatrix} X_{t-1} \\ \delta_{t-1} \end{bmatrix} + \begin{bmatrix} \varepsilon_t^x \\ \varepsilon_t^\delta \end{bmatrix}$$

which is linear in the state variables. Assuming

$$\begin{bmatrix} \varepsilon_t^x \\ \varepsilon_t^\delta \end{bmatrix} \sim N\left\{ \begin{bmatrix} 0 \\ 0 \end{bmatrix}, \begin{bmatrix} \sigma_1^2 & \rho_1\sigma_1\sigma_2 \\ \rho_1\sigma_1\sigma_2 & \sigma_2^2 \end{bmatrix} \right\},$$

the state-variable process is also Gaussian. This completes the factor specification for the two-factor version of the Schwartz model.

In the three-factor Schwartz model, dynamics for the risk-free rate are introduced. Since the short rate is now a state variable, there is no need to eliminate r implicitly by defining $\mu = r - \frac{1}{2}\sigma_1^2$. (When estimating the two-factor model there will only be two free parameters in the intercept of the state equation, standing in for $r - \frac{1}{2}\sigma_1^2$ and $\kappa\hat{\alpha}$, respectively.) Now the spot price process drift can be reset to $(r - \delta)dt$ so that the complete system becomes (in continuous time):

$$\begin{aligned}
dX &= (r - \delta)dt + \sigma_1 dZ_1 \\
d\delta &= \kappa(\hat{\alpha} - \delta)dt + \sigma_2 dZ_2 \\
dr &= \phi(m - r)dt + \sigma_3 dZ_3.
\end{aligned}$$

The discrete time version is

$$\begin{aligned}
X_t &= X_{t-1} - \Delta t \delta_{t-1} + \Delta t r_{t-1} + \sigma_1 dZ_1 \\
\delta_t &= \kappa\hat{\alpha}\Delta t + (1 - \kappa\Delta t)\delta_{t-1} + \sigma_2 dZ_2 \\
r_t &= \phi m \Delta t + (1 - \phi\Delta t) r_{t-1} + \sigma_3 dZ_3
\end{aligned}$$

so the entire system may be expressed as a linear, Gaussian evolution with

$$\begin{bmatrix} X_t \\ \delta_t \\ r_t \end{bmatrix} = \begin{bmatrix} 0 \\ \kappa\hat{\alpha}\Delta t \\ \phi m \Delta t \end{bmatrix} + \begin{bmatrix} 1 & -\Delta t & 1 \\ 0 & 1 - \kappa\Delta t & 0 \\ 0 & 0 & 1 - \phi\Delta t \end{bmatrix} \begin{bmatrix} X_{t-1} \\ \delta_{t-1} \\ r_{t-1} \end{bmatrix} + \begin{bmatrix} \varepsilon_t^X \\ \varepsilon_t^\delta \\ \varepsilon_t^r \end{bmatrix}$$

and system variance

$$\begin{bmatrix} \sigma_1^2 & \rho_1\sigma_1\sigma_2 & \rho_3\sigma_1\sigma_3 \\ \rho_1\sigma_1\sigma_2 & \sigma_2^2 & \rho_2\sigma_2\sigma_3 \\ \rho_3\sigma_1\sigma_3 & \rho_2\sigma_2\sigma_3 & \sigma_3^2 \end{bmatrix}.$$

I make two simple modifications to the three-factor Schwartz model. First, since the market price of convenience yield risk is a quantity of such keen interest, it would be interesting to ask if compensation for the risk of holding commodity inventories changes over time. Second, it is generally known that the one-factor Vasicek model fails to capture longer-term variations in interest rates, since rates are assumed to converge to a fixed long-run mean. If the long-run mean is allowed to change over time, more complicated term structures of interest rates may be reproduced. Accordingly, I include the market price of convenience yield risk λ and the long-run mean of the interest-rate process m as additional state variables, modeling them as simple diffusions evolving independently of the other state variables so that the expanded system equation becomes:

$$\begin{bmatrix} X_t \\ \delta_t \\ r_t \\ \lambda_t \\ m_t \end{bmatrix} = \begin{bmatrix} 0 \\ \kappa\alpha\Delta t \\ 0 \\ 0 \\ 0 \end{bmatrix} + \begin{bmatrix} 1 & -\Delta t & 1 & 0 & 0 \\ 0 & 1-\kappa\Delta t & 0 & -\Delta t & 0 \\ 0 & 0 & 1-\phi\Delta t & 0 & \phi\Delta t \\ 0 & 0 & 0 & 1 & 0 \\ 0 & 0 & 0 & 0 & 1 \end{bmatrix} \begin{bmatrix} X_{t-1} \\ \delta_{t-1} \\ r_{t-1} \\ \lambda_{t-1} \\ m_{t-1} \end{bmatrix} + \begin{bmatrix} \varepsilon_t^X \\ \varepsilon_t^\delta \\ \varepsilon_t^r \\ \varepsilon_t^\lambda \\ \varepsilon_t^m \end{bmatrix}$$

with system variance

$$\begin{bmatrix} \sigma_1^2 & \rho_1\sigma_1\sigma_2 & \rho_3\sigma_1\sigma_3 & 0 & 0 \\ \rho_1\sigma_1\sigma_2 & \sigma_2^2 & \rho_2\sigma_2\sigma_3 & 0 & 0 \\ \rho_3\sigma_1\sigma_3 & \rho_2\sigma_2\sigma_3 & \sigma_3^2 & 0 & 0 \\ 0 & 0 & 0 & \sigma_4^2 & 0 \\ 0 & 0 & 0 & 0 & \sigma_5^2 \end{bmatrix}.$$

Model-Implied Prices and the Observation Equation Equilibrium log futures prices in the three-factor model are a linear function of the three primitive state variables

$$\ln F(X,\delta,r,T) = X - \frac{1-e^{-\kappa T}}{\kappa}\delta + \frac{1-e^{-\phi T}}{\phi}r + C(T)$$

with

$$\begin{aligned} C(T) = {} & \frac{\left(\kappa\hat{\alpha} + \sigma_1\sigma_2\rho_1\right)\left(\left(1-e^{-\kappa T}\right) - \kappa T\right)}{\kappa^2} \\ & - \frac{\sigma_2^2\left(4\left(1-e^{-\kappa T}\right) - \left(1-e^{-2\kappa T}\right) - 2\kappa T\right)}{4\kappa^3} \\ & - \frac{\left(\phi m^* + \sigma_1\sigma_3\rho_3\right)\left(\left(1-e^{-\phi T}\right) - \phi T\right)}{\phi^2} \\ & - \frac{\sigma_3^2\left(4\left(1-e^{-\phi T}\right) - \left(1-e^{-2\phi T}\right) - 2\phi T\right)}{4\phi^3} \\ & + \sigma_2\sigma_3\rho_2\left(\frac{\left(1-e^{-\kappa T}\right) + \left(1-e^{-\phi T}\right) - \left(1-e^{-(\kappa+\phi)T}\right)}{\kappa\phi(\kappa+\phi)}\right. \\ & \left. + \frac{\kappa^2\left(1-e^{-\varphi T}\right) + \phi^2\left(1-e^{-\kappa T}\right) - \kappa\phi^2 T - \phi\kappa^2 T}{\kappa^2\phi^2(\kappa+\phi)}\right). \end{aligned}$$

For simplicity, I have not introduced new terms into the pricing equation to account for any priced risk that might be implied by letting λ and m^* vary. However, the manner in which these variables enter the intercept gives us a pricing equation which is now nonlinear in the expanded set of state variables. Whereas this would be a fatal complication for the batched version of the Kalman filter, it presents no problems for our online estimation method described below.

Based on the model-implied price, we can measure pricing error and obtain a score for simulated states and parameters based on the likelihood for use in resampling. Writing the log model-implied price as $\hat{f}$, we will evaluate

$$\mathcal{N}\left[y_t - \hat{f}(X, \delta, r, T), \sigma_y^2\right]$$

where y_t is a futures price observation and σ_y^2 is a pricing model variance determined a priori.

ONLINE STATE-SPACE MODEL ESTIMATES OF DERIVATIVE PRICES

I estimate the Schwartz model in the modified three-factor version presented above, using data on Brent crude oil futures from January 2000 to December 2013. The futures are continuous series for contracts with 1 to 12 months remaining to expiration, as compiled by Bloomberg. Because estimation itself presents several important analytical issues, I focus on estimation to the detriment of other pricing questions like model comparisons and forecasting performance.

In his original paper, Schwartz himself estimates only a reduced version of his three-factor model. The parameters of the interest rate process are set to constant values obtained in a separate estimation. As a result, specification errors in the interest rate process spill over into estimates of the convenience yield, since this is the only free element of the state dynamics available to fit the term structure of the forward curve. For purposes of my SMC estimates, I model the interest rate process explicitly. While this will mitigate errors in estimating the convenience yield, it does not ensure that errors will be eliminated, or that the interest rate parameters obtained will be useful for understanding the interest rate process. Ideally, the interest rate state estimates would also be controlled by observations on the yield curve and interest rate derivatives, where relevant information is available without the confounding information of commodity price dynamics and convenience yields. The relatively short horizon of the futures prices (12 months) also presents a handicap.

In addition, the difference in the time periods covered by our estimates raises questions about the evolution of model parameters. Schwartz finds meaningful changes in parameter estimates when comparing results from the earlier subperiod to the later subperiod of his data. As I pointed out in Chapter 6, SMC estimates are not designed to accommodate parameter drift, in contrast to DLM estimates. The divide between states and parameters is a sharp divide. It would be possible, in principle, to make all parameters into states that are subject to drift. Propagating the state equation would then involve a nonlinear transformation of the state variables via a locally linear approximation. It is also possible to explicitly reintroduce parameter drift by a discounting operation. As my lengthy time period increases the likelihood of parameter changes, I will investigate both static and dynamic versions of the model, as well as the evolution of pricing errors to look for systematic pricing errors.

Estimation with the Liu-West Filter

The modified three-factor Schwartz model is estimated by the Liu-West filter, a sequential Monte Carlo method for combined state and parameter estimation with nonlinear and non-Gaussian processes. The primary functional steps in the Liu-West filter are resampling the state and parameter vectors, propagating parameters, and propagating states.

As discussed in Chapter 6, the Liu-West filter uses an initial resampling step to fight sample impoverishment and increase adaptivity. Auxiliary variables for the resampling step are obtained in this implementation of the filter by propagating the state equation using the previous iteration's values for parameters and states. Importance weights are then obtained by evaluating the likelihood function with the auxiliary state variables and the previous iteration's parameter values. As the estimation covers a relatively long time period, sample impoverishment presents a real risk to the success of the estimation strategy.

Following Johannes, Polson, and Stroud (2009, p. 2790), I use a normal likelihood with zero mean and a prespecified variance of $(0.15)^2$. The variance is an a priori estimate of errors in the observed price due to market microstructure noise, transaction cost limits to arbitrage, asynchronous data, or staleness in pricing. Alternatively, it may be regarded as a prespecified tolerance level that trades off more exact fit for more continuous state estimates. The likelihood is evaluated at the pricing error implied by each draw from the simulated state-parameter vector. Given values for all states and parameters, the model-implied price is calculated, and the actual price is subtracted.

Since there are 12 observed prices at every time step, the likelihood is actually a joint likelihood. For independent and identically distributed observations, the joint log likelihood will just be the sum of the individual log likelihoods, and this is the solution I have implemented. However, this is not the only possible choice. One might choose to give greater weight to estimates that reproduce certain futures expirations more closely than others. One may also specify different observational error variances at each contract maturity to reflect differences in liquidity or different tolerances for mispricing, or a dependency structure for observational errors across the forward curve.

The likelihoods obtained for each draw in the prior state-parameter particle set become the weights for sampling an index, and the sampled indices are used to resample the particle set. Then new draws of the parameter and state subvectors are taken.

Drawing from the parameter vector presents certain difficulties. The Liu-West filter produces parameter draws from a multivariate normal kernel density mixture. However, not all parameters are necessarily defined everywhere on the real line, like the marginal distributions of the multivariate normal distribution. Some are defined only on a half-interval to be strictly positive or strictly negative. Others are defined on a closed interval. Still others have to satisfy certain joint relationships. We would like to preserve these restrictions on the parameter space whenever they are salient.

The three-factor Schwartz model presents instances of all cases. The variance terms must all take on positive values. The correlations must remain between -1 and $+1$. And the disturbance matrix for the state vector must be positive definite so that the state vector can be propagated in simulation. Not only do such restrictions keep code from breaking, but they also make the algorithms more efficient by confining the search for parameters to high-probability regions of the parameter space.

Parameter values that must be non-negative are mapped to the entire real line using the natural logarithm function, which is inverted back to the non-negative domain by the exponential function. Parameters that are bounded on both sides are remapped to the [0,1] interval, projected onto the real line by the logit transform $q = -\log\left(\frac{1}{p} - p\right)$ and recovered by the logistic transform $p = \frac{\exp(q)}{1+\exp(q)}$. Further remapping to arbitrary closed intervals is achieved by a basic linear transformation. Provided these transforms are applied on either side of sampling from the parameter vector, the sampled parameter draws will maintain the one- or two-sided restrictions imposed a priori.

The new parameter draws are then appended to the resampled state vector, and the combined values are used to simulate from the state equation. A new resampling step moves the search toward those values that best adapt the particle filter. Likelihoods are computed in the same way, and resampling is achieved based on the weight ratio

$$p\left(y_{t+1} \mid (x_{t+1}, \theta_{t+1})^{(i)}\right) \Big/ p\left(y_{t+1} \mid x_t^{(k_1(i))}, \alpha\left(x_t^{(k_1(i))}\right), m^{(k_1(i))}\right).$$

These posterior draws become the prior draws for the next cycle of the particle filter.

I coded the particle filter in Matlab. For efficiency, each stage of the algorithm is packaged as a stand-alone function that is called at each iteration of the loop. (Compiling the code would likely yield further gains.) With the particle approximation set to $N = 50{,}000$, the algorithm requires a little less than three seconds per time step with a quad-core processor running at 2.5 GHz. While the implied run times for daily data over many years can be quite long, a model that has already gone through the initial learning stages can clearly be updated at a modest computational cost. One only needs to store the previous day's particle set and feed in the new day's prices. The opportunity for intervention created thereby should not be ignored, either.

Prior Information

In a model with several states and parameters, the careful specification of prior information places useful restrictions on the parameter space that can help to identify model parameters. We have already discussed in connection with the Liu-West filter implementation the use of transformations to confine parameters to a closed interval or an open half-interval. We can go further to focus the search on certain regions or subintervals, applying existing knowledge about reasonable parameter and state outcomes.

We begin with the priors for the states. The log spot price factor x_0 ought to have a value close to the log of the one-month futures price. In a contango market, it will be below the one-month price, and (possibly significantly) above the one-month price when there is backwardation. The convenience yield δ_0 and short-term interest rate r_0 are treated as being uniformly distributed from 0 percent to 20 percent and 0 percent to 10 percent per annum, respectively, given the level of interest rates and the regular presence of backwardation in the oil futures market. The range of the long-run interest rate m_0^* is constrained to be between 4 percent and 8 percent, while the prior for the market price of convenience yield risk λ_0 is relatively vague, ranging from 0 percent to 100 percent per annum.

The priors for the states imply corresponding priors for the elements of the state covariance matrix. Variances for spot prices, convenience yields, and interest rates are centered at $\sigma_1^2 = (50\%)^2$, $\sigma_2^2 = (50\%)^2$, and $\sigma_3^2 = (4\%)^2$, respectively. Since correlations between these factors and the other two factors are assumed to be zero, the upper left 3×3 submatrix of the covariance matrix can be modeled independently of the lower right 2×2 submatrix. In order to obtain coherent samples for the parameters of the upper left submatrix, I simulate draws from an inverted-Wishart distribution with the above variances on the diagonal and very low degrees of freedom (10). Choosing such a low value for the degrees of freedom ensures a wide range of candidate covariances is observed.

For each inverted Wishart matrix draw the variance values are recovered from the diagonal and used, in turn, to recover the values for the correlations using the decomposition $\Sigma = \mathbf{DRD}$, where $\mathbf{D}$ is a square matrix with standard deviations on the diagonal and $\mathbf{R}$ is a correlation matrix. Going forward, if parameter draws fail to produce a valid (i.e., positive definite) covariance matrix, off-diagonal values are set to zero, which may result in some shrinkage of the correlation estimates as the algorithm proceeds. I complete the prior specification for the covariance matrix by positing that the price of convenience yield risk and the long-term level of interest rates will be relatively slow-moving processes. For these state variables, I used an inverted gamma prior that produces volatilities in the 0 to 3 percent per annum range.

It remains to specify the long-run value of the convenience yield α, the rate of mean reversion in the convenience yield process κ, and the rate of mean reversion in the convenience yield process ϕ. Using uniform distributions for each, I posit $\alpha \in [0, 0.4]$, $\kappa \in [0, 10]$, and $\phi \in [0, 0.4]$. The last prior surrounds Schwartz's a priori estimate of $\phi = 0.2$, just as $m_0^* \in [0.04, 0.08]$ surrounds his estimate for the long-run level of interest rates. Note that specifying the prior distribution is reinforced by the way parameters are drawn in the Liu-West filter. The transformations I employ ensure that these parameters remain restricted to these domains, while also ensuring positive volatilities and correlations on $[-1, 1]$.

Estimation Results

I begin by estimating the model over two subperiods of the data. The first subperiod covers January 2000 to December 2002, a time of very low oil prices, while the second subperiod covers January 2012 to December 2013, a time of persistently elevated oil prices. The results are summarized in a collection of time series plots of the state and parameter estimates produced by the model. For each state or parameter presented, the 25th, 50th, and 75th percentiles of the distribution are plotted as a summary of the particle set. See Figures 8.1 to 8.14.

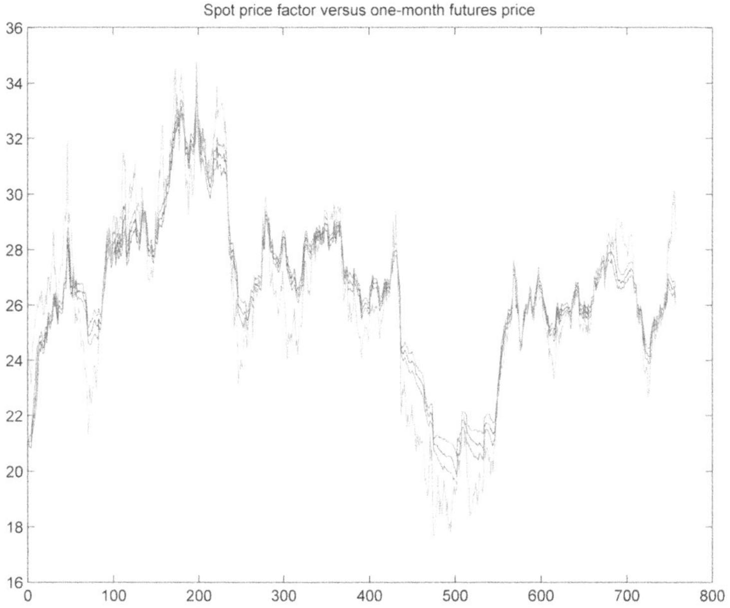

FIGURE 8.1 Spot Price Estimates and One-Month Futures Price, Fixed Parameters, 2000–2002

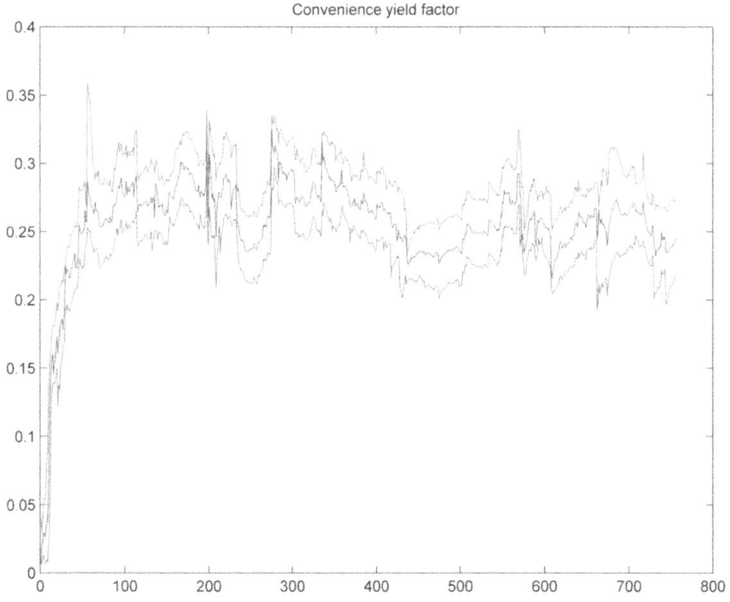

FIGURE 8.2 Convenience Yield State Variable Estimates, Fixed Parameters, 2000–2002

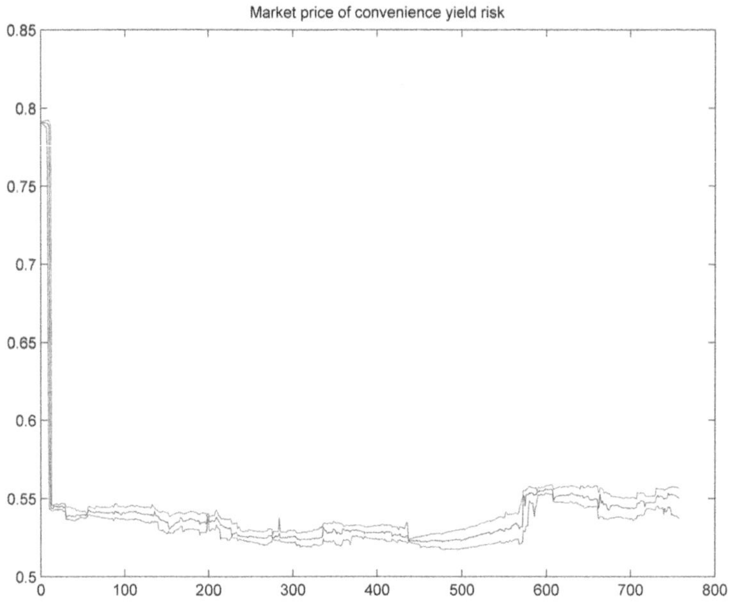

FIGURE 8.3 Market Price of Convenience Yield Risk, Fixed Parameters, 2000–2002

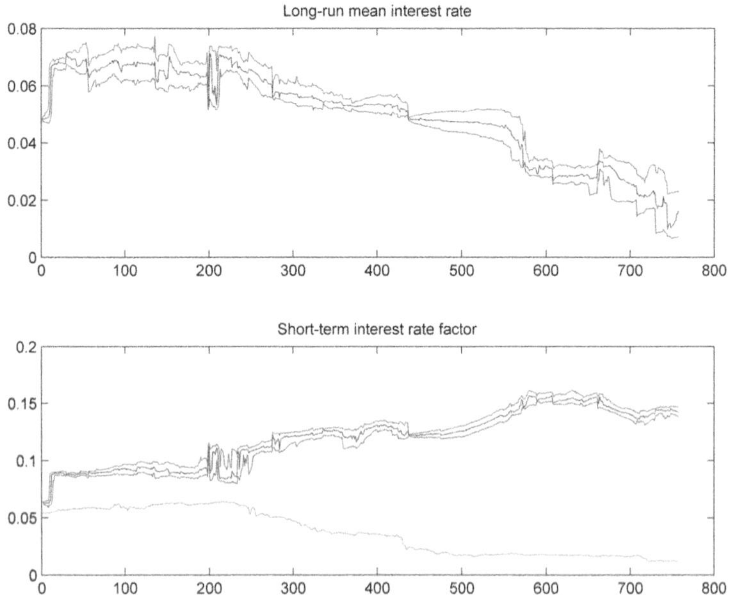

FIGURE 8.4 Long- and Short-Term Interest Rate Estimates, Fixed Parameters, 2000–2002

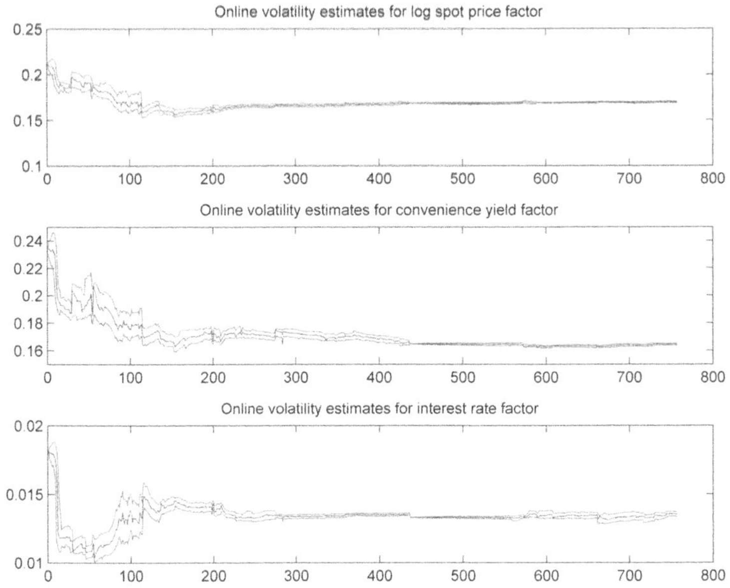

FIGURE 8.5 State Variable Volatility Estimates, Fixed Parameters, 2000–2002

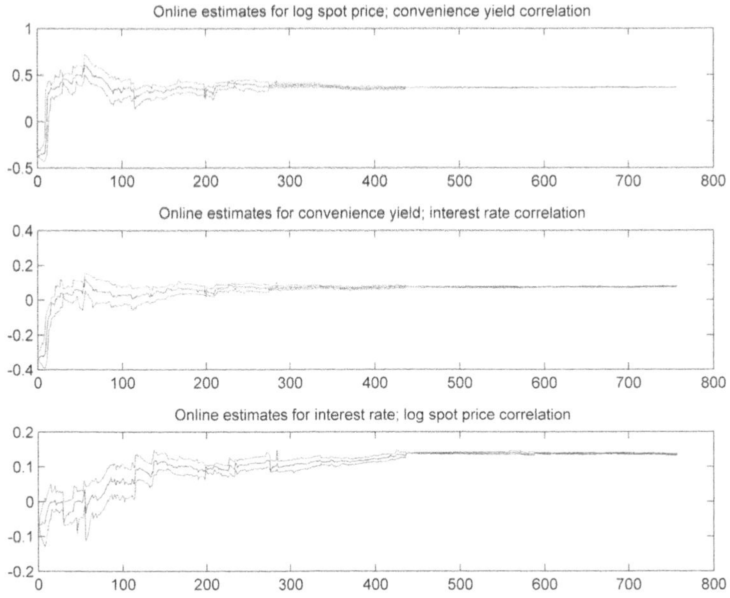

FIGURE 8.6 State Variable Correlation Estimates, Fixed Parameters, 2000–2002

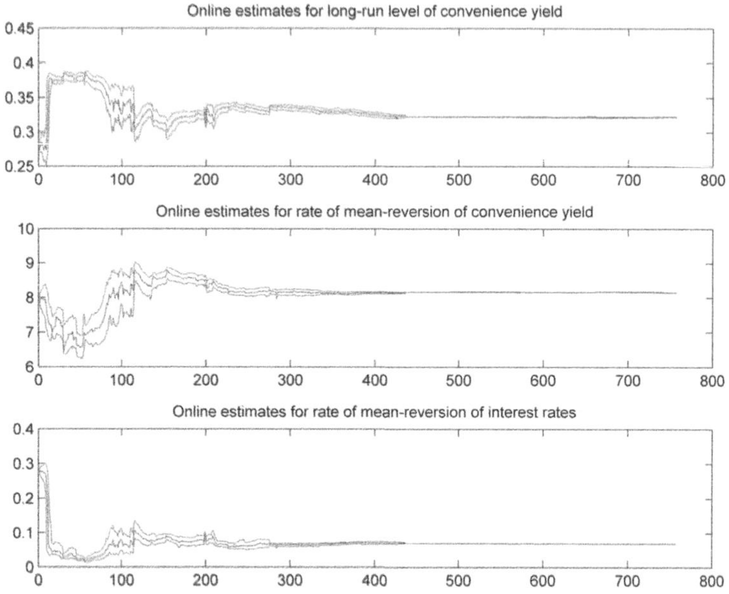

FIGURE 8.7 Long-Run Convenience Yield and Mean-Reversion Rates, Fixed Parameters, 2000–2002

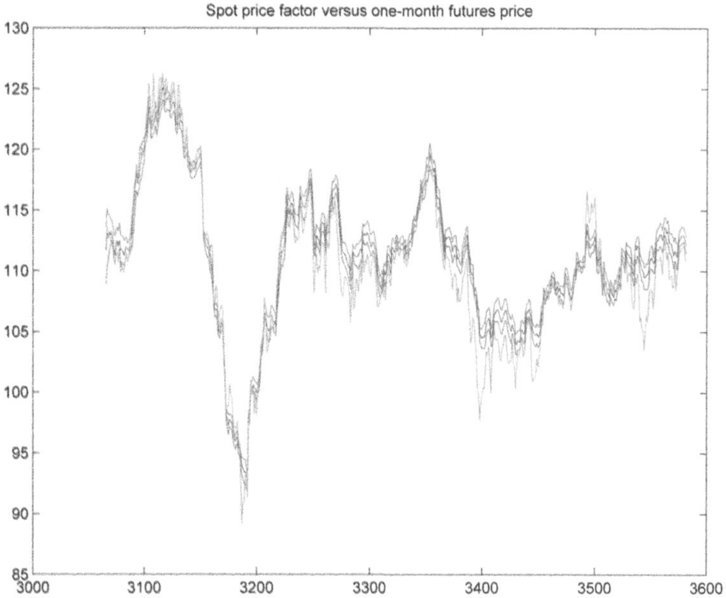

FIGURE 8.8 Spot Price Estimates and One-Month Futures Price, Fixed Parameters, 2012–2013

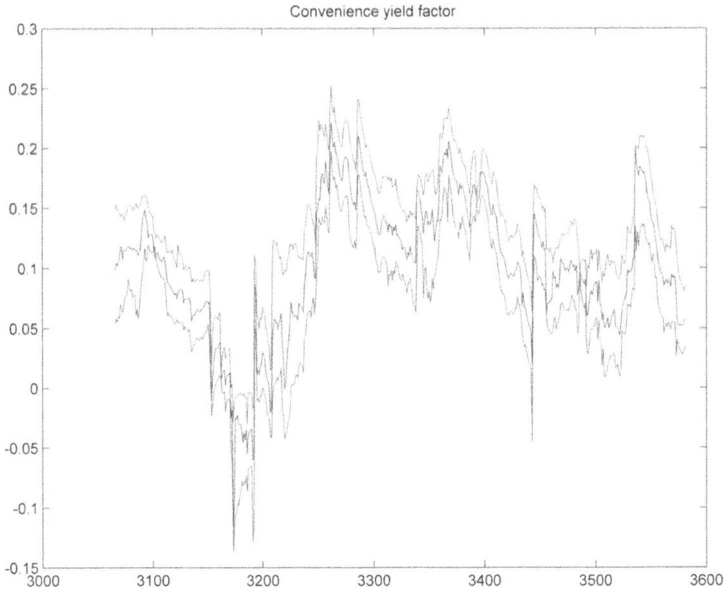

FIGURE 8.9 Convenience Yield State Variable Estimates, Fixed Parameters, 2012–2013

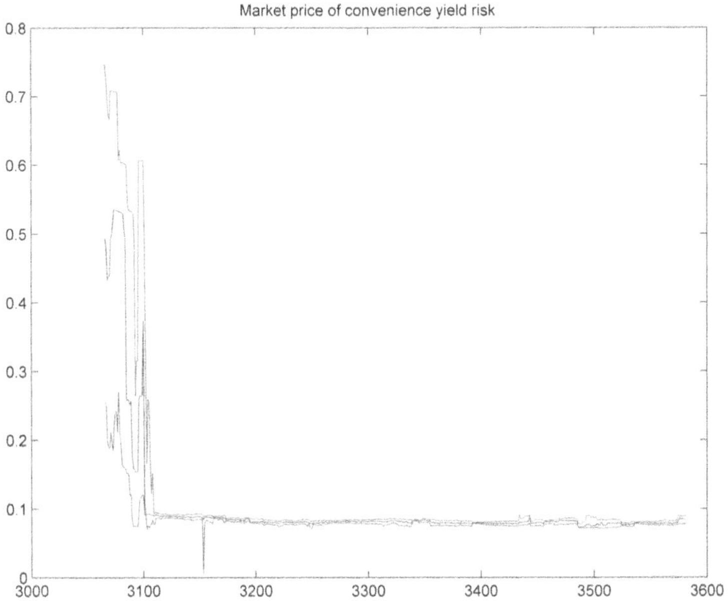

FIGURE 8.10 Market Price of Convenience Yield Risk, Fixed Parameters, 2012–2013

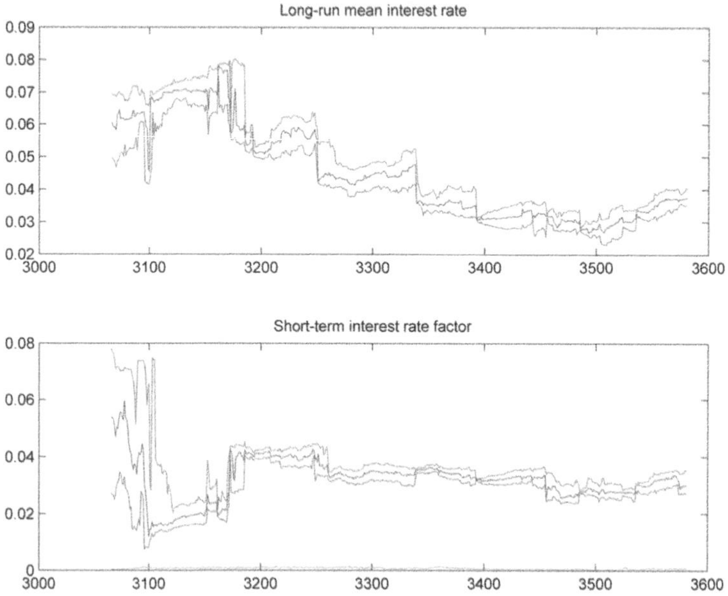

FIGURE 8.11 Long- and Short-Term Interest Rate Estimates, Fixed Parameters, 2012–2013

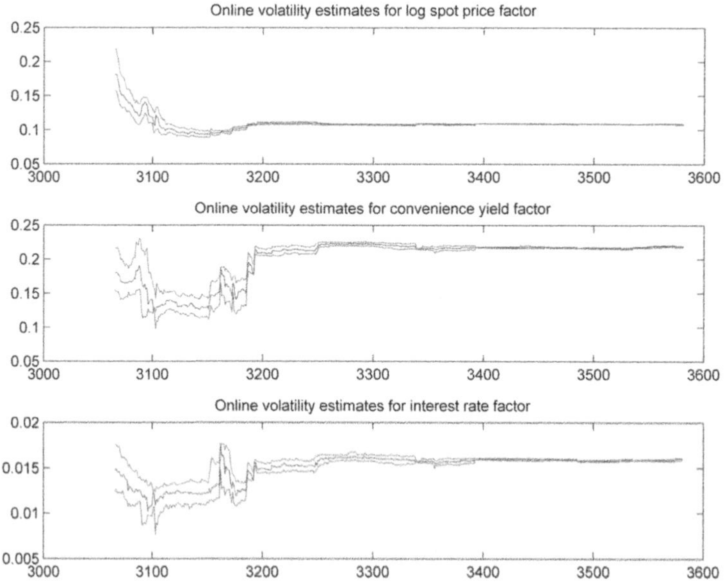

FIGURE 8.12 State Variable Volatility Estimates, Fixed Parameters, 2012–2013

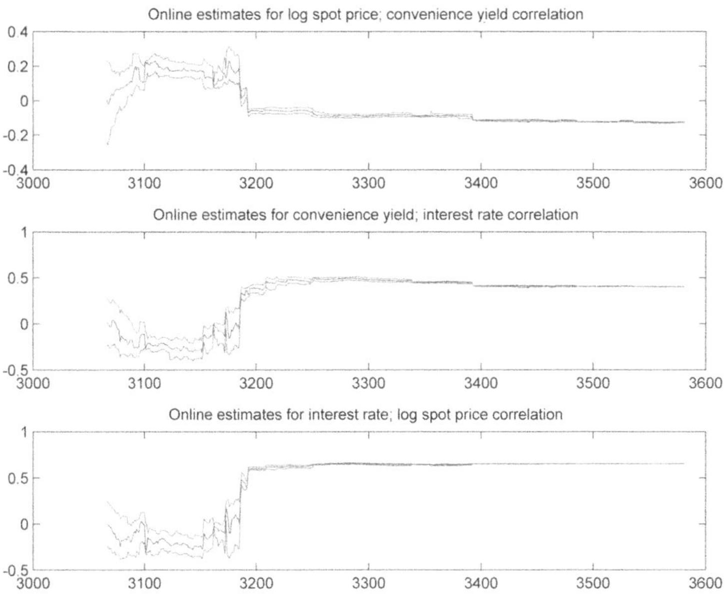

FIGURE 8.13 State Variable Correlation Estimates, Fixed Parameters, 2012–2013

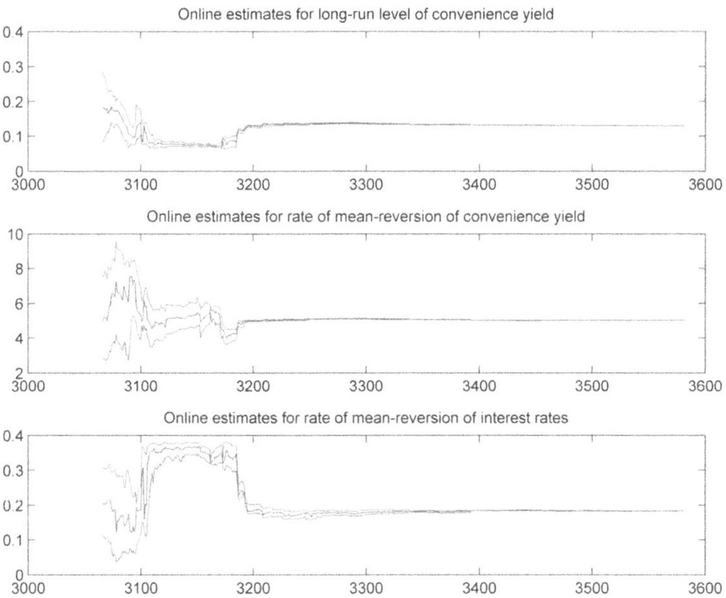

FIGURE 8.14 Long-Run Convenience Yield and Mean-Reversion Rates, Fixed Parameters, 2012–2013

In the Schwartz model the object of primary interest is the stochastic convenience yield process. In addition to extracting the latent convenience yield factor, we are interested in the long-run mean of the convenience yield α and the speed of mean-reversion κ in the convenience yield process. For both subperiods our estimates of the latent convenience yield factor are generally positive. From January 2000 to December 2002, the level of the convenience yield is usually in the 15 percent to 25 percent range, whereas a level of roughly 5 percent to 15 percent prevails in the January 2012 to December 2013 period. The uncertainty associated with the estimates varies through time, as one would expect. Note the sharp fall in the convenience yield in the first subperiod, which coincides with a drop in oil prices from September 24, 2001, forward. (With roughly 250 business days in a year, September 2001 falls between 400 and 450 on the horizontal axis.) Fears of a global recession made it undesirable to hold stocks of oil. After convenience yields reached a low point, there is an evident period of uncertainty before convenience yields regained their earlier levels. A period of weak demand is also evident in depressed convenience yields at the beginning of 2001. In the second subperiod a sharp peak in the convenience yield coincides with geopolitical fears in the Middle East and problems in the North Sea.

The long-run level of the convenience yield before adjustments for risk is approximately 30 percent in the first subperiod and 15 percent in the second, consistent with Schwartz's three-factor model estimate of 25 percent. Strong mean-reversion in the series is evident. The estimates of roughly 5.0 for κ are considerably higher than Schwartz's and correspond to a shock half-life of about seven weeks. Our estimate for the market price of convenience yield risk is quite high in the first subperiod (0.55), but much lower in the second period (0.15), framing Schwartz's estimate of 0.353.

There are also clear weaknesses in the estimation of the interest rate process parameters. While the estimates for the long-term level of interest rates are not implausible, short-term rate estimates are off the mark, which can be seen by comparison to the three-month Treasury rate plotted alongside the rate factor r. In both periods the estimates for short-term interest rates are excessively high. In spite of these problems with the level of interest rate factors, however, the differences between the rates will be decisive for the drift. Thus, it is somewhat encouraging that the estimates for the rate of mean reversion in the rate process are consistent with other studies at 0.3 and 0.2, respectively. The interest rate volatility estimates are also reasonable.

Weaknesses in filtering the short-term interest rate translate into weaknesses in the log spot rate process, as the log spot rate drift is jointly determined by the interest rate and the convenience yield. Plots of the spot price factor alongside the one-month futures price show a lack of responsiveness in periods where the level and steepness of the forward curve change significantly. This also explains why the volatility of the spot rate process does not exceed the volatility of the convenience yield process in either subperiod, and why the correlation between convenience yield and spot rate shocks is relatively low.

Despite these reservations about our results, they have some positive aspects when compared to Schwartz's original paper. We have implemented the model with a completely online orientation, thereby avoiding the use of later data in obtaining estimates early in the period. Constant model quantities settle down to constant values in estimation. We have obtained estimates of the state variables that acknowledge the uncertainty associated with the states, and we have seen that the uncertainty can be considerable and time-varying. In addition, notwithstanding the manifest problems of estimating the interest rate process online, we have avoided assuming foreknowledge of interest rates. As a result, we have confronted an aspect of model risk sidestepped in the original model implementation. Our estimates of the convenience yield factor also appear to be quite good, as they tend to remain positive and to vary in a reasonable way with fundamental market developments. Schwartz's estimates are often sharply negative, though they do track market developments in a reasonable way.

Still, it is clear that improvements can be made. Looking at the estimates of the fixed model parameters, adaptivity is lost after roughly 450 observations in the January 2000 to December 2002 subperiod and 250 observations in the January 2012 to December 2013 subperiod. The loss of adaptivity in the first subperiod coincides with the September 2001 price shock, whereas adaptivity disappears from the second subperiod as geopolitical tensions subsided and oil prices and convenience yields fell sharply in early 2013.

The sharp change in state and parameter values results in an immediate reduction in the number of distinct candidate values included in the parameter particle sets. Variation in the parameter subvector of the particle sets is eliminated, fixing parameter values from that point forward. Thus, once parameter values are essentially fixed, adjustments in the states will be constrained by the estimate of the state covariance matrix. If state volatility estimates are too low, the latent state variables will not be able to adjust adequately to cover variation in market prices afterward. Achieving ongoing flexibility in the parameterization of models has been an overarching goal of our modeling enterprise, so we explore what can be done to preserve parameter flexibility in the face of changing market conditions.

Estimation Results with Discounting

For the sake of a better oil market model, as well as the project of building more flexible models in general, we would like to reintroduce drift in the parameter set using techniques similar to the discounting methods introduced in Chapters 4 and 5. The obvious target for discounting is the covariance matrix of parameters, $h^2\mathbf{V}$. A first thought would be to introduce parameter-specific discount factors and compute $h^2\Delta^{-1/2}\mathbf{V}\Delta^{-1/2}$ by analogy with components of the DLM. However, this does not solve our problem. The discount factors will increase the elements of the parameter covariance matrix at each time step. But for reasonable discount factor values they won't offset the eventual convergence of parameter values to a narrow set of values. Discounting a matrix that converges to zero will still bring online learning to a halt, albeit on a slightly delayed schedule. Accordingly, we prefer to add a matrix $\mathbf{\Omega}$ to the parameter covariance matrix $h^2\mathbf{V}$ to obtain $h^2\mathbf{V}+\mathbf{\Omega}$. The matrix $\mathbf{\Omega}$ may be considered the long-run minimum parameter uncertainty. As $\mathbf{V}$ goes to zero only $\mathbf{\Omega}$ remains. I will begin by experimenting with a diagonal $\mathbf{\Omega}$ where all nonzero elements are equal to $(0.01)^2$, implying an information loss of 1 percent at each time step. (Actually, our fixed-model estimates used a minimal parameter disturbance term of 0.001 to avoid having the algorithm stop altogether from sample impoverishment.) See Figures 8.15 to 8.28.

In our previous model of Brent crude futures from January 2000 to December 2002, learning about parameters essentially stopped after 450 observations. When parameters are allowed to vary, learning continues throughout the sample period. Moreover, several global changes have been enabled by relaxing the fixed parameter constraint. The market price of convenience yield risk is found to be much higher than in the static parameter case. The convenience yield process is more strongly mean-reverting (a value of about 9.0 implies a half-life of about four weeks for shocks), but also less volatile and associated with a higher market price of risk. Mean-reversion in the interest rate series is less pronounced, with estimates of the short-term interest rate factor falling considerably below previous estimates. Finally, some variation in factor volatilities and correlations can be seen over the entire period.

The January 2012 to December 2013 period shows similar evidence of ongoing learning when parameters are allowed to vary. The long-run level of the convenience yield increases slowly through the period, and the rate of mean-reversion for the convenience yield process settles at a much lower level than previously estimated. The correlation between the spot price and the convenience yield increases steadily, and the factor volatilities show meaningful evolution over the early part of the time period. The market price

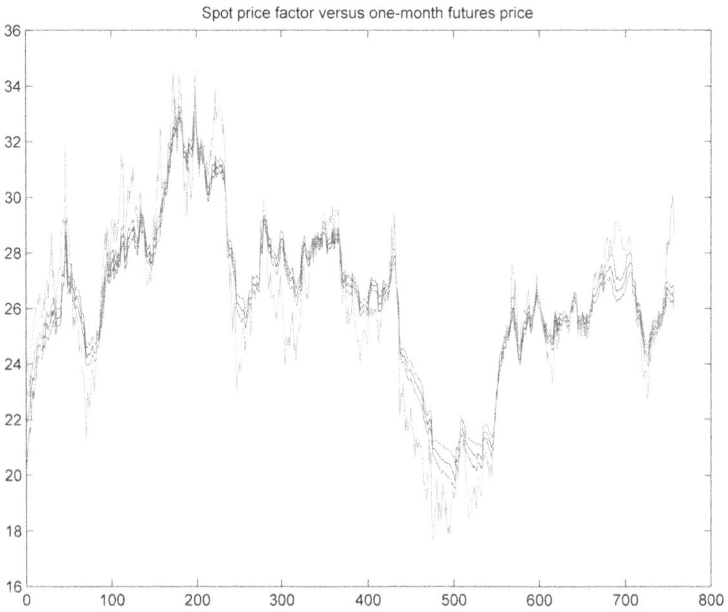

FIGURE 8.15 Spot Price Estimates and One-Month Futures Price, Flexible Parameters (1%), 2000–2002

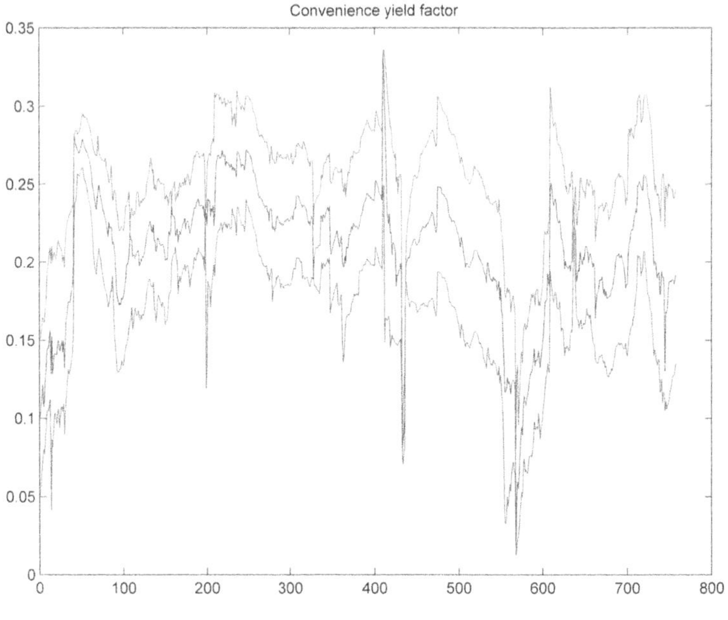

FIGURE 8.16 Convenience Yield State Variable Estimates, Flexible Parameters (1%) 2000–2002

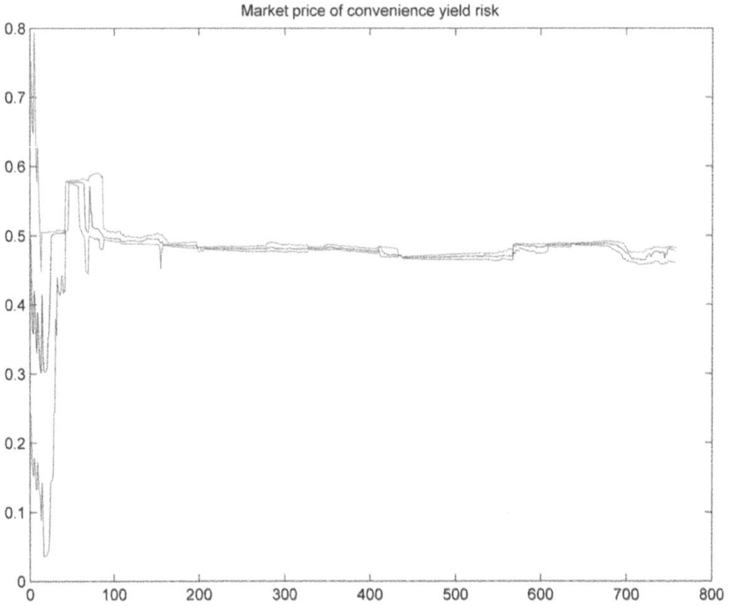

FIGURE 8.17 Market Price of Convenience Yield Risk, Flexible Parameters (1%) 2000–2002

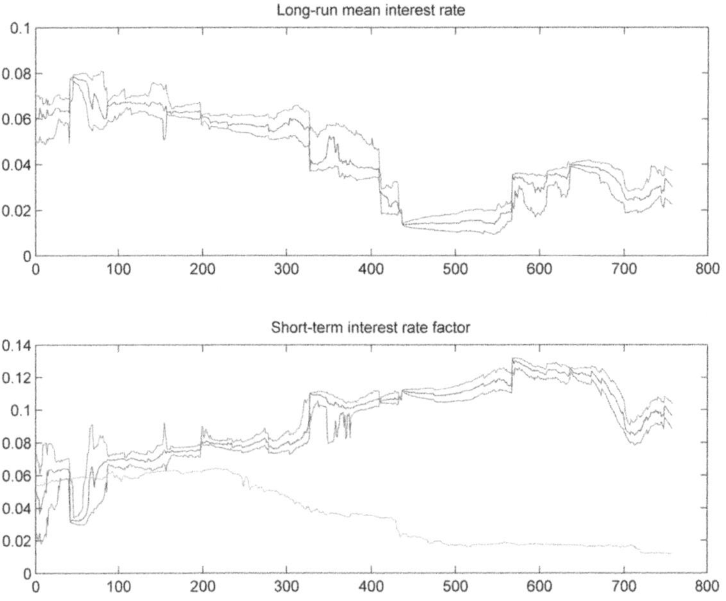

FIGURE 8.18 Long- and Short-Term Interest Rate Estimates, Flexible Parameters (1%) 2000–2002

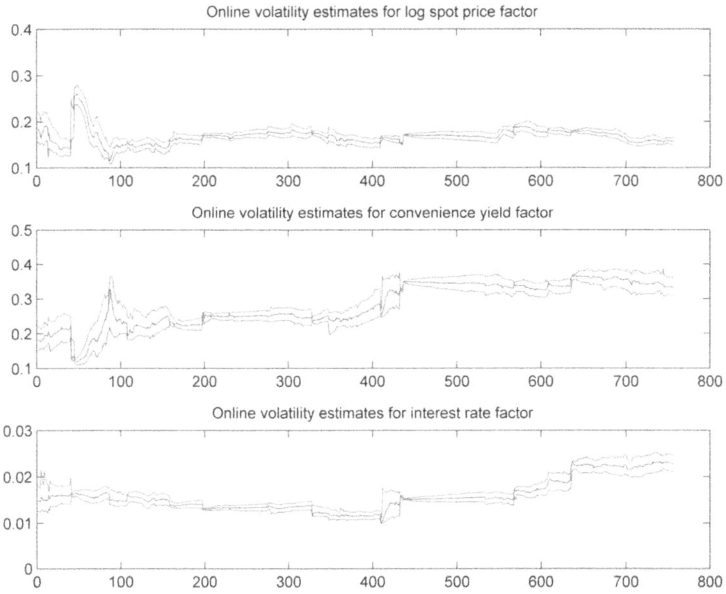

FIGURE 8.19 State Variable Volatility Estimates, Flexible Parameters (1%) 2000–2002

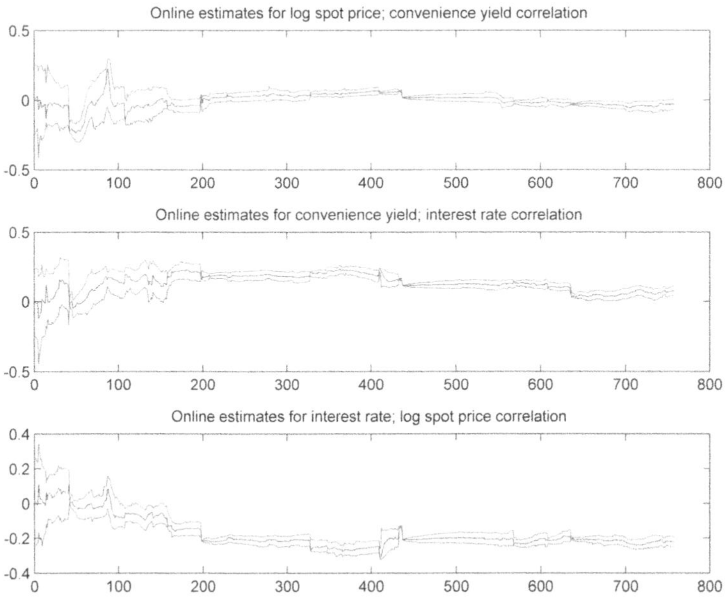

FIGURE 8.20 State Variable Correlation Estimates, Flexible Parameters (1%) 2000–2002

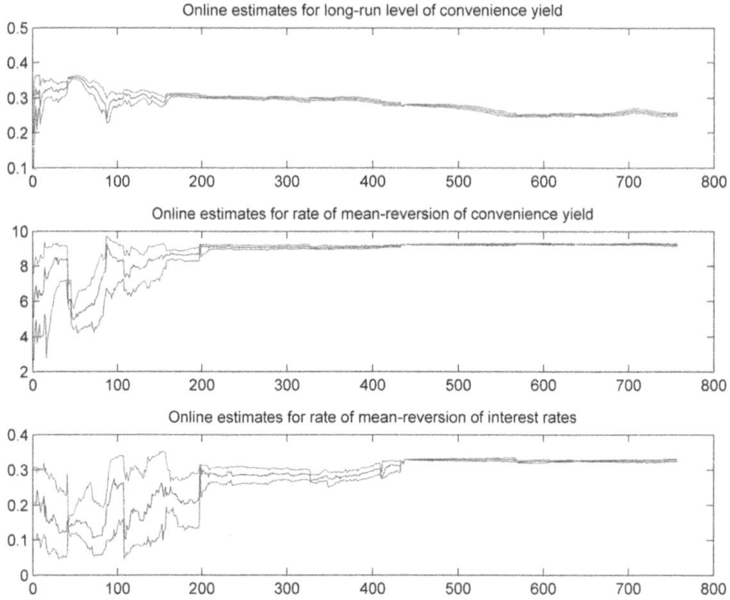

FIGURE 8.21 Long-Run Convenience Yield and Mean-Reversion Rates, Flexible Parameters (1%) 2000–2002

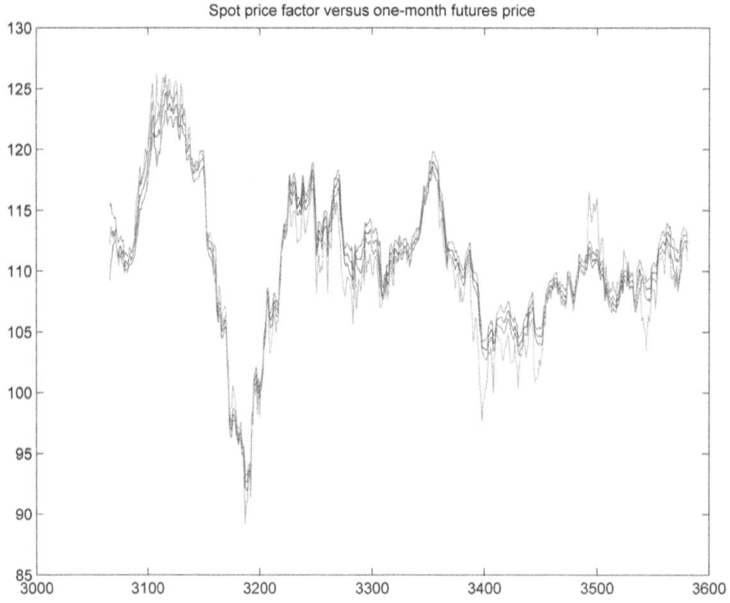

FIGURE 8.22 Spot Price Estimates and One-Month Futures Price, Flexible Parameters (1%) 2012–2013

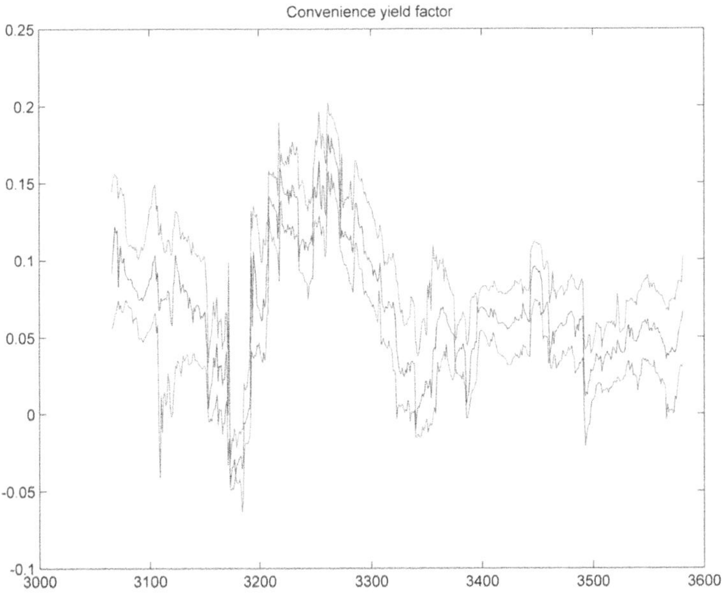

FIGURE 8.23 Convenience Yield State Variable Estimates, Flexible Parameters (1%) 2012–2013

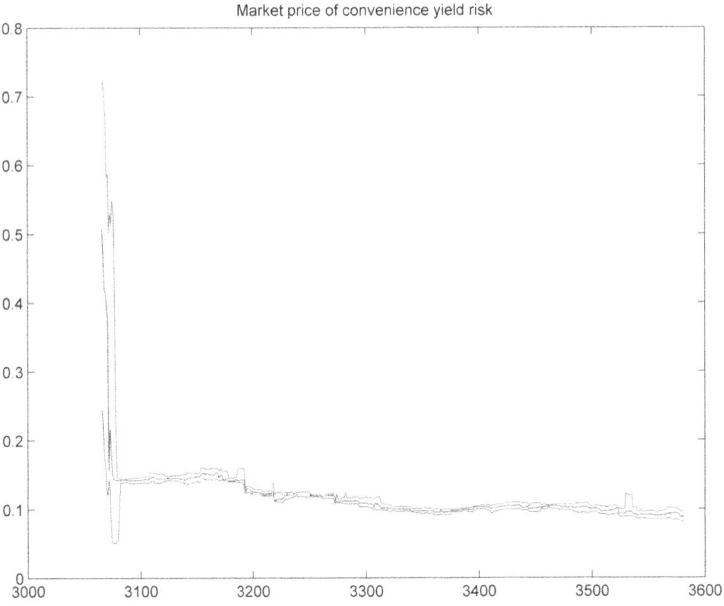

FIGURE 8.24 Market Price of Convenience Yield Risk, Flexible Parameters (1%) 2012–2013

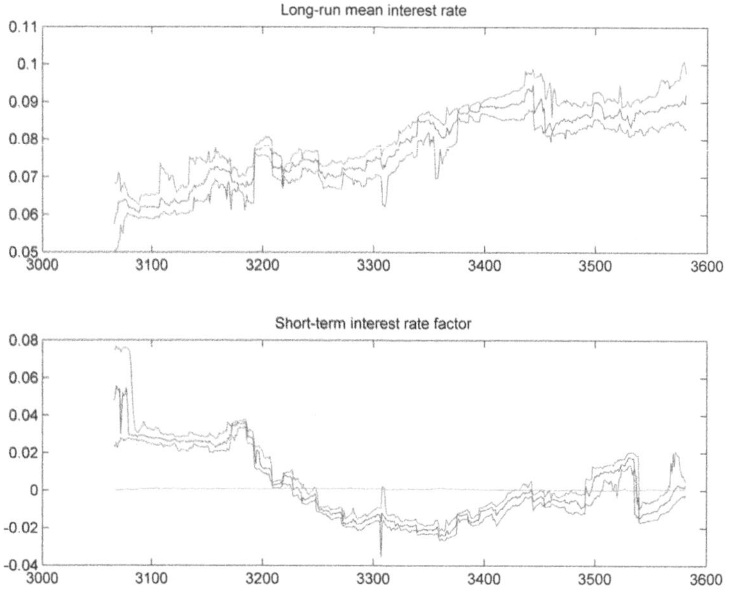

FIGURE 8.25 Long- and Short-Term Interest Rate Estimates, Flexible Parameters (1%) 2012–2013

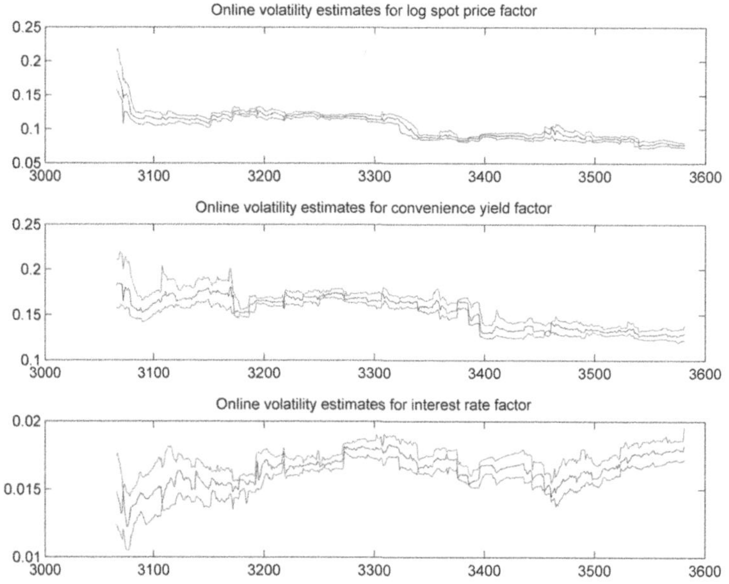

FIGURE 8.26 State Variable Volatility Estimates, Flexible Parameters (1%) 2012–2013

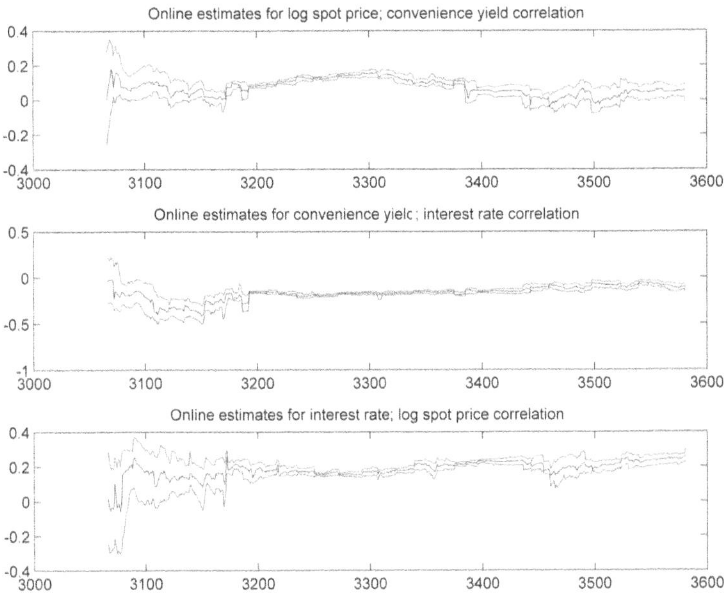

FIGURE 8.27 State Variable Correlation Estimates, Flexible Parameters (1%) 2012–2013

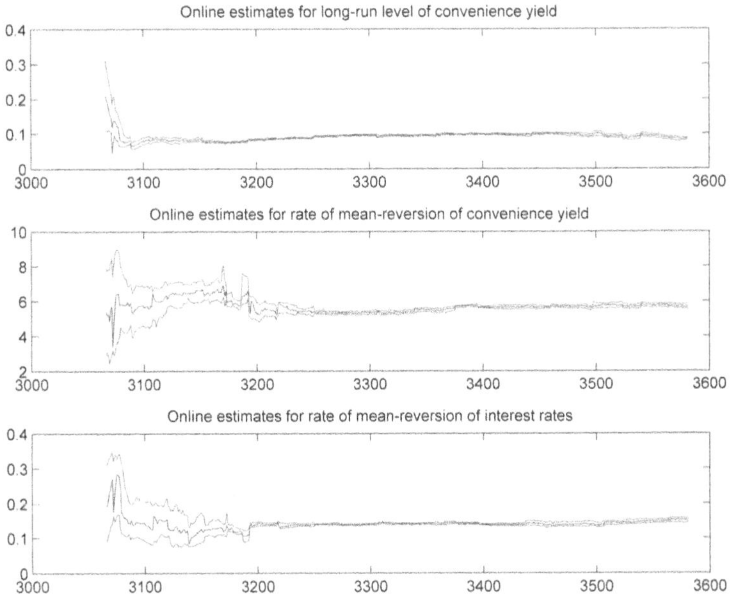

FIGURE 8.28 Long-Run Convenience Yield and Mean-Reversion Rates, Flexible Parameters (1%) 2012–2013

of convenience yield risk settles in at a low value consistent with the fixed parameter estimates obtained previously. See Figures 8.29 to 8.35.

Encouraged by the results of discounting with $\mathbf{\Omega}$ for the two subperiods of the data, we attempt sequential estimation over the entire time period, from January 2000 to December 2013. To allow for greater variation over this longer time frame and the increased risk of particle set impoverishment, I increase the parameter variance along the diagonal to $(0.02)^2$. Model estimates suggest that the two periods examined previously reflect a relative calm on either side of very turbulent developments. Convenience yields climb with the beginning of war in Iraq, but soon stabilize and drift downward, turning negative as prices fall at the onset of the credit crisis and worldwide recession in 2008. Note that the pattern of convenience yields in each subperiod is consistent with previous estimates. The long-run level of the convenience yield follows the same basic trajectory as the convenience yield state. Volatilities and correlations change meaningfully for all of the state variables.

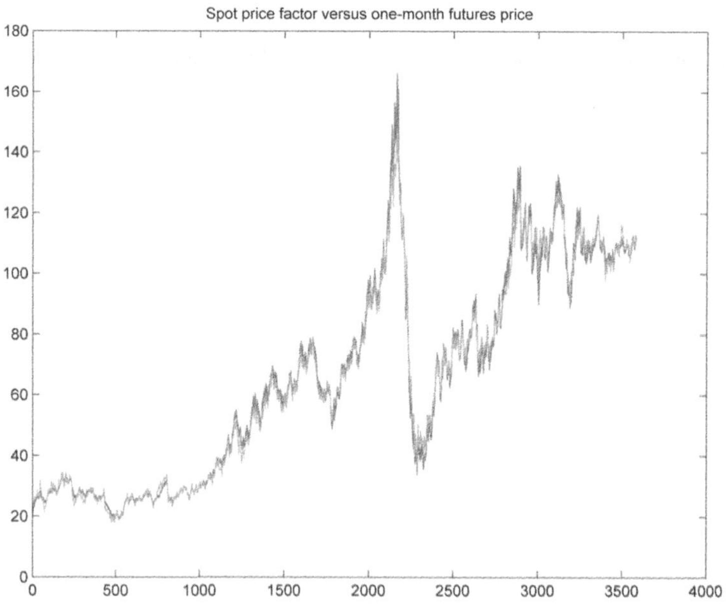

FIGURE 8.29 Spot Price Estimates and One-Month Futures Price, Flexible Parameters (2%) 2000–2013

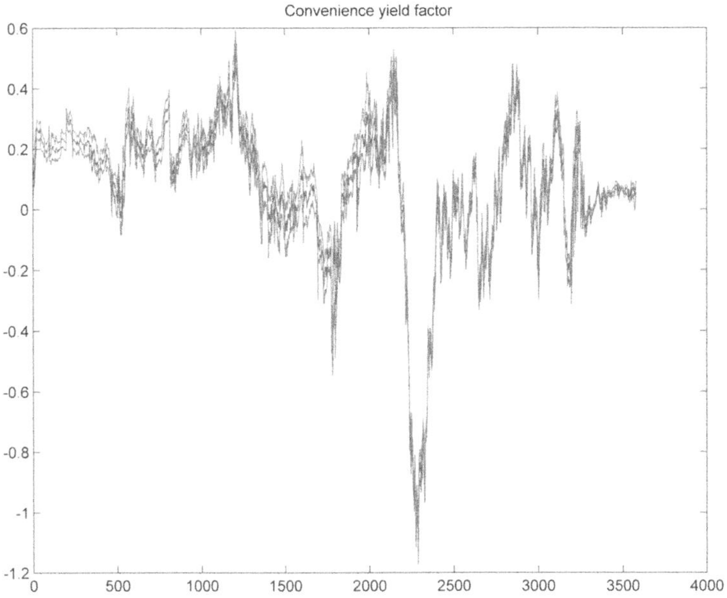

FIGURE 8.30 Convenience Yield State Variable Estimates, Flexible Parameters (2%) 2000–2013

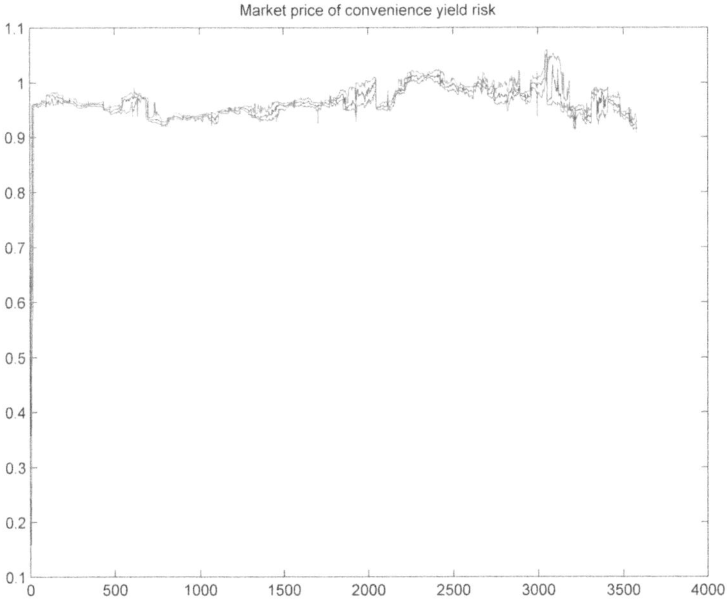

FIGURE 8.31 Market Price of Convenience Yield Risk, Flexible Parameters (2%) 2000–2013

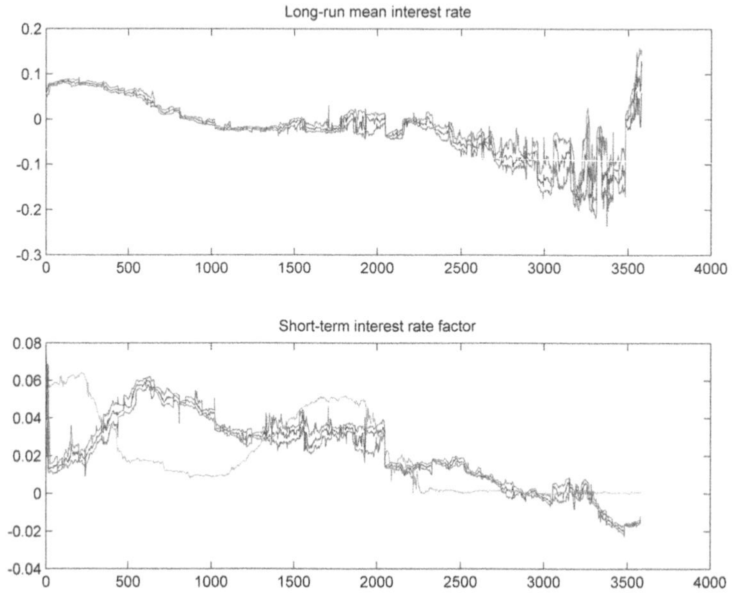

FIGURE 8.32 Long- and Short-Term Interest Rate Estimates, Flexible Parameters (2%) 2000–2013

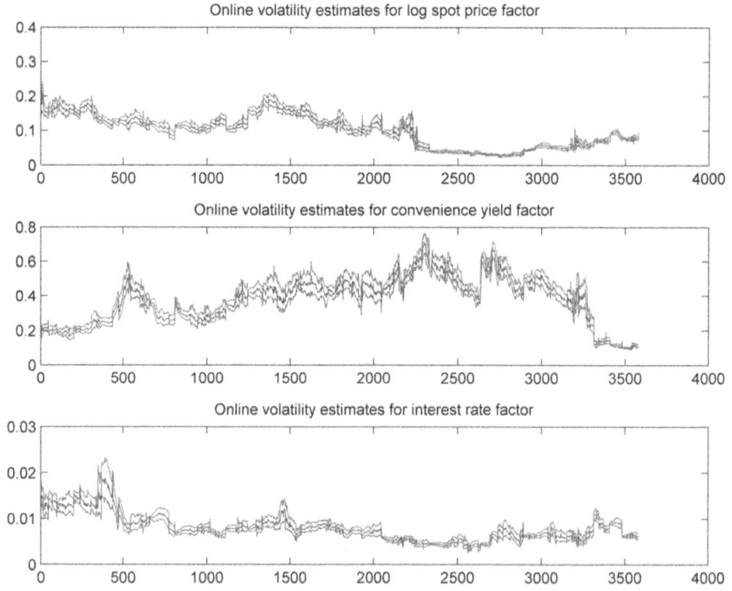

FIGURE 8.33 State Variable Volatility Estimates, Flexible Parameters (2%) 2000–2013

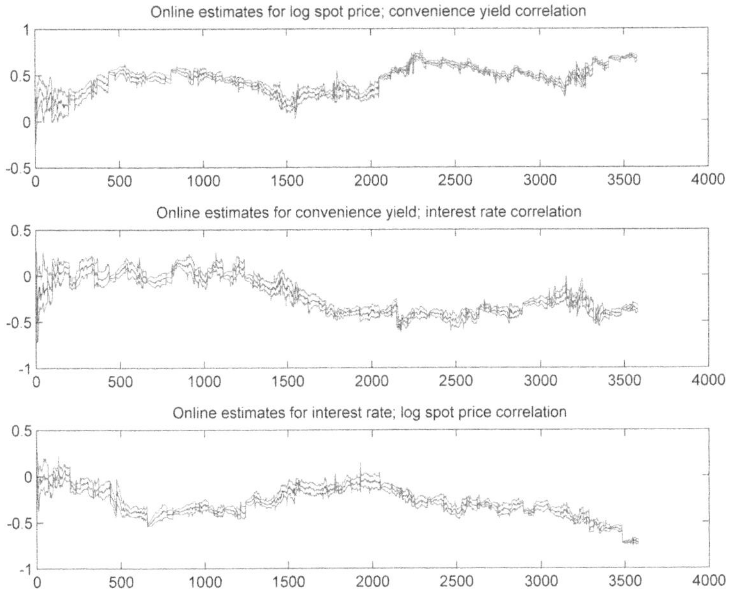

FIGURE 8.34 State Variable Correlation Estimates, Flexible Parameters (2%) 2000–2013

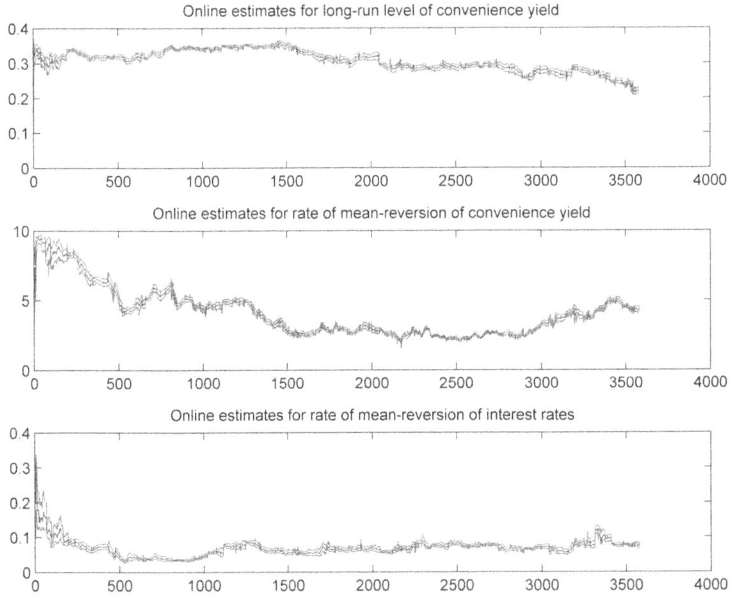

FIGURE 8.35 Long-Run Convenience Yield and Mean-Reversion Rates, Flexible Parameters (2%) 2000–2013

The long period also yields the most interesting results with regard to the market price of convenience yield risk. Whereas estimation in the two subperiods suggested that the market price of risk fell from approximately 0.6 in 2000–2002 to roughly 0.15 in 2012–2013, inclusion of the intervening period leads to a completely different conclusion. The constraint on the parameter space imposed by the historical experience accumulated prior to the second subperiod turns out to be very meaningful in this case. The prior information available in January 2012 is far more precise for this long model run than when estimation begins in January 2012 with a relatively vague prior for the market price of risk. Accordingly, we are left with the intriguing economic conclusion that current oil prices reflect increased risk to holding inventories of oil, for which the market commands greater compensation. Were one to experiment with different rates of information loss for the model parameters, it might be possible to draw other conclusions.

Certainly, other information could be brought to bear in refining the model estimates. Volatilities at each futures contract maturity are described by the same model parameters as futures prices, so changes in prices as well as price levels could be processed by the model in a similar fashion. The variance of model pricing errors could be updated by an auxiliary model rather than fixed at an arbitrary level (0.15^2). And as suggested before, yield curve information would help to better identify the parameters of the interest rate process. Though combining each source of information in a joint likelihood invites many different modeling choices, the possibility of improving inferences by considering multiple corroborating information sources is an exciting prospect not available in the classical time series analysis toolkit.

Hedging with the Time-Varying Schwartz Model

Table 8.1 presents the root mean square errors (RMSEs) of the model prices at each tenor of the forward curve, for each simulated version of the model. The errors reflect inadequacy in the pricing model, the tolerance specified for market microstructure noise, and the forecast uncertainty associated with sequential estimation. This degree of pricing error, which would not be acceptable for market-making purposes, is the price paid for a coherent and stable hedging strategy.

Recalling the expression for the futures price, the partial derivatives of the futures price with respect to the state variables can be seen to be functions

TABLE 8.1 RMSEs for Schwartz Model Estimates

Future	2000–2002 Fixed	2012–2003 Fixed	2000–2002 1% Discounted	2012–2003 1% Discounted	2000–2013 2% Discounted
1	1.2726	1.6945	1.2913	2.1873	2.4816
2	0.9706	1.4719	1.0084	1.7036	1.9721
3	0.7689	1.2848	0.8198	1.3979	1.5870
4	0.6147	1.1042	0.6592	1.1979	1.2831
5	0.4788	0.9230	0.5096	1.0413	1.0379
6	0.3775	0.7877	0.3873	0.9149	0.8557
7	0.3315	0.7415	0.3089	0.8388	0.7665
8	0.3485	0.7892	0.2892	0.8504	0.7890
9	0.4094	0.9193	0.3156	0.9707	0.9151
10	0.4940	1.1053	0.3700	1.1748	1.1136
11	0.5840	1.3285	0.4309	1.4417	1.3582
12	0.6805	1.5818	0.4939	1.7570	1.6375

Data source: Brent crude futures data from Bloomberg; author's calculations.

of the rates of mean-reversion κ and ϕ:

$$\ln F(X,\delta,r,T) = X - \frac{1-e^{-\kappa T}}{\kappa}\delta + \frac{1-e^{-\phi T}}{\phi}r + C(T)$$

$$\begin{aligned}
C(T) = {} & \frac{\left(\kappa\hat{\alpha} + \sigma_1\sigma_2\rho_1\right)\left(\left(1-e^{-\kappa T}\right) - \kappa T\right)}{\kappa^2} \\
& - \frac{\sigma_2^2\left(4\left(1-e^{-\kappa T}\right) - \left(1-e^{-2\kappa T}\right) - 2\kappa T\right)}{4\kappa^3} \\
& - \frac{\left(\phi m^* + \sigma_1\sigma_3\rho_3\right)\left(\left(1-e^{-\phi T}\right) - \phi T\right)}{\phi^2} \\
& - \frac{\sigma_3^2\left(4\left(1-e^{-\phi T}\right) - \left(1-e^{-2\phi T}\right) - 2\phi T\right)}{4\phi^3} \\
& + \sigma_2\sigma_3\rho_2\left(\frac{\left(1-e^{-\kappa T}\right) + \left(1-e^{-\phi T}\right) - \left(1-e^{-(\kappa+\phi)T}\right)}{\kappa\phi(\kappa+\phi)}\right. \\
& \left. + \frac{\kappa^2\left(1-e^{-\varphi T}\right) + \phi^2\left(1-e^{-\kappa T}\right) - \kappa\phi^2 T - \phi\kappa^2 T}{\kappa^2\phi^2(\kappa+\phi)}\right)
\end{aligned}$$

On the assumption that volatilities, correlations, and other parameters are constant, the relevant partial derivatives for an oil futures hedging strategy are those with respect to the state variables. Given three oil hedging instruments and values of the partial derivatives for all three instruments, a system of equations can be solved that matches the state-variable sensitivities of the hedge to the target portfolio. Schwartz shows that the composition of a hedge portfolio constructed in this manner changes relatively little for wide ranges of state values, suggesting a durable hedge with low transaction costs. Similar results would follow from the model estimates and analysis given here, particularly because our estimated rates of mean-reversion closely follow Schwartz's. Because risk information is carried from one period to the next, the implied hedge ratios will change more slowly and more smoothly from day to day than if models were simply recalibrated from period to period.

The stability of the hedging strategy developed by Schwartz depends on the assumption of constant model parameters. When there is significant variation in model parameters, consideration should be given to expanding the set of hedging instruments and numerically evaluating derivatives of the futures price with respect to key parameters. We have observed meaningful changes in volatilities, correlations, and state-variable dynamics whenever we have allowed parameters to evolve. The horizon over which the hedge has to remain durable will be decisive. When the horizon for hedging an exposure is long, allowing for the possibility of model parameter changes allows model risk to be hedged along with market risk.

In this respect, the Schwartz model estimates we have developed are quite good. For horizons of three and two years, respectively, when we allowed static model parameters to drift, parameter estimates remained fairly constant for long periods. When parameters did drift, they did so in a controlled way, with occasional odd jumps in state-variable volatilities and correlations. Thus, hedging with the Schwartz model appears to offer the desirable qualities first mentioned in Chapter 3: Most of the meaningful variation is mediated through the state variables, and the range of possible parameter drift is reasonably well-confined.

Connection with Term-Structure Models

The formulation of the Schwartz model has a close affinity with the way models of the term structure of interest rates have developed in recent years. The class of affine term-structure models (Piazzesi 2010), for example, captures latent linear factor dynamics with general disturbances and solves for bond prices as a function of the latent factors. Many well-known term structure models are nested within the affine model as special cases

(Duffie 2001, pp. Chapter 7). While closed-form expressions for bond prices are only available within the one-factor Vasicek model, the one-factor Cox-Ingersoll-Ross model, and the two-factor independent square root model of Chen and Scott, prices can be found by numerically solving differential equations for the other affine term structure models. Solving differential equations for all simulated state and parameter values will be computationally costly. But with this single technical complication, the structure of the preceding analysis can be taken over essentially intact from the Schwartz model.

MODELS FOR PORTFOLIOS OF ASSETS

The logical conclusion of the state-space modeling approach for asset prices would be a process that reproduces the prices of an entire universe of instruments from a suitably specified system of latent risk factor processes.

Consider, for example, a generalized Schwartz model of the nonferrous base metals complex (aluminum, nickel, tin, zinc, and copper). A state vector for the complex would include spot prices and convenience yields for all metals, along with a common set of interest rate factors. The state vector would then be sufficient to price all derivatives based on the metals, while shedding light on correlations between spot prices and convenience yields within the complex. The latter correlation structure would help to imply a more efficient hedging strategy for exposures across the complex.

It is not hard to go beyond this initial view to a more inclusive modeling strategy encompassing other classes of commodities, interest rate–sensitive instruments, equity-based instruments, and whatever other exposures exist in one's portfolio. As the number of instruments increases, the number of needed factors may be reduced (if, for instance, two factors capture most of the risk in a particular class of instruments) or augmented (if further aggregation enables the estimation of new effects, similar to panel-data models).

Provided a reasonably low-dimensional state vector can be discovered to describe the pricing of a diverse portfolio, the corresponding system dynamics would be all of the information necessary to simulate alternative outcomes for the entire portfolio, and therefore to measure the range of possible gains and losses in the portfolio over various horizons. In other words, the discipline of Bayesian state-space modeling with sequential Monte Carlo estimation would enable flexible, online estimation of enterprise value at risk (VaR). This endgame differs from classical exercises based on principal components analysis or factor mappings in several important respects. First, the uncertainty associated with factors and state equation estimates may be given its due in simulation exercises, capturing elements of model risk that are generally ignored. Repeated draws from a posterior particle set will capture the joint distribution of states and parameters, obviating any choice of estimators and capturing the full range of anticipated outcomes. Existing methods, by contrast, only randomize over states. Second, the underlying risk factors need not be observed. Indeed, we have assumed from the outset when using SMC methods that all risk factors will be latent. Current methods in production routinely identify risk factors with available hedging instruments, which can introduce identification error and the possibility of unspanned risk. Principal components analysis can identify latent factors, but only after the fact, in contrast to the real-time estimates furnished by the particle filter.

This brings us to the third virtue of particle filter methods: Estimates of all modeled quantities can be obtained online, with relatively short starting runs of data. Conventional VaR estimates depend on congruence between the immediate future and the sample of data chosen for calibrating risk models. Online Bayesian estimates capture variation in market conditions leading up to the point at which a VaR forecast is made.

Finally, in a state-space approach combined with arbitrage-free asset-pricing models, one can avail oneself of the considerable structure imposed by pricing models, in contrast to the very reduced-form agnosticism normally practiced in risk modeling. In addition, financial instrument portfolios could be priced globally and coherently, taking into account common factor exposures in a way overlooked when individual values are simply added up. Such a system would be an admirable goal for a financial institution. But it is too much to elaborate fully in a short book.

PART

Four

Bayesian Risk Management

CHAPTER 9

From Risk Measurement to Risk Management

Financial firms measure risk with the intention of managing it more wisely. It is now time for us to make the transition from measurement to management. The first three sections of this book have been dedicated to risk measurement. It is worth reviewing the results of those sections first to revisit the many ways Bayesian risk measurements can supply useful information for risk management, and to provide a synthetic view of the Bayesian approach to the models used in finance and risk management.

The second and final part of this chapter argues that a genuinely Bayesian form of risk management accompanies Bayesian risk measurement. I describe a process of risk governance for firms operating in environments of incomplete information based on the controlled deployment of prior knowledge throughout the organization. When prior knowledge is explicitly formulated and communicated through a firm's risk systems, senior management can maintain decentralized control of the firm's risk-taking activities via the effect that prior knowledge has on posterior estimates and model probabilities. The results of ongoing sequential learning may also be compared retrospectively to management's priors as a means of corroborating or falsifying conjectures about markets or new ventures. Thus, Bayesian risk management represents a fundamental contribution to the rational management of the firm in situations characterized by sparse, incomplete, and even contradictory information.

RESULTS

By formulating and applying sequential Bayesian methods to the analysis of financial time series, we have exposed a number of "degrees of freedom" available in the model-building enterprise. A given phenomenon may be articulated by multiple models with varying degrees of memory. Within any particular model, varying degrees of parameter and model uncertainty will prevail. Accordingly, efforts to specify and implement new candidate models, even for markets that appear to be well understood, are well spent.

In contrast, the way risk modeling is usually undertaken begins to appear downright conventional, in the sense that models in production generally conform to an arbitrary standard. The existence of conventions facilitates communication and coming to understanding, but at the price of a diminished sensitivity to the underlying reality. Indeed, for the conventions generally used to be correct, the future must always look like the past.

Time Series Analysis without Time-Invariance

We took as our point of departure the implicit claims about the world made by the assumption of ergodic stationarity at the foundation of classical time series methods. Classical methods require the identity of data-generating processes over time for a number of purposes. Chief among these purposes is the putative reduction of sampling error needed to distinguish static parameter estimates and achieve an acceptable degree of fit to the data. Taking as our clue the evident inability of models built on such foundations to discern changes in the business cycle and the market environment generally, we became suspicious about the claims of continuity underlying such models. We likewise began to suspect that their apparent fit to the data was exaggerated simply by the practice of pooling data from different time periods without any sensitivity to the conditioning information available at the time the data were observed.

Accordingly, we set out to discover means for investigating financial time series data that would not depend on the assumption of an invariant data-generation process hidden away somewhere in "nature." Absent such an assumption, we could no longer depend on observed data as forming samples or short realizations of a stochastic process that may have developed otherwise. Arguments based on the law of large numbers could no longer be applied to our model estimates. Nor could it be assured that model parameters would inevitably converge to their "true" values, that we could make definitive statements about the integrity of our prior knowledge, or that anything meaningful could be said about the adequacy of models, particularly for purposes of constructing forecasts. Indeed, we saw much of the classical time series modeling enterprise on the verge of collapse.

Preserving Prior Knowledge We began rebuilding on Bayesian foundations in Chapter 2 with an extended discussion of prior knowledge in model building and its importance for the choice of estimators that are, in many respects, the key numerical result of any statistical modeling exercise.

We argued that classical methods treat prior knowledge in a severe manner, either preserving it completely intact or discarding it altogether in favor of a single point estimator. In place of classical estimators we developed a discussion of Bayesian estimators that emphasized the continuity of prior knowledge and information obtained from the data. Information from both sources was seen to be pooled in the probability distributions now used to describe model parameters. When reduction of the distributions to a single number was desired, we saw the interconnectedness of prior knowledge and the loss function in framing decisions about estimators.

The key result of Chapter 2 was the discovery that probability distributions for model parameters could be used to carry prior knowledge and information about the data without loss of fidelity. Prior information remains embedded in parameter distributions. It cannot be discarded; it can only be drowned out by an overwhelming amount of disparate information introduced by more data or alternative priors. This insight about *parameters as carriers of inferences* would later be developed to a much higher degree with the introduction of state-space models. The preservation of prior knowledge in posterior parameter distributions also ensures that sequential Bayesian inference does not treat information as profligately as classical hypothesis tests or the equally standard practice of regularly recalibrating classical time series models. Indeed, we showed the rate of information loss could be introduced and controlled as another model parameter in our discussion of discounting in Chapter 4.

The choice of estimators is not the only way that classical time series methods throw away useful information. They also throw away information that cannot be encompassed by the currently preferred model specification. We saw that Bayesian methods, by contrast, furnished a means for entertaining multiple models simultaneously, and that information captured by each model could be superposed to provide blended forecasts and approximate irregularly distributed phenomena that cannot be sorted out through further conditioning. Assigning probabilities to models on the basis of their forecast accuracy also gave us a ready means for discussing model risk in a coherent way.

In connection with model uncertainty we tackled the problem of model complexity. The relative merits of alternative models, just like the choice of Bayesian estimators, were shown to be interconnected with the nature of prior knowledge introduced in each model. More complex models can be supported either by better conformity with the joint distribution of the data or by providing a vehicle for the introduction of more-nuanced prior knowledge. Accordingly, the choice between competing models of different degrees of complexity is not a matter of testing a restriction with the aid of the data. A model that captures the knowledge and experience of traders and risk managers more effectively may be more successful in "letting the data speak."

Our discussion of model uncertainty led us to a new problem: In what way are financial models statistical in nature? The extension of our notion of model risk to a wide class of practical models turns on this question, as does the veracity of our claims that meaningful uncertainty persists even where such models are apparently well-calibrated to current market data. We saw that a mere acknowledgment of the possibility of measurement error was sufficient to introduce model and parameter uncertainty into the discussion of the arbitrage-free models at the center of financial engineering.

We argued further that practitioners tend to overparameterize their models in their quest to match market prices exactly, with a corresponding loss of insight into the market dynamics posited to lie at the foundation of such models. Our discussion led us to separate the problem faced by market makers (matching the current constellation of prices exactly) from the problem faced by risk managers (understanding the joint movements of prices over short- and medium-term horizons). The tools that ensure the absence of arbitrage in the immediate term will not, in general, be useful tools for understanding and managing the risk exposures of the firm in the longer term.

Information Transmission and Loss Chapters 2 and 3 canvassed the question of how information is best captured from financial data, but it was not until Chapter 4 that we tackled the problem of how such information may be carried from one point in time to another. Thus, it was in Chapter 4 that we first arrived at a provisional solution to the problem of divorcing time series modeling from the assumption of a time-invariant data-generation process. Classical time series methods were shown to coincide with a process of sequential Bayesian inference that never loses information accumulated from the data. In order to adapt to new data at odds with the old data, the process of sequential inference needed a way to forget accumulated inferences at a certain rate. The possibility of multiple candidate models indexed by different rates of information loss lets us remain agnostic about the "correct" rate of information loss, while the explicit recognition of parameter uncertainty puts feelers out for changes in the data, allowing anomalous observations to pull the accumulated inference to different regions of the parameter space.

The recognition of information loss through the device of discounting was also shown to set a boundary on the precision of inferences and to cap the weight given to the data at a certain effective sample size. Instead of handicapping our ability to make more definitive statements about time series processes, these consequences of discounting were seen to be our protection against an ignorant certainty borne from treating all data as manifestations of an identical process. We argued that the apparent loss of precision is the price paid for vigilance: If we want to be alert to changes in the marketplace, we can never pull in our feelers completely. Our purpose is to furnish methods that remain alert for phenomena that classical methods regard as rare and deviant—recessions and crises, for instance, as well as the more diffuse but pervasive phenomenon of "structural change."

Bayesian State-Space Models of Time Series Thus equipped with the elements of a modeling strategy for discontinuous markets, we set out in Chapters 5 and 6 to refine our technique. The use of parameters as carriers of inference was opened up in an explicitly dynamic context by the concept of a state space on which time-varying parameters are defined and evolve. The problem of sequential inference on model parameters was redefined as the problem of filtering latent states with the aid of observed data. The filtering problem led us to the question of adaptation, or the problem of efficiently forming a posterior inference about a latent state with the aid of observed data. This feedback step was shown to be crucial in ensuring the integrity of ongoing learning about states, and controlling the ongoing search over the state space for values that best represent the observed data.

Dynamic linear models were our first proving ground for state-space ideas, showing how a fully adapted filter could be devised with the aid of a linear, Gaussian model formulation. We expanded on the modular construction of dynamic linear models enough to show that traditional time series concerns about trends and seasonality could be accommodated without claiming thereby that some kind of time-invariant residue would fall out afterward. More important, we found that a relatively small set of recursive calculations could be performed to develop inferences about a financial time series observation by observation. While we had done this in a simple way before in Chapter 4 by writing hyperparameter updates for a single observation in discounted Bernoulli and normal linear regression models, the filtering recursions of the DLM provided a technically rigorous way of learning and revising beliefs from the data step by step. Thus, at this point it became possible for us to dispense with batched treatments of time series all together in favor of online, sequential methods. We emphasized that this new sequential orientation avoided imputing future information to past inferences, erasing another pretense of knowledge embedded in classical time series techniques. Further, we pointed out why filtered and smoothed estimates would not coincide with batched estimates except for the rare and deviant case in which the latent states do not vary at all.

In Chapter 6, we reached the highest level of our technical development by showing how sequential Monte Carlo simulation methods extend the dynamic state-space modeling framework to nonlinear and non-Gaussian models, which are found in abundance in finance. We showed in particular how adaptivity may be best maintained without the direct feedback of the DLM. In addition, we introduced the problem of combined parameter and state learning. The DLM bracketed the problem by defining parameter matrices in such a way that all quantities to be filtered out would be states—the parameters were known a priori.

Sequential Monte Carlo methods allow for the possibility that fixed but unknown parameters govern the state evolution process and can be learned from the data just as states are. The juxtaposition of absolutely fixed parameters with variable states presented a problem not resolved technically until Chapter 8: Any fixed quantity in the state-space model will restrict its ability to adapt to the data, while implicitly falling back on the false premise that certain aspects of market phenomena are knowable to any desired degree of accuracy. Nevertheless, any obstacles presented by fixed model parameters can be addressed by a variation on the discounting techniques we have used to such great effect already.

Real-Time Metrics for Model Risk

Our search for methods to handle discontinuous time series thus led to a sequential Bayesian state-space time series framework that draws on parameter uncertainty, model uncertainty, and possible rates of information loss as additional degrees of freedom to capture variation in financial time series. These extra degrees of freedom also furnish ready indicia of model performance and its other side, model risk. Thus, while sequential learning about financial time series goes on observation by observation, we obtain information about model performance at the same frequency. Breakdowns in a model may be registered by increased parameter uncertainty, sharp changes in a latent state, the shift in posterior model probability from one candidate model to another, or a sudden increase in the rate of information loss signaled by posterior model probabilities within a class of otherwise-identical models. These changes can be seen in real time; they do not require large samples of data on either side of the breakdown for detection and confirmation. Current protocols for backtesting, model challenges, and other strategies for vetting models fail to supply such information on such a regular and timely basis. The solution to the problem of financial time series is also the solution for managing model risk: Assume fallibility, update regularly, acknowledge all forms of uncertainty, and entertain multiple candidate models. These prescriptions for model risk management and the sequential Bayesian means to carry them out represent the second major achievement of the analysis above.

To appreciate the handling of model risk in terms of changes in parameter uncertainty and abrupt changes in states, it is helpful to recall the discussion of the DLM from Chapter 5. In the feedback step that produces the posterior state estimates, the direction in which the mean is revised, as well as the posterior variance of the state estimator, depends on a quantity called the Kalman gain. When data are observed that are surprising based on the prior state estimate, the Kalman gain will move the mean to compensate for the forecast error, while also increasing the variance of the state estimator. Sequential Monte Carlo methods operate in the same way. Surprising observations can significantly reweight the candidate particle set in a way that leads parameter and state searches into new regions of the parameter and state spaces. Our observations on sample impoverishment, as well as the decisions in Chapter 8 to artificially increase the variance of the parameter draws in the particle set, were intended to ensure that enough variability was maintained to allow these shifts in direction and uncertainty to occur.

Shifts in posterior model probabilities likewise signal breakdowns in model performance and, if models are indexed in this way, changes in the optimal rate of information loss. Increased rates of information loss signal quickly changing markets that favor models with a greater degree of flexibility. Since more-adaptive models will tend to have greater parameter and state variances than their less-adaptive counterparts, risk measures will tend to increase during quickly changing markets. In other words, beyond the increased risk signaled directly by the model, an additional cushion of measured risk will arise from the increased dispersion of the model estimates.

It would be nice to have the ability to forecast recessions and crises. But until we are able to do that, the model risk metrics canvassed herein offer the best-available solution. Increased parameter uncertainty, sharp changes in a latent state, and shifts in posterior model probabilities within a sequential modeling framework supply real-time indications that markets are no longer operating as they have before, and force decision makers to recognize increased levels of risk. Such indications are superior to modeling efforts based on discerning the probability of a regime change, because they do not require the shift in market dynamics to look like other shifts seen in the past. When abrupt changes in models are observed, the best response for an organization is not necessarily to shut down or reduce exposures. Instead, the firm should redouble its efforts to gather more information. Knowledge gleaned from sources other than the available data can be used to intervene in prior distributions, or new models can be introduced into the set of candidates. Thus, our indicia of model risk are real-time signals that our existing knowledge base is less effective in anticipating market outcomes, and that we should either search for better information or trim risk exposures to a level commensurate with the reduced level of understanding.

Adaptive Estimates without Recalibration

A different demonstration of the success of our enterprise is furnished by the empirical explorations of Chapters 7 and 8. We chose two problems at opposite ends of the spectrum of model complexity. On the one hand, we chose to model single- and multiple-asset volatilities, which can be accomplished respectably merely by specifying an appropriate probability distribution. On the other hand, we estimated a model of an entire forward curve, which entailed discerning latent states and parameters under the risk-neutral measure with the aid of an arbitrage-free pricing formula. Thus, we have two cases at much different levels of complexity aimed at learning about two different probability measures. Both were framed as problems of sequential inference, heightening the degree of difficulty.

On the whole, the results of our empirical investigations were highly successful. The estimates we obtained online were not so different from conventional estimates as to make us doubt their correctness, but different enough that they made deficiencies in the standard techniques evident. In the single-asset volatility case, the Bayesian methods performed well with regard to the number of VaR exceptions generated, while also making plain that recalibrating GARCH models results in parameter changes and breakdowns in forecasting performance. Multivariate volatility was shown to have a finer structure when it was decomposed into factors and weightings. And our estimates of the Schwartz model using Brent crude futures showed that meaningful variations in parameters regarded as fixed can occur over periods for which such models are typically estimated. Each of these findings has direct consequences for risk reporting, asset allocation, and hedging, respectively.

It can also be said that the techniques used are significantly easier to implement than their counterparts in the literature, while sidestepping the problems inherent in batching time series data. The sequential Monte Carlo approach to the Schwartz model used in Chapter 8 could easily be repurposed for other situations where simulated maximum likelihood, the method of simulated moments, and other highly demanding econometric techniques currently hold sway. Besides the gain in transparency, the online methods permit flexibility that cannot be had otherwise, and begin to provide useful results on relatively small runs of data, particularly when good prior knowledge is available.

Deliberately absent from the empirical results are any of the usual claims made for the superiority of econometric techniques, such as reduced variances or in-sample goodness of fit. We have done this for several reasons. In each case we have implemented a process of sequential inference in a way that it can continue without supervision. However, in most practical situations an analyst would intervene at various points to introduce new information not based on the data. Thus, the results demonstrated lack one of the most useful inputs that can be brought to bear on the problem. Secondly, the usual properties of estimators espoused in classical econometrics become meaningless in a Bayesian context. The properties of being unbiased and efficient, which are desired in the classical context, lose their justification once they are divorced from the assumption of ergodic stationarity. Our discussion of loss functions made clear that unbiasedness is not a desirable property if losses are asymmetric. And when parameter variances are deliberately increased because adaptivity is desired, the property of being a minimum-variance estimator is not desirable, either.

Econometric methods are also compared based on the fit they provide to the data in- and out-of-sample. By design, sequential methods provide an out-of-sample fit over the range of data that classical methods would consider in-sample: Whereas classical methods have the benefit of later observations in fitting earlier periods of the data, sequential methods use only the information available at the time the data are observed. A comparison of both methods out-of-sample leads to a different impasse: One somehow has to choose apposite in-sample data for the classical method. The impossibility of making such claims in a theoretically rigorous way is a central premise of our enterprise. Further, when forecasting, the most desirable property is not necessarily the accuracy with which a method forecasts from period to period, but the degree to which the method corrects itself if the method does not forecast accurately. In stable markets even a naïve model may give superior out-of-sample performance, but it will be useless if conditions suddenly change. Thus, instead of arguing that Bayesian estimates are "better" on any of these artificial proving grounds, we have preferred to highlight the range of information furnished, the timeliness of the information furnished, and their ability to show variation where classical methods hold things fixed.

The conditional approach of online estimation offers a very simple but far-reaching challenge to many of the shibboleths of asset pricing. Whenever statistical moments appear in a pricing formula, it is now possible to put time subscripts on them and be explicit about the information sets employed, including prior information sets. Different estimators can be tried out to capture alternative loss function specifications. The extra degrees of freedom opened up by sequential Bayesian analysis permit new tests of old questions in finance, which may lead to surprising new answers.

PRIOR INFORMATION AS AN INSTRUMENT OF CORPORATE GOVERNANCE

Within the field of behavioral microeconomics, Bayesian updating is taken as the paradigm of rational information processing in order to furnish a standard of comparison for empirical instances of information processing by individuals. (See, for example, Tversky and Kahneman 1974 and Tversky and Kahneman 1982.) The same standard of rationality could easily be extended to the firm.

An exceptionally imaginative book by David Harper (1996) conceives of the entrepreneurial firm as an organ for learning about market demand through a process of conjectures and refutations. Those firms that are most effective at learning which conjectures are refuted by experience and which are borne out are most likely to survive and prosper. A Bayesian system of risk measurements and sequential updating can make such a learning process operational within financial services firms.

Suppose several entrepreneurs (traders) seek to make money in a market about which each of them has an identical set of models and data. In the absence of prior information, each should come to the same conclusions when attempting to measure risk in the market. If these entrepreneurs are to come to different conclusions about the market, it can only be because they possess heterogeneous prior information. We saw in Chapter 2 that different priors imply different hypotheses about the market. Hypotheses are updated upon observing the data. Depending on the nature of the hypothesis and the relative weight given to it, the posterior distributions will register the extent to which the data are consistent with the hypothesis.

Hypotheses expressed as informative prior distributions thus can have two functions. First, they can reduce the posterior variance of certain estimates, suggesting that risk is lower in a certain domain than the data would suggest on their own. The apparent reduction in risk serves as an allocative signal: Invest more in those activities that have a lower posterior variance. Prior information thus can be an instrument of governance, signaling priorities by communicating a kind of conjectural knowledge. The ability to signal priorities in this way also suggests a need for control of the propagation of prior information in organizations.

Prior distributions can also be compared to posterior distributions as a means of subsequently checking the veracity of speculations. *Ex post* reconciliations such as these may be more useful in identifying exceptional performance than other forms of measurement, as each initiative can be captured as a hypothesis and measured against the data. In each case, it will be abundantly clear whether certain actors have insight into the market or not.

The careful use of prior information in an organization enables a dynamic of conjectures and refutations by which the firm may be rationally steered with feedback from market data. Thus, it is an instrument of governance par excellence.

Much has been written about risk governance at the board level and the concomitant need to communicate risk appetites throughout the organization as a means of directing focus. Most organizational goals can easily be restated in terms of risk. Instead of communicating a desired end result, make a statement about growth rates and risk; then let downstream decisions organize around that information. Just as firms use internal transfer pricing to communicate scarcity of organizational resources, they could easily deploy prior information to communicate changes in their risk appetites.

Discipline is required in making such a gestalt shift. Take a pedestrian declaration of strategy from senior management: to be at the top of the league tables for syndicated loans in leveraged buyouts, for example. Rephrased in terms of risk appetites: Syndicated loans for leveraged buyouts offer less default risk per point of excess spread than other bank lending opportunities. Such loans supply less exposure to ultimate drivers of default risk than other available lending opportunities. In the latter formulation, no specific goal is communicated, but a portfolio optimization exercise will assign greater weight to leveraged loans.

The Black-Litterman approach to asset allocation follows this general pattern (Black and Litterman 1991). A portfolio manager's view is melded with a market-equilibrium allocation to arrive at a result that tilts in a direction consistent with the manager's thesis. Instead of choosing directly to overweight certain stocks or market sectors, the portfolio manager inputs optimistic excess return assumptions or favorable risk characteristics, and lets the optimization routine arrive at a consistent allocation decision.

The portfolio management analogy can be pushed further. An asset manager would typically first set sector allocations, and then have submanagers build portfolios within the scope of these mandates; perhaps the process reaches another level deep in the hierarchy. Lower levels are unable to disturb the control decisions made above their heads. A similar pattern of governance can be made to prevail in financial firms generally. One has to decide on either a set of sectors or a collection of factors that most completely determines the outcomes possible within the business. For a bank, one can choose to allocate capital among loans, securities investments, trading operations, and capital market transactions; alternatively, senior management can put the greatest effort into articulating views about interest rates, credit risk, volatility in over-the-counter dealer markets, and the valuation of publicly traded firms. The latter specification has the advantage of leaving new business possibilities open by mapping onto the set of fundamental risk factors; the former unifies the top-level strategy of the business with the economic capital problem. In either case, no distinction between risk governance and strategy is necessary, so long as all are agreed on the optimization problem being solved.

Assigning responsibility at the highest levels for the most consequential statements of prior knowledge ensures that posterior estimates cannot be manipulated by employees to suit their own purposes, while also signaling a degree of deliberation and judgment on questions of risk from senior management. We have seen how prior knowledge influences the form of posterior parameter estimates and the choice of models, and while erroneous aspects of prior knowledge can be "unlearned" with the aid of data, prior knowledge can be decisive, particularly in the early stages of entering a market or a line of business. It is here in the management of new ventures that the elicitation, control, and revision of prior knowledge through a Bayesian risk management framework is most valuable.

At other echelons of the financial firm, communicating trading theses in terms of prior information allows for careful appraisal of the strategy's prospects and a clear statement of what market outcomes can signal refutation of the thesis. The swap spread trades that sank Long-Term Capital Management could have been formulated as prior knowledge about a rate of mean-reversion. The natural gas seasonal spread trades that were the undoing of Amaranth could have been framed as a statement about the amplitude of a seasonal price cycle. It would then be the work of sequential inference to determine whether the data continue to bear out such theses about model parameters and states. The ability to reconcile prior knowledge to posterior model estimates holds the promise of enabling an extremely disciplined approach to risk-taking and risk management by precisely framing the conditions under which a trading thesis or business strategy will be abandoned.

Bayesian risk management is thus a strategy for the decentralized management of a firm in an environment of dynamic uncertainty, by quantifying and sharing disparate bits of information within the firm in a controlled and mathematically rigorous way. We have laid out the elements necessary for such a system to operate and have shown the kind of results it can produce. It remains for forward-thinking firms to put it into practice.

References

Allen, Linda, Jacob Boudoukh, and Anthony Saunders. *Understanding Market, Credit, and Operational Risk: The Value at Risk Approach* (Hoboken, NJ: Wiley-Blackwell, 2003).

Barndorff-Neilsen, Ole. "Hyperbolic Distributions and Distributions on Hyperbolae." *Scandinavian Journal of Statistics* 5, no. 3 (1978): 151–157.

Berger, James O. *Statistical Decision Theory and Bayesian Analysis*, 2nd ed. (New York: Springer-Verlag, 1985).

Bernardo, Jose M., and Adrian F. M. Smith. *Bayesian Theory* (Chichester: John Wiley & Sons, Ltd., 2000).

Black, Fischer. "Studies of Stock Price Volatility Changes." Proceedings of the 1976 Meetings of the American Statistical Association, Business and Economical Statistics Section (1976a): 177–181

Black, Fischer. "The Pricing of Commodity Contracts." *Journal of Financial Economics* 3 (1976b): 167–179.

Black, Fischer, and Robert Litterman. "Global Portfolio Optimization." *Financial Analysts Journal* 48 (1992): 28–43.

Bollerslev, Tim, Robert F. Engle, and Daniel B. Nelson. "ARCH Models." Chapter 49 in Robert F. Engle and Daniel L. McFadden, eds., *Handbook of Econometrics*, Vol. IV (Amsterdam: North-Holland, 1983), 2959–3038.

Box, George E. P., and Gwilym M. Jenkins. *Time Series Analysis: Forecasting and Control* (San Francisco: Holden-Day, 1970).

Carter, C. K., and R. Kohn. "On Gibbs Sampling for State Space Models." *Biometrika* 81 (1994): 541–553.

Carvalho, Carlos M., Michael S. Johannes, Hedibert F. Lopes, and Nicholas G. Polson. "Particle Learning and Smoothing." *Statistical Science* 25, no. 1 (2010): 88–106.

Chib, Siddhartha, and Bakhodir Ergashev. "Analysis of Multifactor Affine Yield Curve Models." *Journal of the American Statistical Association* 104 (2009): 1324–1337.

Chincarini, Ludwig B. *The Crisis of Crowding: Quant Copycats, Ugly Models, and the New Crash Normal* (Hoboken, NJ: John Wiley & Sons, 2012).

Culp, Christopher L. *Risk Transfer: Derivatives in Theory and Practice* (Hoboken, NJ: John Wiley & Sons, 2004).

Dowd, Kevin. *Beyond Value at Risk: The New Science of Risk Management* (Chichester: John Wiley & Sons, 1998).

Duffie, Darrell. *Dynamic Asset Pricing Theory*, 3rd ed. (Princeton, NJ: Princeton University Press, 2001).

Eberlein, Ernst, and Ulrich Keller. "Hyperbolic Distributions in Finance." *Bernoulli* 1, no. 3 (1995): 281–299.

Engle, Robert F. *Anticipating Correlations: A New Paradigm for Risk Management* (Princeton, NJ: Princeton University Press, 2009).

Fama, Eugene F. "The Behavior of Stock Market Prices." *Journal of Business* 36 (January 1965): 34–105.

Fama, Eugene F., and Kenneth R. French. "Multifactor Explanations of Asset Pricing Anomalies." *Journal of Finance* 51, no. 1 (March 1996): 55–84.

Fisher, Franklin. *Disequilibrium Foundations of Equilibrium Economics* (Oxford: Cambridge University Press, 1983).

Fleming, J., C. Kirby, and B. Ostdiek. "The Economic Value of Volatility Timing." *Journal of Finance* 56, no. 1 (2001): 329–352.

Friedland, Bernard. *Control System Design: An Introduction to State-Space Methods* (Mineola, NY: Dover Publications, 2005 [1986]).

Frühwirth-Schnatter, Sylvia. "Applied State-Space Modeling of Non-Gaussian Time Series Using Integration-Based Kalman Filtering." *Statistics and Computing* 4 (1994): 259–269.

Gamerman, Dani, and Hedibert F. Lopes. *Markov Chain Monte Carlo: Stochastic Simulation for Bayesian Inference* (Boca Raton, FL: Chapman & Hall/CRC Press, 2006).

Gordon, N. J., D. J. Salmond, and A. F. M. Smith. "A Novel Approach to Non-Linear and Non-Gaussian Bayesian State Estimation." *IEEE Proceedings F* 140, no. 2 (1993), 107–113.

Green, T. Clifton, and Stephen Figlewski. "Market Risk and Model Risk for a Financial Institution Writing Options." *Journal of Finance* 54 (1999): 1465–1499.

Hamilton, James D. *Time Series Analysis* (Princeton, NJ: Princeton University Press, 1994).

Harper, David. *Entrepreneurship and the Market Process: An Enquiry into the Growth of Knowledge* (London: Routledge, 1996).

Harrison, P. J. "Exponential Smoothing and Short-Term Forecasting." *Management Science* 13 (1967): 821–842.

Harrison, P. J. "Short-term Sales Forecasting." *Applied Statistics* 15 (1965): 102–139.

Hayashi, Fumio. *Econometrics* (Princeton and Oxford: Princeton University Press, 2000).

Hendry, David, and Bent Nielsen, *Econometric Modeling: A Likelihood Approach* (Princeton, NJ: Princeton University Press, 2007).

Hoeting, Jennifer A., David Madigan, Adrian E. Raftery, and Chris T. Volinsky. "Bayesian Model Averaging: A Tutorial." *Statistical Science* 14, no. 4 (1999): 382–417.

Hull, John C. *Options, Futures, and Other Derivatives*, 6th ed. (Upper Saddle River, NJ: Prentice Hall, 2005).

Jaynes, E. T. *Probability Theory: The Logic of Science* (Oxford: Cambridge University Press, 2003).

Johannes, Michael, and Nicholas G. Polson. "Markov Chain Monte Carlo." In T. G. Anderson, et al., eds. *Handbook of Financial Time Series* (Berlin: Springer-Verlag, 2009a), 1001–1013.

Johannes, Michael, and Nicholas G. Polson. *Bayesian Computation: Markov Chain Monte Carlo and Particle Filtering* (Princeton, NJ: Princeton University Press, forthcoming).

Johannes, Michael, and Nicholas G. Polson. "MCMC Methods for Financial Econometrics." Chapter 1 in Yacine Aït-Sahalia and Lars Peter Hansen, eds., *Handbook of Financial Econometrics, Vol. 2: Applications* (Amsterdam: North-Holland, 2009b), 1–72.

Johannes, Michael S., Nicholas G. Polson, and Jonathan R. Stroud. "Optimal Filtering of Jump Diffusions: Extracting Latent States from Asset Prices." *Review of Financial Studies* 22, no. 7 (2009): 2759–2799.

Johnson, Norman, Samuel Kotz, and N. Balakrishnan. *Continuous Univariate Distributions*, Vol. 2, 2nd ed. (New York: John Wiley & Sons, 1995).

Jorion, Philippe. *Value at Risk: The New Benchmark for Managing Financial Risk*, 3rd ed. (New York: McGraw-Hill, 2006).

Kalman, Rudolf. "Contributions to the Theory of Optimal Control." *Boletin Societa Matematica Mexicana* 5 (1960): 102–119.

Khandani, Amir, and Andrew Lo. "What Happened to the Quants in August 2007?" MIT Working Paper, 2007.

Knight, Frank. *Risk, Uncertainty, and Profit* (Boston: Hart, Schaffner & Marx; Houghton Mifflin Company, 1921).

Koop, Gary. *Bayesian Econometrics* (Chichester: John Wiley & Sons, 2003).

Leamer, Edward. "Model Choice and Specification Analysis." Chapter 5 in Zvi Griliches and Michael D. Intrilligator, eds. *Handbook of Econometrics*, Vol. 1 (Amsterdam: North-Holland, 1983), 285–330.

Liu, Jane, and Mike West. "Combined Parameter and State Estimation in Simulation-Based Filtering." In A. Doucet, N. de Freitas, and N. Gordon, eds., *Sequential Monte Carlo in Practice* (New York: Springer-Verlag, 2001: 197–223).

Lopes, Hedibert F., and Nicholas G. Polson. "Bayesian Inference for Stochastic Volatility Modeling." In Klaus Bocker, ed., *Rethinking*

Risk Measurement and Reporting: Uncertainty, Bayesian Analysis and Expert Judgment, Vol. II (London: Risk Books, 2010), 31–68.

Lopes, Hedibert F., and Ruey E. Tsay. "Particle Filters and Bayesian Inference in Financial Econometrics." *Journal of Forecasting* 30 (2011): 168–209.

Lütkepohl, Helmut. *New Introduction to Multiple Time Series Analysis* (Berlin: Springer-Verlag, 2004b).

Lütkepohl, Helmut. "Univariate Time Series Analysis." In Helmut Lütkepohl and Markus Krätzig, eds., *Applied Time Series Econometrics* (Oxford: Cambridge University Press, 2004a), 8–85.

Maddala, G. S., and In-Moo Kim. *Unit Roots, Cointegration, and Structural Change* (Oxford: Cambridge University Press, 1998).

Madigan, David, and Adrian E. Raftery. "Model Selection and Accounting for Model Uncertainty in Graphical Models Using Occam's Window." *Journal of the American Statistical Association* 89 (1994): 1535–1546.

Malevergne, Yannick, and Didier Sornette. *Extreme Financial Risks: From Dependence to Risk Management* (New York: Springer, 2005).

Mandelbrot, Benoit. "The Variation of Certain Speculative Prices." *Journal of Business* 36 (October 1963): 394–419.

Mina, Jorge, and Jerry Yi Xiao. *Return to RiskMetrics: The Evolution of a Standard* (New York: RiskMetrics, 2001).

Pitt, Michael K., and Neil Shepherd. "Filtering via Simulation: Auxiliary Particle Filters." *Journal of the American Statistical Association* 94, no. 446 (1999): 590–599.

Piazzesi, Monika. "Affine Term Structure Models." Chapter 12 in Yacine aït-Sahalia and Lars Peter Hansen, eds., *Handbook of Financial Econometrics*, Vol. 1 (North-Holland: Elsevier, 2010), 691–766.

Poirier, Dale J. *Intermediate Statistics and Econometrics: A Comparative Approach* (Cambridge, MA: MIT Press, 1995).

Prado, Raquel, and Mike West. *Time Series: Modeling, Computation, and Inference* (Boca Raton, FL: Chapman & Hall/CRC Press, 2010).

Rebonato, Riccardo, Kenneth McKay, and Richard White. *The SABR/LIBOR Market Model: Pricing, Calibration and Hedging for Complex Interest-Rate Derivatives* (Chichester: John Wiley & Sons, 2009).

Robert, Christian P. *The Bayesian Choice: From Decision-Theoretic Foundations to Computation Implementation* (New York: Springer, 2007).

Rossi, Peter E., Greg M. Allenby, and Robert McCulloch. *Bayesian Statistics and Marketing* (Hoboken, NJ: John Wiley & Sons, 2005).

Schwartz, Eduardo S. "The Stochastic Behavior of Commodity Prices: Implications for Valuation and Hedging." *Journal of Finance* 52, no. 3 (1997): 923–973.

Singleton, Kenneth. *Empirical Dynamic Asset Pricing* (Princeton, NJ: Princeton University Press, 2006).

Storvik, Geir. "Particle Filters for State-Space Models with the Presence of Unknown Static Parameters." *IEEE Transactions on Signal Processing* 50, no. 2 (February 2002): 281–289.

Tversky, Amos, and Daniel Kahneman. "Evidential Impact of Base Rates." In Daniel Kahneman, P. Slovic, and Amos Tversky, eds., *Judgment under Uncertainty: Heuristics and Biases* (Cambridge University Press, 1982), 153–160.

Tversky, Amos, and Daniel Kahneman. "Judgment under Uncertainty: Heuristics and Biases." *Science* 185 (1974): 1124–1131.

West, Mike, and Jeff Harrison. *Bayesian Forecasting and Dynamic Models*, 2nd ed. (New York: Springer-Verlag, 1997).

Index

Printed and bound by CPI Group (UK) Ltd, Croydon, CR0 4YY

23/04/2025

14660921-0002